International Migration
within, to and from Africa in a Globalised World

Edited by

Aderanti Adepoju

NOMRA

Sub-Saharan Publishers, Ghana

First published in Ghana 2010 by
SUB-SAHARANPUBLISHERS
P.O.BOX 358
LEGON-ACCRA
GHANA
Email; saharanp@africaonline.com.gh

© Network of Migration Research on Africa 2010

ISBN: 978-9988-647-42-1

All rights reserved. No part of this publication may be reproduced, stored in a retrieval system or transmitted in any form or by any means electronic, mechanical, photocopying recording, or otherwise without the prior permission of the publishers

Typesetting and cover design by Kwabena Agyepong

Preface

This publication presents contributions by experts drawn from the Network of Migration Research on Africa (NOMRA). It provides a perspective from African scholars on the ramifications of migration within and outside the continent. The authors examine, outline and discuss traditional and emerging migrations within sub-regional groupings; the unwholesome migration in irregular situations by the youth to Europe and also within the continent; the causes and consequences of brain drain; the role of the diaspora in the development of countries of origin, principally through social and economic remittances; institutional frameworks for policy formulation and bilateral agreements between Africa's sending countries and European receiving ones. All these trajectories have been severely disrupted by the ongoing economic recession in both rich countries and poor, and its impact on movement of persons. This is especially the orientation of the concluding chapter.

This volume will be of immense value to researchers and scholars, students and policy-makers, and development partners working on Africa's migration, regional integration, poverty alleviation, and sustainable development.

We wish to acknowledge appreciation of all those associated with this book. First of all, the Dutch Ministry of Foreign Affairs, for providing financial support to NOMRA. Then we owe the staff at headquarters, and especially at its Nigeria's mission, our gratitude for their enthusiastic backstopping role on the project. Biddy Greene painstakingly edited the manuscript and helped format the tables and boxes; NOMRA's Programme Officer, Dupe Kuteyi, kept the authors on track in the preparation of their chapters, and Adunola, my dear wife, inspired me to finalise the manuscript in difficult circumstances and endured sleepless nights watching over me. The authors worked through the sparse data regime to provide readers as comprehensive a picture as was feasible of the traditional and rapidly-changing configurations of Africa's intra-regional and inter-continental migration.

Aderanti Adepoju
Editor

Contents

Preface	3
Abbreviations and acronyms	6

CHAPTER ONE
INTRODUCTION: Rethinking the Dynamics of Migration within, from and to Africa ... 9

CHAPTER TWO
Regional Economic Commissions and Intra-Regional Migration Potential in Africa: Taking Stock ... 46

CHAPTER THREE A
African Skilled Labour Migration: Dimensions and Impact* ... 97

CHAPTER THREE B
Emigration of Skilled Professionals from Africa: Dimensions and Consequences ... 119

CHAPTER FOUR
African Diaspora and Remittance Flows: Leveraging Poverty? ... 137

CHAPTER FIVE
Irregular Migration within and to the Republic of South Africa and from the African Continent to the European Union: Tapping Latent Energy of the Youth ... 169

CHAPTER SIX
Institutional Framework for the Management of Migrants, Data and Information in Africa ... 208

CHAPTER SEVEN
Promoting Managed Migration through Bilateral and Multilateral Agreements between European and African Countries ... 236

CHAPTER EIGHT
Conclusion ... 255

About the Authors ... 259

Abbreviations and acronyms

ACBF	African Capacity Building Foundation
ACP	African, Caribbean and Pacific (countries)
AEC	African Economic Community
ANPPCAN	African Network for the Prevention and Protection Against Child Abuse and Neglect
AU	African Union
CEMAC	Central African Economic and Monetary Community
CERPOD	Centre d'Etudes et de Recherche sur la Population pour le Développement
CICP	Centre for International Crime Prevention
COMESA	Common Market for Eastern and Southern Africa
CSO	Civil Society Organisation
EAC	East African Community
ECA	(United Nations) Economic Commission for Africa
ECCAS	Economic Community of Central African States[1]
ECOWAS	Economic Community of West African States[2]
EDF	European Development Fund
EU	European Union
FDI	foreign direct investment
GDP	gross domestic product
HIV/AIDS	Human immuno-deficiency virus/ Acquired immune deficiency syndrome
HTA	home town association
IDP	internally displaced person
IGO	inter-governmental organisation
ILO	International Labour Organization
IMF	International Monetary Fund
IMP	International Migration Policy Programme
INSEE	Institut National de la Statistique et des Études Économiques[3] (France)
IOM	International Organization for Migration
IT	information technology
MDGs	millennium development goals
MIDA	Migration for Development in Africa
MIDSA	Migration Dialogue for Southern Africa

1 The ECCAS countries are Angola, Burundi, Cameroon, Central African Republic, Chad, Democratic Republic of the Congo, Equatorial Guinea, Gabon, Republic of the Congo, Rwanda, São Tomé & Príncipe.
2 The ECOWAS countries are Benin, Burkina Faso, Cape Verde, Côte d'Ivoire, Gambia, Ghana, Guinea, Guinea Bissau, Liberia, Mali, Niger, Nigeria, Senegal, Sierra Leone and Togo.
3 National Institute for Statistics and Economic Studies.

Abbreviations and acronyms

MIDWA	Migration Dialogue for West Africa
MSU	Michigan State University
NAPTIP	National Agency for Prohibition of Traffic in Persons and Other Related Matters (Nigeria)
NCFR	National Commission for Refugees (Nigeria)
NELM	new economics of labour migration
NEPAD	New Partnership for Africa's Development
NOMRA	Network of Migration Research on Africa
NGO	non-governmental organisation
NHS	National Health Service (UK)
OAU	Organisation of African Unity
ODA	official development aid / overseas development assistance etc.
ODCCP	Office of Drug Control and Crime Prevention (UN)
OECD	Organisation for Economic Co-operation and Development[4]
PRSP	poverty reduction strategy paper
RCP	regional consultative process
REC	regional economic community/ Regional Economic Commission
RQAN	Return of Qualified African Nationals
SADC	Southern African Development Community[5]
SADCC	Southern African Development Coordination Conference
SAMP	Southern African Migration Project
SSA	sub-Saharan Africa
SOPEMI	Systeme d'Observation Permanente sur les Migrations[6]
UEMOA	West African Economic and Monetary Union
UK	United Kingdom (of Great Britain and Northern Ireland)
UKNMC	UK Nursing and Midwifery Council
UN	United Nations
UNCHR	United Nations Commission on Human Rights
UNDP	United Nations Development Programme
UNDPI	United Nations Department of Public Information
UNECA	United Nations Economic Commission for Africa
UNFPA	United Nations Population Fund
UNHCR	United Nations High Commissioner for Refugees
UNICEF	United Nations Children's Fund
UNIFEM	United Nations Development Fund for Women

---

4 The OECD countries are Australia, Austria, Belgium, Canada, Czech Republic, Denmark, Finland, France, Germany, Greece, Hungary, Iceland, Ireland, Italy, Japan, Korea, Luxembourg, Mexico, Netherlands, New Zealand, Norway, Poland, Portugal, Slovak Republic, Spain, Sweden, Switzerland, Turkey, United Kingdom, United States.

5 The SADC countries are Angola, Botswana, Democratic Republic of the Congo, Lesotho, Madagascar, Malawi, Mauritius, Mozambique, Namibia, Seychelles, South Africa, Swaziland, Tanzania, Zambia and Zimbabwe.

6 Continuous Migration Monitoring System.

UNICRI	United Nations Interregional Crime and Justice Research Institute
UNODC	United Nations Office on Drugs and Crime
UNOWA	United Nations Office for West Africa
US/USA	United States of America
USAID	United States Agency for International Development
WOTCLEF	Women Trafficking and Child Labour Eradication Foundation

CHAPTER ONE

INTRODUCTION: Rethinking the Dynamics of Migration within, from and to Africa

Aderanti Adepoju

Background

Countries in Africa today are weighed down by rapid population and labour force growth, declining agricultural productivity, rapid and compressed urbanisation, rural exodus to large cities whose economies are too fragile to absorb large numbers of new workers, general poverty, and widespread unemployment. Internal, intra-regional and international migration take place within diverse political, socio-ethnic and economic contexts. Many countries are concurrently experiencing challenges and opportunities related to the emigration of skilled professionals, diaspora links with countries of origin, and migrants' remittances from within and outside Africa. Emigration pressure is fuelled by unstable politics, ethno-religious conflicts, poverty, and rapidly-growing populations. Distinctive forms of migration characterise the different sub-regions: labour migration from western and central Africa to other locations within the region, as well as to the countries of the OECD (Organisation for Economic Co-operation and Development) and the oil-rich countries of the Middle East; refugee flows within eastern, and increasingly in western, Africa; labour migration from eastern and southern African countries to southern Africa, and cross-border clandestine migration of seasonal workers and nomads in West and East Africa.

Unlike in other world regions, these migrations are complex and dynamic, and again unlike in other world regions, are largely intra-regional, complex and dynamic. This is reflected in increasing female migration, diversification of migration destinations, transformation of labour flows into commercial migration, and the emigration of skilled health and other professionals from Africa. Coupled with trafficking in human beings and the changing map of refugee flows, these are the key migratory configurations that require innovative research, but at present most countries lack synchronised migration policies and programmes, as well as appropriate data bases to inform such policies.

In the twenty-first century, Africa has come to a crossroads economically, politically and demographically. It is a region of great diversity in terms of history, culture, colonial experience, socio-political systems, population size, ecology and patterns of development. It is a continent of contradictions: rich in resources, its peoples are becoming poorer by the day. The poorest continent in the world, resources deviated to repay external debts deprive countries of the ability to solve their own problems. Efforts by several countries to restructure their economies, privatise state-controlled entities, devalue their currencies, and open their markets to share in the global economy have been disappointing.

Over the past decade, many African countries have been moving, albeit sluggishly, to multiparty systems of governance. Fewer countries are ruled by the military, including those – Mauritania and Guinea Conakry – that have reverted to military rule since 2006. After decades of devastating mismanagement, corruption, and human rights abuses associated with one-party systems, conditions that forced much-needed skilled professionals to go into exile in droves, popular participation is at last taking firm root.

Today, most of Africa's youth are unemployed. The annual population growth, the fastest in the world, is expected to double within a generation, doubling the number of youths compared to the general population. Ethnic conflicts that create incessant refugee flows, displace populations and stall efforts to eradicate poverty, are also likely to increase. Distressful economic and living conditions continue to trigger the emigration of skilled and unskilled persons – men and women alike. Achieving sustainable livelihoods, food security, peace and stability, is essential not only for sustainable development, but also to induce these emigrants, professionals in particular – the engine of growth and development – to return to their countries.

Africa's disillusioned, unemployed youth faces difficult choices between being apprenticed to a trade, farming, or going to school, only to join, at the end of it, the queue of job-seekers roaming the streets, seeking unsuccessfully for months for even lowly-paid jobs. For most, migration in pursuit of higher education or wage employment is urban-centred, although that may be preparatory to migrating abroad. By migrating, many youths simply exchange misery without hope for misery with hope. The informal sector's incapacity to absorb the rapidly-growing number of job seekers compels potential migrants to find alternative destinations, and to be ready to do any odd jobs anywhere – but increasingly outside their home countries. Since the late 1980s, when the region experienced negative economic growth and a deteriorating well-being of its people, such migration has been strictly for survival; as the effects of economic restructuring bite harder, migration has become a coping mechanism of the last resort.

Unemployment in Africa's urban areas is essentially among youth. Initially localised among primary school leavers in the early 1960s, the pool of the unemployed now includes secondary school leavers as well as university graduates who constitute a dormant labour force, socially and economically dependent and disillusioned. Sadly the majority of youths are illiterate. Less than half of the school-age population do in fact go to school, and thousands drop out annually, resulting in low transition rates between educational levels. With only a few exceptions, fewer girls than boys have access to schools, and far fewer obtain diplomas. Uneducated young girls are severely constrained in employment markets.

Dramatic changes in the economic fortunes have adversely undermined the abilities of families to meet basic needs. One of the consequences is the weakening and disintegration of family control over youth, who turn to the street, seeking even lowly-paid jobs for months without success. In desperation, most of these youths become easy prey to scams, or risk their lives in hazardous journeys to countries of the North, assisted by bogus agencies, in search of the illusory green pastures. Trafficking in irregular migrants, previously a rare phenomenon, is on the increase as young persons become involved in daredevil ventures to gain entry into Europe. Individual stowaways risk their lives hidden on ships going to southern Europe, or, recently, as far away as eastern Asia. Many others seek political asylum, citing abuse of human rights in their home countries. For most non-urban youths in pursuit of higher education or employment, migration towards towns and often thence to other countries is inevitable. For a few, such migration is to attain socio-economic mobility, but for the large majority, it is strictly for survival (Adepoju 2006).

The limited size of internal markets, and especially the disadvantageous position of African countries in the new era of globalisation, impact on migration dynamics in various ways. Agricultural subsidies in OECD countries, especially the USA and Europe, have a negative effect on the income of farmers in the region, drastically affecting the livelihood of ten million cotton growers and their families (OECD 2004). Most of these people are now migrating to the cities, in a desperate bid for survival. Also the high OECD tariffs and technical barriers to trade cost Africa billions of dollars yearly in lost exports – much-needed revenue which could have been used for development and for employment generation.

The preoccupation among researchers with the question of motivation (why people migrate) tends to obscure the other side of the picture – indeed a large part – which deals with the question of non-mobility, that is why most people do *not* migrate from the rural environment, or from their home countries. Nevertheless, although the majority of Africans do not in fact migrate, those who do are becoming increasingly desperate, exploring diverse destinations through formal and informal entry points (Adepoju & Hammar 1996).

Migration data and research

Until the 1960s, efforts to interpret Africa's population dynamics were constrained by a scarcity of accurate data. By the '70s and '80s, however, national censuses and surveys were generating solid new data sets that helped planners place population issues, in the forefront of development agendas – albeit at varying levels of confidence.

Data on migration within and outside Africa is patchy, but slowly improving. Among the earlier studies are the census-based demographic analyses of migration in West Africa, the survey of Mali, Mauritania and Senegal by the Sahel Institute and the OECD in 1982, and the seven-country survey of migration and urbanisation in West Africa, coordinated by the Centre d'Etudes et de Recherche sur la Population pour le Développement (CERPOD) in 1993. (The countries covered in this survey were Burkina Faso, Cote d'Ivoire, Guinea, Mali, Mauritania, Senegal and Nigeria.) The IOM/UNFPA[1] research project on Emigration Dynamics in Developing Countries (1992–1996) included sub-Saharan Africa (with the author as research team leader), its key objectives being to construct a conceptual framework with a multi-disciplinary perspective, and to increase knowledge in countries of origin and reception concerning emigration dynamics in poor countries (Adepoju 1995).

In 2003, the Southern African Migration Project (SAMP) conducted a 'potential skills base survey' – a study of skills-in-training to assess the emigration intentions and potential of the future labour force in six southern African countries (SAMP,n.d.). The 2004 EUROSTAT project, coordinated by the Netherlands Interdisciplinary Demographic Institute, covered two receiving OECD countries and five sending countries, two of them – Ghana and Senegal – being in West Africa. This work, on the push and pull factors of international migration, examines the pressure on emigration intentions in different cultural, geographical and economic settings. The University of Sussex's Centre for Migration Research has been engaged in gathering qualitative and quantitative materials on international migration from Ghana and Cote d'Ivoire, complemented by in-depth interviews and focus groups in the UK, France and the USA (Black et al 2004).

It is essential that the information obtained from these surveys be analysed and coordinated in the near future, to enhance their usefulness for development-friendly migration policy formulation.

Leading issues in migration within and from Africa

The emigration of highly-skilled professionals, including doctors, nurses, paramedical personnel, teachers, lecturers, engineers and technologists, has been a contentious issue between rich and poor countries. This development had its antecedents in the 1960s when African countries engaged in unprecedented educational expansion. Emigration was later spurred by deteriorating economic, political and related factors, including lack of job satisfaction and a system in which efficient input was not recognised or rewarded. Uganda led the way in both volume and rapidity of exodus of its skilled manpower, as highly educated

---

1 International Organization for Migration/United Nations Population Fund.

people were forced to migrate to Kenya, South Africa, Botswana, Europe and North America (Adepoju 1991). For similar reasons, the vast majority of Somali, Ethiopian and Zambian graduates have been working overseas. The conditions which sparked off emigration from these countries later gripped Kenya. The bonding system and travel clearance demands imposed on Tanzanian, Ugandan and Kenyan professionals and civil servants to restrict their emigration did little to stem the tide (Oucho 1998).

Twelve of the thirty OECD countries – Australia, Belgium, Canada, France, Germany, Ireland, Italy, the Netherlands, Portugal, Spain, the UK and the USA – are all major recipients of Africa's skilled professionals, due largely to the colonial legacy. Between 1960 and 1987, for instance, Africa lost 30 per cent of its highly-skilled nationals, mostly to Europe; between 1986 and 1990, an estimated 50 to 60 thousand middle and high-level managers emigrated as local socio-economic and political conditions deteriorated. Since then, about 23 000 qualified academic staff have been emigrating each year in search of better working conditions (IOM 2003). In 2002, 18 per cent of Nigerian doctors worked abroad. Although total immigration from sub-Saharan Africa to the USA is relatively small in comparison with the total inflow and stock of immigrants to that country, the sub-Saharan Africa immigrants consist primarily of highly educated people, especially those from Ghana, South Africa and Nigeria.

Until the early 1980s, few African professionals, especially Nigerians, saw emigration as a rewarding option – because local working conditions were attractive and internationally competitive. However, the biting effects of economic restructuring, authoritarian military rule and the fluctuating economic situation fuelled large-scale emigration, especially of skilled people, pushing many professionals to market their skills internationally. Widespread unemployment and inadequate openings for admission into Nigeria's tertiary educational institutions were the deciding factors for a large proportion of visa applicants.

Of the estimated 4 million sub-Saharan Africans living in rich OECD countries, more than 100 000 (2½ per cent) are professionals. This is about the same as the number of expatriate professionals employed by aid agencies as part of an overall aid package, at a cost to the region of about $4 billion. This level of loss denies the region the optimum utilisation of the skills of its diaspora (United Nations 2003). About 23 000 university graduates and 50 000 executives leave sub-Saharan Africa annually; about 40 000 of them with PhD degrees now live outside Africa. For Nigerians and Zambians, highly-skilled professionals constitute about a half or more of expatriates living in OECD countries; 20 per cent of the nationals of Benin, Tanzania, Zimbabwe, Cameroon, Lesotho, Malawi and South Africa in the diaspora are highly-skilled professionals.

Rich countries have contributed to the 'brain drain' crisis by creating a fatal flow of health professions from the region. More Ethiopian doctors are practising in Chicago than in Ethiopia; over half of Malawian nurses and doctors have emigrated, and more Malawian doctors practise in Manchester, UK, than in Malawi; and 550 of the 600 Zambian doctors trained in medical school over the last decade have emigrated. If statistics are to be trusted, Ghana has lost 50 per cent of its doctors to Canada, Britain and the USA. Three-quarters or more of Zimbabwe's doctors have left the country since the early 1990s and half of its social health workers have relocated abroad since 2001. In 2005 more than 16 000 nurses and about 12 500 doctors from the region were registered to work in Britain (UKNMC 2005). A very similar scenario holds for the education sector.

Specialists in new technologies, engineering, medicine and healthcare are a small proportion of the emigrants from Africa, but they cost the region in a variety of ways and far beyond their numbers, not least because of the lost opportunity for the training of replacement cohorts. Tertiary educational institutions lack experienced leaders to train those required for development activities and to undertake research for development. The large exodus of doctors has impacted negatively on the training of new doctors as well as on the quality of health services delivery. The driving force is the wide differential in incomes: a trained nurse in Uganda earns $US38 per month and a doctor $67 per month, while their colleagues in the USA could earn about $3000 and $10 000, respectively.

External factors are also to blame for the negative impact of government policies on the exodus of skilled professionals. The fiscal policies imposed by international financial institutions (IMF, World Bank) that restrict provision for health and education by poor countries often have adverse effect on the brain drain phenomenon. This is the case in Kenya where, for instance, in the face of a shortage of 5 000 nurses in public facilities, 6 000 nurses are either unemployed or working outside the health sector because of a freeze on recruitment. It is imperative for governments to improve working conditions and enhance productivity through higher remunerations, revamp dilapidated equipment and infrastructure and promote workers' rights in order to retain highly-skilled workers.

There is, however, another change taking place. In many regions of the South, brain drain is being gradually transformed into brain circulation. Highly-skilled professionals, pressured to leave their countries by uncertain economic conditions, have found China, India, Taiwan, South Africa and Botswana attractive alternatives to Europe, North America and the Gulf States, thus transforming the erstwhile brain drain from Africa, into brain circulation within Africa and to other regions of the 'global South'. In Rwanda and Burundi, over a quarter of the teachers come from the Democratic Republic of Congo (DRC); the acute shortage of doctors in South Africa following the emigration of white doctors shortly before majority rule in 1994 forced the government to recruit foreign doctors, especially from Zimbabwe, the DRC and Cuba (Johns 2001).

Both brain drain and brain circulation originate largely from the same group of countries, which have invested heavily in human resources development: Ghana, Uganda, Nigeria and Kenya. The patterns of internal and intra-regional migration for these countries are similar, with highly educated men and women, who were employed in urban-centred skill-short areas – tertiary institutions, industries and parastatals – in their home countries, taking up similar posts in the destination countries. A similar pattern can be seen further South: during the past decade, Botswana has evolved from a migrant-sending to a migrant-receiving country, attracting skilled professionals, a movement fuelled largely by political stability, a fast-growing economy, prudent economic management and a small largely unskilled local labour force (Lefko-Everett 2004).

Diaspora

The migrant-diaspora-return continuum and its linkages are both strong and pervasive in Africa. During their sojourn abroad, migrants maintain contact by visiting and by sending money home (Koser 2003). Many African migrants, including those residing in developed countries, do not intend to stay indefinitely, and actualise their vision of a permanent return to home by keeping their wives and children in their countries of origin – these resident families in effect becoming 'hostages' to guarantee the migrants' return. Migrants thus lead dual lives, socially and economically, by maintaining families, land and other resources at their home-place.

The diaspora can promote the flow of trade, capital and technology back to countries of origin, and can also be active in transnational transactions (Block 2005). Migrants can acquire skills, save capital to be productively invested in ventures back home, and boost local productivity by introducing modern techniques into farming or local enterprises – as has happened in Mali and Senegal.

African diasporas are active in political advocacy; in Nigeria and Ghana charity and cultural exchange help new arrivals adapt and insert themselves into labour markets. They also mobilise members' capital for community development projects at home. Another example was a group of Nigerian doctors in the USA who planned to establish state-of-the-art hospitals in Nigeria to cater for the health needs of local people who would otherwise have had to seek treatment abroad at exorbitant cost (Adepoju 2004). Another example is the case of MIDA-Ghana's health project for strengthening the Ghanaian health sector. Migrants from Ghana in the Netherlands (and the UK), together with the local Ghanaian Embassy and the Netherlands Embassy, and in collaboration with the health sector in Ghana, have developed strategies for involving Ghanaian health professionals in the Netherlands and the UK in supporting the implementation of return of talent in the health sector in Ghana. In Benin, where more Beninoise doctors are resident in France than in their own country, migrant associations encourage migrant doctors to engage in voluntary work in Benin for one month in a year.

Migrant remittances

Migration is an increasingly important survival mechanism, and impacts at the family, community and national levels. At the community level, remittances from hometown associations serve as platforms for improving education, health and infrastructural facilities and recreation centres – responsibilities that should fall to municipal authorities – thus benefiting all households, not only those of migrants. In poor communities that lack the basic services normally provided by government, migrants' remittances pay for or supplement the pressing needs for better housing, funds to pay school fees and access to basic health services (Adepoju 2004).

At the national level, migrant remittances constitute an important source of foreign exchange. For example for Burkina Faso, Lesotho and Eritrea nationals working abroad remit huge sums of money home, thus easing credit constraints (Sander & Maimbo 2003). As well as external remittances there are also those in cash and kind flowing from urban residents – internal migrants – to their rural origins, which are largely unrecorded.

There are many ways in which remittances can benefit poor households: by sustaining living conditions, as in Lesotho and Mali; when used to pay for education and health care, as in Nigeria and Cape Verde; for the purchase of land and improvement in its productivity through irrigation schemes, as in Mali and Senegal; or for maintenance and improved housing, as in Ghana. Emigrants from Cape Verde are located in twenty-five countries across the globe, and migrant remittances are indispensable for sustaining households back home (Carling 2002). France's annual aid to Mali of $50 million is about the same as the amount remitted by Malians resident in France. Malian migrants in France have built schools and health clinics, paid for road repairs, and invested in small business enterprises in their home communities.

Remittances are also used in anticipation of migrants' return, being an important and dependable insurance, for example for building houses or setting up small enterprises in preparation for this event (IMP 2003). Returning migrants invest mainly in trading, refurbished or new buildings and high-yielding real estates. The work they participate in thus generates jobs and incomes – for example for those, including family members, who are engaged in the labour-intensive construction industry.

Not all remittances are routed via official channels, on account of heavy transaction costs. The costs of money transfers for small transactions are exorbitant – sometimes as much as 20 per cent – astronomical in comparison with the costs of bank transfers within industrial economies. But the alternative of using informal channels may be risky. Regular migrants, who are able to depend on their legal status at destination, can use a variety of channels to send money home. Irregular migrants who are vulnerable, exploitable and subject to uncertainty and insecurity, normally opt for informal channel of remittances for fear of apprehension and deportation (Van Doorn 2002). Senegalese emigrants have adapted the indigenous, trust-based traditional courier system (Kara International Exchange) and networks of traders, visiting relations and associates to send money home. This process is prompt, avoids exchange rate fluctuations and costly transfer charges, and overcomes the bottleneck of poor accessibility to remote rural areas.

Remittances can be a cause of migration, as well as a result. The demonstration effect of remittances and ostentatious expenditures by home-visiting migrants often prompt the emigration of youths to urban areas and, when they fail to find viable employment opportunities there, to richer and more attractive-seeming countries.

The discourse now in Africa is how to make remittances work productively for poor recipients, communities and countries: how to reduce transaction and transfer costs, minimise transfer risks, and enhance the domestic environment for investment. All stakeholders – governments, financial institutions, regulatory agencies, hometown associations, migrant communities, researchers and development institutions – should work in concert in exploring opportunities and minimising obstacles for remittance flow, and in particular in lobbying for low-cost transfer services and less stringent regulations, in order to increase its productive use.

Increasing female migration

Forced to do more with less, and propelled by the economic crisis, families are developing a variety of survival strategies, including autonomous female migration. Anecdotal evidence reveals an increase in migration by women, who had traditionally remained at home, while men moved around in search of paid work. The improved access of females to education and training opportunities has enhanced their employability locally and across national borders. In many parts of the region, the emergence of migrant females as bread-winners puts pressure on traditional gender roles within families. The gendered division of family labour has been upset by the loss of male employment through urban job retrenchment and structural adjustment, forcing women to seek additional income-generating activities to support the family. Such family survival strategies in the face of harsh domestic economic conditions, and changing gender roles, create new challenges for research and public policy.

In addition, a significant proportion of female migrants are educated women who move independently to fulfil their own economic needs; they are no longer simply joining a husband or other family member. No longer confined by national borders, professional women – both single and married – now engage in international migration. Married women leave their spouses behind with the children, who, in a reversal of responsibilities, are looked after by their fathers, or by other female members of the family. The remittances these women send home are a lifeline for family sustenance. This phenomenon of independent female migration constitutes an important change, and clearly can imply a turn-around in traditional gender roles, again creating new challenges for public policy.

Globalisation has introduced new labour market dynamics, including a demand for highly-skilled health care workers. Professional women – nurses and doctors – have been recruited from Nigeria, Ghana, Kenya, Malawi, Zimbabwe, South Africa and Uganda to work in Britain's National Health Service and in private home care centres. Earlier on, women were recruited to work in Saudi Arabia and Kuwait, often as nurses and domestic servants, leaving their spouses and children behind at home. For example, since 1990, when about 5000 female nurses were interviewed in Lagos for job placements in the USA and Canada, many more have been migrating, taking advantage of the network of colleagues already established (Adegbola 1990).

Once set in motion, the migration of skilled females has taken root in the UK as well, with nurses and midwives admitted through the UK Nursing and Midwifery Council (UKNMC 2005). Statistics from the UKNMC show that, from a trickle of nurses and midwives recruited from Zimbabwe, Ghana, Zambia, Botswana and Malawi in 1998/99, the number continued to rise steadily till 2004/2005. Overall, the number of nurses and midwives in the UK who came from sub-Saharan Africa rose from 915 in 1998/99 to 3789 in 2001/2002, then declined erratically to 2546 by 2004/2005. An unknown number of migrant women were recruited by private agencies to work in care homes for the elderly. Highly-skilled women migrants are however in the minority compared overall to their male counterparts who dominate the IT and business sectors.

Trafficking

As fewer migrants are able to find remunerative work in traditional regional destinations, circulation and repeat migration have expanded to a wide variety of OECD destinations. Restrictions on migration to OECD countries are, however, forcing young people to enlist the services of bogus agents, thus increasing irregular migration. Faced with strict immigration control measures and tightened barriers to legal entry in what has become a fortressed Europe, desperate youths are exploited by unscrupulous agents with promises of passages to Italy, Spain and France. Many use Libya, Morocco and Algeria as transit countries in the hazardous journey through the Sahara desert and across the Mediterranean to southern Europe. Hundreds of irregular immigrants and trafficked persons, both men and women, but mostly youths, originate from or transit through several cities in West Africa en route to Spain, but end up stranded in Las Palmas and Morocco, living in tin shanties. Those who survive are regularly apprehended and deported (Adepoju 2005).

As in the situation of regular migration, trafficking in people also takes place within, from and to Africa. The trafficking map is complicated, involving diverse origins within and outside the region. Trafficking in young children from rural areas to capital cities has increased in recent years. This includes cross-border trafficking, especially from Mali, Benin, Burkina Faso, Togo and Ghana to Côte d'Ivoire's commercial farms, as well as from and through eastern Nigeria for moving to Gabon, Equatorial Guinea, Côte d'Ivoire, Congo and Nigeria to work as domestic servants, or in the informal sector, or on plantations (UNICEF 2000). Parents are often forced by poverty and ignorance to enlist their children, hoping to benefit from their wages and sustain their families in deteriorating economic situations. Castle and Diarra (2003) warn that, in the case of West Africa, there remains a lot of grey area between child labour, child abuse, child migration and child trafficking.

Trafficking in women and children is a simmering problem in southern Africa, especially in Lesotho, Mozambique, Malawi, South Africa and Zambia. South Africa is destination for regional and extra-regional trafficking activities. Women are trafficked from refugee-producing countries, through the network of refugees already set up in South Africa. Children are trafficked to South Africa from Lesotho's border towns. In Malawi, women and girls are trafficked to northern Europe and to South Africa. Besides these configurations, women are also trafficked from Thailand, China and Eastern Europe to South Africa (IOM 2003). Trafficked victims from southern China enter South Africa through Johannesburg or across land borders from Lesotho or Mozambique, using tourist visas, study permits or false passports, and are forced to work in the sex industry. Trafficked victims from eastern Europe include Russian and other eastern European women lured to South Africa with offers of jobs as waitresses or dancers (Martens et al 2003).

Women are also trafficked from Ethiopia, Uganda and Kenya especially to Italy, Germany, Spain, France, Sweden, the UK and the Netherlands, for commercial sex; and children are trafficked for domestic labour, sexual exploitation and pornography. Conflicts, family dislocation and disintegration expose many children, especially young girls, and women to traffickers. The prolonged conflicts in Sierra Leone, Uganda and Liberia are believed to have exposed some women, victims of the civil war, to trafficking scams and bogus agents who exploit their dire situations with promises of lucrative work abroad. As a result of poverty, rural-urban migration, unemployment, broken homes, displacement and peer influence, women often fall prey to traffickers through offers of further education, marriage and remunerative jobs. Poor women who wish to migrate to rich countries may simply be looking for better job opportunities in order to assist their families. Some of them obtain huge loans to procure tickets, visas and accommodation, only to find on arrival that the promises were false, and their passports are seized by the traffickers to forestall their escape. Many of these women are stranded and helpless, but the absence of any judicial framework limits attempts by law-enforcement agencies to prosecute and punish perpetrators and their accomplices for trafficking crimes.

The lure of South Africa

Migration to South Africa was and remains a survival strategy for poor households from sending countries, and Zimbabwe, formerly the 'food basket of Africa', has become a failed state. Decades of conflict and poverty have made Mozambique a dominant source of immigrants into South Africa. Lesotho, a very poor country, is perhaps the most dependent on labour migration to South Africa; at its peak, about 50 per cent of Basotho working in the mines and on the farms of South Africa, attracted 51 per cent of the GDP through migrant remittances and deferred pay (Milazi 1998). During the apartheid era, skilled professionals, drawn especially from Ghana and Uganda, and trickles from Nigeria, migrated clandestinely to South Africa to work mainly as teachers, university professors, doctors and engineers – in contrast to the traditional immigrants who were mostly unskilled farm labourers and mine workers (Adepoju 2006).

Majority rule in South Africa in 1994 was followed by a new wave of immigrants, from Africa and especially from Eastern Europe. From West Africa came highly-skilled Nigerian and Ghanaian professionals, finding employment at universities and in other skilled workplaces. These professionals have, to some extent, been replacing the skilled white engineers and doctors who emigrated to Australia, Canada, Britain and the USA. South Africa is thus concurrently a recipient and a sender, and perhaps also a transit country, exporting skilled migrants, especially doctors, nurses, and engineers to Europe, North America and Australia.

As well as receiving highly-qualified professionals, post-apartheid South Africa has also seen a vastly increased influx of informal workers: tradesmen from Senegal and Mali, including street vendors and small traders, have ingeniously invigorated the informal sector through their aggressive commercial acumen and also by engaging locals. Previously barred under the apartheid regime, these entrepreneurs have joined their counterparts from the then Zaire, and Zimbabwe, to swell the informal sector. Many immigrants from Mozambique enter the country without proper documentation, and others – from Nigeria, Sierra Leone, Ethiopia and Zambia – frequently overstay their legal residency (Crush 1999). Many of these are deported by the South African government, but simply turn round and re-enter the country – again illegally, and often with the help of 'guides' who know the clandestine routes. In an effort to reduce the waves of Zimbabwean asylum seekers, the majority of whom are in reality economic migrants, South Africa announced on 4 May 2009 that Zimbabweans could travel to the country on a 90-day visitor's permit and apply to do casual work during their stay (*Cape Times*, 5 May 2009).

Official statistics indicate that 16 000 highly-skilled South Africans emigrated between 1994 and 2001, but the real numbers may have been under-enumerated. It is believed that about one half of South Africans living in rich countries have higher-education degrees. According to figures from the national Education

Department, the number of foreign students in South Africa's 23 public universities rose sharply from 12 577 in 1994 to 53 733 in 2006, and a quarter of these are postgraduates (University World News n.d.). Two out of three international students are from SADC member countries.

The health sector has been the most strikingly affected by migration – both inwards and outwards. Other sources (e.g. Horowitz & Kaplan 2001) indicate that between 70 and 100 doctors emigrate from South Africa every year, and that about 10 per cent of hospital doctors in Canada are South Africans. The number of South African nurses in the UK's National Health Service (NHS) rose sharply from about 600 in 1998/99 to well over 2 000 in 2001/2002. The resulting acute shortage of doctors has forced the South African government to recruit foreign doctors, especially from Zimbabwe and Cuba, the latter to work in the under-served rural areas where newly qualified doctors have since 1999 had to participate in community services (Johns 2001). In 1997, Nelson Mandela's criticism of Britain as an active recruiter of doctors and nurses from South Africa prompted the UK Ministry of Health to issue guidelines to all NHS employers in November 1999, asking them to refrain from active recruiting, especially from South Africa and the Caribbean (Buchan & Dovlo 2004). However, the problem with ethical codes lies in their enforcement: only 59 per cent of private sector recruitment agencies in the UK signed the 2001 code; non-NHS employers and recruitment agencies continue to recruit from South Africa, while also increasing recruitments from Nigeria, Ghana and Zimbabwe (Buchan 2002; Bach 2003). The South Africa–UK Memorandum of Understanding on the Reciprocal Educational Exchange of Healthcare Personnel of October 2003 included clauses for active cooperation in monitoring recruitment agencies accredited by the UK government (Republic of South Africa 2004; 2005).

Bilateral and multilateral agreements and regional consultative processes

Migration management involves the development of a comprehensive policy framework which takes into account the many urgent issues: the direct and indirect impacts of sectoral policies on trade, investment, employment, health and so on; comprehensive and coherent migration management policy formulation and its implementation; research in partnership with policy makers; and intra-agency collaboration and synergy between sectoral policies (see Chapter 6 of this book). The aim of migration dialogue is to engage all stakeholders – policy makers, politicians, civil society, the media, migrant associations, divergent constituencies – who often have conflicting interests in matters of migration management (IOM 2002).

Migration cannot be effectively managed by unilateral action: bilateral relations need to be forged between the countries sending and receiving migrants within and outside Africa, and also, in this context, multilateral arrangements between sub-regional economic unions and OECD countries. Sub-regional economic organisations are potential avenues for multinational cooperation and policy development regarding migration – more so where these are dominated by the economies of a single country, and where movements of people have been directed to these core countries. Examples of this are Botswana and South Africa in southern Africa, Gabon in central Africa, Kenya in eastern Africa, and Côte d'Ivoire and Nigeria in West Africa. In reality, the prosperity of many of these 'magnet' countries was built by migrant labour – cocoa and coffee plantations in Ghana and Côte d'Ivoire, mines and agriculture in South Africa, forestry and oil in Gabon. Resource-rich but labour-short countries such as Botswana, Gabon, Côte d'Ivoire and Libya rely heavily on immigrant labour (Adepoju 2000).

Policy and programmes

There are daunting challenges with respect to all forms of migratory flows, but especially regarding irregular migration, human trafficking, and the emigration of skilled professionals. The situation calls for the development of a co-ordinated implementation of policies and programmes and a comprehensive framework to address issues of migration. The problems posed by migration, circulation, permanent residence and settlement – and the policy responses to them – are quite different for each migratory configuration within the different sub-regions, and even within individual countries, and are seemingly intractable.

There is no formal forum in Africa specifically for the discussion of migration matters by all stakeholders – in particular the media and the public – as a continuous process, in order to avoid the misrepresentations, ignorance and xenophobia that currently surround the issue of migration. Discourses on migration, especially from the receiving end, are full of anxiety, misconceptions, myths and prejudices, and are often fed on xenophobia. In that context, the positive aspects of migrants as agents of development in source and destination countries needs to be made far more widely-known, and more explicit. Dialogue and consultations among the various stakeholders, to discuss common approaches to their migration concerns and interests, share ideas, and enhance understanding and cooperation in migration management could lead to the development of a coherent policy framework for the management of migration.

As Afolayan observes in Chapter 6, in many countries the institutional capacity required to manage migratory flows and for effective policy formulation and implementation is weak, and must be strengthened through capacity building – the training and retraining – of officials. At the national level, collaboration between and within agencies of government dealing with migration matters is essential but rarely exists at the moment. The key role of trade relations, and especially the short and long term effects of bilateral and multilateral trade agreements on migration, is not yet evident or appreciated by many migration stakeholders and should be explicitly recognised while conducting trade negotiations.

The African Economic Community and NEPAD (New Partnership for Africa's Development) both advocate programmes to foster labour mobility within and between the countries of the region, as well as sustained development of the region (see Chapter 2). For countries that remain ambivalent regarding the principle of free movement of persons and reluctant to modify domestic laws and administrative practices, now is the time to realign national laws with sub-regional treaties to facilitate intra-regional labour mobility, establishment and settlement. Lessons learnt from ECOWAS (the Economic Community of West African States) in creating a borderless sub-region should be replicated by other sub-regional organisations. Although migration is, increasingly, a global phenomenon, migration in Africa remains largely regional and should be addressed – at least immediately – within NEPAD's framework. In this way NEPAD could strengthen regional economic groupings and play a larger role in the management of intra-regional labour migration. As already mentioned, intra-regional migrations are generally directed towards only a few countries within sub-regional economic unions, and are usually dominated by the economies of a single country. In view of the controversial nature of the migration debate in parts of Africa, especially in southern Africa and the Maghreb, a regional dialogue and consultative approach is urgently required to help balance the interests of sending-and receiving-countries and migrants alike.

A major challenge now facing the region is how to retain, attract back and effectively utilise the rare skills of its nationals, as is required for national development. The Homecoming Revolution[2], a non-profit online initiative begun in 2004, encourages and assists South Africans living abroad to return home, offering a range of practical help and advice, backed up by financial and business services. Ghana's Homecoming Summit held in Accra in 2001 encourages the diaspora to return with offers of incentives, including favourable local investment opportunities and tax-relief for returnees (Ghanaian Government 2001). The Ghanaian Dual Citizenship Regulation Act was promulgated in 2002 and a Non-Resident Ghanaians Secretariat was set up in May 2004, the latter to promote links with the diaspora and to encourage their return. The Nigerians in Diaspora Organisation in Europe, the Americas, Asia and Africa mobilises and promotes cooperation and networking among Nigerians in diaspora to promote national development and is building a database of diaspora Nigerians with professional skills.

Leaders in Ethiopia, Ghana, Mali, Kenya, Nigeria, Uganda and Senegal, among others, are increasingly interested in promoting migrant remittances for investment purposes, and are using their embassies to disseminate information on domestic investment opportunities to their nationals abroad, encouraging them to return with offers of incentives. The boom in the domestic real estate

---

2 http://www.homecomingrevolution.co.za/

market has encouraged many Ghanaians abroad to remit money home and has also created local jobs with multiplier effects on income and consumption among the resident population.

African leaders must address the push factors that spurred the brain drain – conflicts, political instability, abuses of human rights, poor remuneration and deteriorating working environments, job insecurity and so on – so that potential returnees can expect to work in environments conducive to productivity, with due reward for effort. In addition, health sector reform should be pursued with vigour to ensure that the skills needed for national socio-economic development are effectively utilised. Poverty alleviation and employment generation for the teeming unemployed youth population should be the cornerstone of the region's development agenda. More importantly, governments must invest in job creation to make investments in social capital pay off, and ensure mutually beneficial trade relations with rich countries to improve living conditions, stimulate economic growth, and generate employment opportunities. They should also institute incentive-based tax regimes to attract migrants' remittances and ensure their productive, employment-generating investment.

As Adepoju emphasises in Chapter 7, bilateral and multilateral agreements between countries sending and receiving migrants should address the issue of depleting Africa of its scarce skilled-manpower resources. It is important that residential laws of rich countries be made flexible, to give skilled professionals the opportunity of relocating without losing their residence rights in those countries. Information about the regulations guiding entry, residence and employment abroad should be disseminated to potential emigrants in countries having, or likely to have, a significant potential emigrant population. In addition, emotive public reactions based on 'immigration myths' – that immigration is massive, with immigrants swarming into receiving OECD countries (Heran 2004) – should be treated with caution as they are often not based on empirical data.

African societies and individuals have traditionally been hospitable to strangers, welcoming them and sharing their limited resources with them. This is no longer the case in many countries. Increasingly, political leaders have resorted to the use of ethnicity and religion to reclassify long-standing residents as non-nationals – for example, in Côte d'Ivoire, a major country of immigration in West Africa. During tightly contested elections leaders are wary of the presence of large numbers of immigrants within their shores, fearing that they might swing the vote along ethnic or religious lines in favour of the opposition (Adepoju 2002). Events in Côte d'Ivoire show how changes arising from a liberal immigration policy can impact negatively on the migration space, stability and development of a country. Aliens are scapegoats in periods of economic recession and are accused of stealing jobs from nationals, stigmatised as criminals (for example in Botswana and South Africa) (Campbell 2003). Indeed South Africa, a major destination of intra-regional migration, has become increasingly xenophobic. Press and politicians fan public discontent, driving a wedge between immigrants and locals clamouring for the latter's expulsion. In May 2008, the orchestrated attacks on immigrants in South Africa in Pretoria and Cape Town shocked the world – many were killed or forced to leave their abode. Migrants are uniformly blamed for untested negative aspects of migration, and extensive public education is required to halt the hostility against immigrants and showcase the positive aspects of migrants as agents of development in both source and destination countries.

To ensure a coherent migration policy, current data-collection methods must be reviewed, updated and expanded, and the key agencies responsible for migration matters need to coordinate their activities more transparently and more effectively. At the moment, information on the stock and flow of emigrants from the region is more readily available in the destination countries than it is in the countries of origin. Countries of origin need to institutionalise the collection of data on internal, intra-regional and international migration, and to endeavour to keep track of the number and characteristics of their nationals emigrating abroad. A modest start has begun in SADC (the Southern African Development Community) with the 2000 round of censuses that collected information on cross-border migrations.

Today, no country of the world remains unaffected by international migration flows – as origin, transit or destination for migrants, or all three simultaneously. The movements of people are global processes. Globalisation facilitates movement of components such as capital, information and technology, but frowns on that of labour. As economic and political processes evolve, and the global economic recession deepens, the major challenge is how to make migration work productively for migrants, and also for origin and destination countries, and societies and families at home. On-going financial and economic crises have led to millions of job losses resulting from closures of factories and other enterprises in rich countries. Policy dialogue on migration is thus at a crossroads, not least because diverse actors and stakeholders in poor and rich countries, and a variety of constituencies and interest groups have genuine, even if conflicting, interests. In poor and rich countries, economic and demographic factors underline current debate and policy on migration. Rich countries need immigrants to cope with prevailing economic and demographic imperatives: unskilled, sometimes undocumented immigrants to do poorly paid, dirty, and dangerous jobs which nationals scorn; and highly-skilled professionals – engineers, doctors and nurses – who are locally in short supply.

The chapters of this book

The key issues introduced in the preceding sections are elaborated in greater depth in the chapters of this volume.

In *Chapter 2, Anthony Barclay* argues strongly that in Africa, human migration has historically manifested itself as an important feature of the socio-cultural, economic and political lives of the people. Currently, while this observation remains valid, the migratory flows, characteristics, trends and processes are more complex and diverse with multifaceted consequences for migrants and for their countries of origin, transit and destination. These consequences impact national development through opportunities for and constraints on peace, security, political advancement and socio-economic growth. Various initiatives are being undertaken to understand the complexity of the migration-development nexus and to explore possible ways of maximising positive effects and minimising negative ones.

Given the regional and global dimensions of migration, it is widely acknowledged that effective management of migration is imperative not only at the country level, but also at regional and international levels. At the regional level, regional organisations are expected to play a major role in the process. From this perspective, Barclay takes stock of the potential and progress of, and constraints on, some of the initiatives of regional organisations over the period since they were established, highlighting the cases of the ECOWAS Commission and SADC. He also examines the role of the African Union (AU) and the implications for the African Economic Community (AEC) as envisaged under the 1991 Abuja Treaty within the context of intra-regional migration and development in Africa.

The substantive issues discussed by Barclay include: (a) an historical overview of intra-regional migration in Africa, highlighting the levels, trends, characteristics, causes and other factors – including gender dimensions – that define the nature of African intra-regional migration; (b) theoretical and empirical views on the implications of and potential for development through intra-regional migration; and (c) the role and functions of some of the Regional Economic Communities (RECs) in the migration-development nexus management process with respect to intra-regional migration, and their achievements, constraints and opportunities.

At the regional management level, most of the treaties and protocols of the RECs advocate for or stipulate the freedom of movement of people, and certain guarantees for residence and establishment, including access to and management of other factors of production. Some RECs – in particular in the ECOWAS countries, and to a lesser extent in SADC – have made more progress than others in the promotion of intra-regional migration. Despite the progress made, there are still significant on-going challenges. For example, some of the instruments for promoting intra-regional migration have either not been effectively brought into force or the implementation of the programmes and operational mechanisms needed to have them fully functional is fraught with difficulties.

According to Barclay, these challenges have been, and are likely to continue to be, conditioned by political fluctuations, socio-economic circumstantial pressures and mistrust of some governments by other governments in member states. Other constraints observed are due to human, financial and similar capacity inadequacies, as well as the lack of enforcement mechanisms to ensure compliance with agreed decisions. Furthermore, the general problems of multiple memberships, inadequate translation of regional economic community goals into national plans and budgets, general laxity in programme implementation, and ineffective continental coordination exacerbate the problems of intra-regional migration.

As a way forward, Barclay argues that the prospects are not as bleak as sometimes portrayed. First, he says, it is encouraging to note that on the national level, despite some political and economic setbacks in a few countries, there is a general positive trend. In many countries there is a steady consolidation of peace and democracy, greater political inclusiveness, an expanded voice of the people, greater public sector accountability, and improved economic management. Second, progress is also being made at the regional level, albeit slowly and sometimes with fluctuations due to historical, political and socio-economic setbacks. An important consideration however is that there is heightened awareness in Africa, at the highest level, of the critical need for enhanced intra-regional migration as a pre-requisite for the realisation of the AEC. In that context, concerted efforts should be made to accelerate the process by consolidating the achievements and steadfastly addressing the lingering and emerging constraints of the RECs.

From this context, Barclay proposes that the following actions be undertaken: (a) increase support for and utility of gender-sensitive and results-oriented regional consultative processes on intra-regional migration; (b) strengthen internal and external efforts to reinforce and sustain human, financial, technical, legal and institutional capacities; (c) develop and institutionalise a robust knowledge-management and statistical information system, on migration in general and intra-regional migration in particular; (d) provide regular support for an African migration-development nexus and related policy-oriented research; (e) intensify and widely promote public awareness campaigns about current and emerging migration issues relevant to evidence-based information on the advantages and disadvantages of migrating, as well as regarding the rights and responsibilities of migrants; (f) institutionalise and strengthen legal measures to deter criminal cross-border activities, including human and illicit drugs trafficking and smuggling; (g) institutionalise measures to eliminate xenophobic and negative exploitative tendencies directed at labour migrants; (h) increase resource-mobilisation efforts and ensure adequate results-based and accountability-based absorptive capacity of the RECs; (i) continuously develop and nurture partnerships and networks with civil society, other non-state actors, the private sector, other continental organisations and the international community; (j) continue to vigilantly pursue poverty alleviation and human development goals.

Away from Barclay's discourse, and with respect to the 'brain drain' discourse, the global migration market allows developed countries to select unilaterally who should be admitted, what skills combinations and income profiles are preferred, and when and for how long migrants may stay – all this without recourse to the countries of origin which incurred human capital investment in the migrants. These highly qualified professionals – specialists in IT, engineering and medicine – whose skills are internationally marketable, are a small proportion of the emigrants but their absence nevertheless costs poor countries in a variety of ways, not least the capacity – already mentioned – to train replacement cohorts. This is especially the case for doctors from Nigeria, Ghana, South Africa and Zimbabwe.

In many African countries today, students are being churned out without the requisite rigour of learning, thereby both stalling development activities and accelerating the collapse of institutions. The outflow of highly-skilled professionals from Africa has resulted in a breakdown in institutions which are now bereft of trained personnel to manage them in an era of development paradigm shifts. In the meantime, aid programmes paradoxically import about 100 000 expatriate professionals with the same skills possessed by Africans in diaspora, at a cost to the region of about $4 billion yearly. The region thereby pays the price of producing the human capital for use by the rich countries; at the same time it is denied the realisation of development goals by the outflow of scarce skilled manpower.

The 2002 estimate of the International Organization for Migration (IOM) and the World Bank was that 3.6 million Africans were living in Europe and North America, including more than 100 000 professionals; that about 23 000 African university graduates, and 50 000 executives leave the region annually, and about 40 000 Africans with PhDs live outside Africa (UN 2003; IOM 2004b). It is estimated that people of foreign origin represent 12 per cent of the highly qualified component of the labour force in the USA, and this may well be true of many countries of Europe today. Probably about a third of researchers and engineers from poor countries work in OECD countries – a significant number indeed and a huge human capital flow produced at great cost by poor countries. The USA 'diversity visa' programme was designed to liberalise immigration by creating entry avenues for new sources of immigration, and Africans with professional, technical and managerial skills have frequently used it to enter that country. As early as the 1990s they numbered about 52 000, making up 7 percent of the total of professional, technical and managerial immigrants to the USA. Understandably, a major challenge facing Africa now is how to retain, effectively utilise and attract back the rare skills of its nationals required for national development.

Chapter 3a is by Ben hadj Abdellatif. He argues that emigration has beneficial effects on the countries of origin as it relieves the labour market, contributes to the balance of payments and financing for development as well as enhancing the skills of returnees. Surveys conducted in Egypt, Tunisia, Morocco and other African countries showed that, having gained knowledge and experience to become entrepreneurs, returning migrants invest in development projects by creating small and medium enterprises at home. Investment in housing, in particular, not only improves the quality of life of those who benefit, but it creates a dynamic local economy and stimulates the proliferation of sectors related to housing – the selling of building materials, construction companies, carpentry and so on. Agriculture has also benefited from migrant remittances, which enable the expansion of agricultural activities and the modernisation of production on family farms. Given their potential contribution to development in all countries, greater participation of migrants in local, regional and national development of their countries of origin should be promoted.

African emigrants rarely sever their ties with home; they hope to return at the earliest opportunity and contribute to the development of their countries – for instance, when Germany offered to retain foreign graduates through the Green Card scheme, less than a third of the quota was taken up at the expiration of the scheme. Informed by this scenario, some foreign international corporations in Europe have launched programmes to recruit Africans in the diaspora to work in their multinational corporations in Africa – a process that Abdellatif believes should be encouraged. Building networks with their colleagues at home enables diaspora scientists to contribute to the development of home countries without residential relocation, but the stiff immigration policies of rich countries preclude many scientists the flexibility to relocate. Indian IT specialists are working for American companies in India – without physical dislocation and with considerable economic mobility. Such possibilities should be encouraged also for specialists in Africa. Networking between professionals in the diaspora and their counterparts in training, technology transfer, information exchange and research projects – principally via the Internet – should be encouraged. But the challenges are daunting: many poor African countries lack the appropriate infrastructure.

African disaporas are active in political advocacy, charity and cultural exchange. For example, the Ghanaian diaspora in the UK have pressed for and received concession from their government allowing them to vote in national elections. As regards activity in the home country, these migrants are actively involved in modernising political processes, as well as helping to reinforce cultural identity, and mobilise members' capital for community development projects.

Lessons learnt from the IOM's Return and Reintegration of Qualified Nationals project, and from Migration for Development in Africa (MIDA) and similar programmes (IOM 2004a) can be useful in evaluating policy interventions aimed both at attracting back and at effectively utilising the skills of Africans in the diaspora. In this context, Abdellatif points out that we need more such evidence-based research to promote country-of-origin development.

Chapter 3b, by T.O. Fadayomi, complements Abdellatif's discussion. He argues that the emigration of skilled professionals from Africa is a phenomenon that started about a decade after most of African countries attained political independence and has been growing from that time up till the present. This phenomenon is the outcome of social, political and economic forces that have shaped the continent since the era of statehood and self-determination. For most of the period since independence, the post-colonial economy of sub-Saharan African states was based on state capitalism, with the dependence on the primary commodities of agriculture and mining, the unimpressive growth of value-added industries and the generally unfavourable terms of trade all leading to a slowness of growth in formal employment, accompanied by inflation and an underdeveloped private enterprise.

The post-independence drive for African self-sufficiency in high-level manpower led to substantial investments in education and a rapid increase in educational facilities and the award of scholarships for foreign acquisition of skills. The outcome has been the production of a large number of graduates out of tune with local employment opportunities. Access to specialisation in developed countries has often led to over-specialisation, reducing professionals' ability to secure challenging jobs in their home countries. Some professionals therefore remain in the developed countries where they did their training, while others return home but after a while seek exit to countries offering greater opportunities.

The pervasive autocratic and military-style regimes across Africa prior to the democratic wave of the early 1990s was another important push factor of emigration of professionals in Africa. It fuelled the desire to emigrate among political opponents, including academics and professionals, who were constantly threatened with arrest and detention. While African professionals were facing repressive regimes and abuses of human rights, especially in the 1980s, the educational system in most African countries had begun a process of decay, mainly due to IMF structural adjustment policies which encouraged further curtailment of public sector employment and de-industrialisation. These policies also curtailed investments in education and health, induced the retrenchment of professionals in the civil service and tertiary institutions, as well as the devaluation of salaries and benefits, and the disintegration of infrastructures in universities and health care delivery institutions. Strengthening the push factors, too, are the immigration laws in the major immigrant countries, which have been selective in attracting skilled manpower to those countries.

While there are no adequate statistics on the emigration of skilled professionals from Africa, the estimated magnitude and patterns of emigration showed that in the 1960s the dominant paths of migration were from Africa to the metropolitan powers with African colonies (or ex-colonies), such as Britain, France, Portugal and Belgium. Other paths led to other important non-metropolitan countries such as those of North America and other countries in Western Europe, where most of the professional skills were acquired. According to the ECA and IOM, an estimated 27 000 skilled Africans left the continent for industrialised countries between 1960 and 1975. In the 1970s, however, major sub-Saharan African oil-producing countries such as Nigeria and Gabon witnessed an economic boom, as did countries like Ivory Coast, which had a large agricultural surplus at the time. These countries became alternative destinations for some of the African skilled migrants who would previously have headed for the metropolitan countries.

The emigration of highly skilled Africans, which started to increase in the 1970s, intensified in the 1980s and 1990s because of worsened economic conditions. As a result, a substantial number of highly-skilled persons joined the stream of migrants from areas where economies had collapsed. Countries such as Nigeria and Zimbabwe, that had not long before been havens for emigrants from other parts of Africa, started themselves to produce skilled emigrants, as their economies declined. In addition to the metropolis, the USA and Western Europe, new destinations opened for African skills in the Gulf States and South Africa. While precise figures for these patterns of emigration are not known, ECA and IOM estimated that at least 20 000 skilled Africans left the continent each year during the 1990s (UN 2003). In a 1995 World Bank study, it was noted that at that time some 23 000 qualified academics were emigrating from Africa each year in search of better working conditions (World Bank 1995). After agitations for improvements in the conditions of service and funding of university education had failed, the poor economic status of teachers and the disintegration of infrastructure in the universities created a launch pad for emigration. Similarly, health professionals emigrated under pressure from unrelenting economic problems and intolerable working conditions. Although the situation witnessed some improvements at the dawn of the new century, the emigration of skilled professionals has not abated.

Given the demand for skilled professionals in the advanced industrial economies, and the institutional support for their immigration there, the migration of skilled African professionals away from their home countries has become inevitable. African governments therefore need to put in place realistic policies to minimise the costs of emigration and maximise the benefits by addressing the underlying causes. Among such intervention policies would be providing research facilities in higher institutions of learning, better conditions of work and pay, and deepening the democratic process to enhance good governance, human rights and the rule of law. As well as this – and as concluded by other authors – Africa needs to adopt an effective management mechanism to make migrant remittances more development-oriented, and to develop appropriate incentives and institutions to engage the diaspora in the transformation of Africa.

From the 1980s, African international migration has been viewed as an important resource for development in African countries in terms of the diaspora and their remittances. These two resources underline the inevitability of diaspora's involvement in, and the flow of remittances to, African countries, mediated by international events and local factors. *In Chapter 4, John Oucho* examines in greater detail the role of the African diaspora and their remittances in leveraging development in African countries. In trying to unravel the impact of diaspora remittances on poverty alleviation, the chapter defines and explains the diversity of the African diaspora; considers the sources, volume and value of migrant and diaspora remittances; attempts to unpack the contribution of the diaspora in homeland development as well as the utilisation of the remittances sent, with particular focus on poverty alleviation; and, finally, analyses whether the diaspora and their remittances do in fact leverage poverty reduction in African countries.

Migrants in different categories in the diaspora play different roles by committing their skills and knowledge to homeland development and by sending remittances which stimulate development and, to a certain extent, reduce poverty. Although the notion of remittances conjures up only the monetary aspect, remittance also embraces non-monetary flows, including social remittances. These can take place in different forms: permanent return to the home country; short-and long-term sabbatical placements due to family circumstances, children's education, mortgages, career advancement and so on; as well as the 'virtual return' of talents and skills described above.

Four African case studies are described by Oucho, representing different types of diaspora and remittances to the countries of origin. Morocco represents northern African emigration to Europe, and Oucho discusses the nature and extent of Moroccan diaspora in homeland development through remittances and other means. Ghana is a classical case of successive generations of diaspora found in different parts of the world, most of whom have an exemplary commitment to Ghanaian development. Somalia exemplifies the way in which a refugee diaspora has sustained its motherland, despite the lack of an operational government at home. Finally there is Zimbabwe, a country where decade-long repression and an unbearable economic crisis have forced the people out of their country, to live elsewhere in southern Africa, and in Europe. Their remittances have, to a large degree, sustained relatives and friends left behind.

Return of the diaspora is another option on which African countries pin their hopes. This, Oucho argues, raises several questions, among them are the nature and infrastructure of the environment in African countries to which the diaspora is expected to return; suspicion or lukewarm relations between the diaspora and nationals back home; and possibilities of virtual return should the IT infrastructure become more reliable in the countries of origin.

In concluding, Oucho outlines several key points. For African countries to harness diasporas and remittances in their development process, they should formulate policies in which they involve the diaspora themselves; improve the investment environment, and be constantly responsive to changes positively affecting utilisation of migrant remittances. African countries need to emulate the policy frameworks and programmes which have emanated from the Latin American region. It should be remembered, too, that there exists ambiguity in analysing the impact of migration and poverty on each other: poverty may induce people to migrate to improve their livelihoods and the migrants may in turn become further impoverished and more vulnerable.

More importantly, as mentioned also by Oucho, future research, policy and programmes concerned with remittances should not neglect the effect of social remittance. In view of the growing importance of migration and development interrelations, Africa requires a series of African Migration Surveys in the mould of the African demographic and health surveys. This is a challenge to the African Union and the Economic Commission for Africa in their quest for implementing migration and development frameworks that are meant to serve their member states. Finally, both internal and international migration and their inherent consequences should be factored into poverty reduction strategy policy and the Millennium Development Goals, thereby making them an integral part of mitigating and eventually eradicating poverty from the African scene.

Chapter 5, by Eugene Campbell, examines the causes, processes and consequences of irregular migration from within Africa to South Africa and from West Africa and the Maghreb to the European Union (EU). Irregular migration, he points out, is not only about crossing international borders without valid documents; it also includes overstaying beyond the period allowed by a visa.

Campbell recalls that irregular migration to South Africa began as early as the 1920s. Government policies restricted non-white migrant labour to South Africa, permitting only work on the mines, and thus triggering irregular labour migration to that country. In West Africa, relatively unrestricted immigration in colonial times was followed in the post-colonial period with efforts by African governments to protect their territories. In Ghana, for instance, many of those deemed 'irregular migrants' in the 1960s were actually descendants of families whose movement to (and stay in) the country had been legal generations before. Generally, economic factors, corruption and poverty are the strongest motivators of irregular migration in West and southern Africa, facilitated by porous borders.

Contemporary issues on irregular migration involve migration to and in South Africa as well as African migration to Europe. However, estimating the number of irregular migrants in South Africa, and from Africa to the EU, is problematic. Figures provided by various sources about South Africa ranged from 2.5 to 4 million in 2004, but with the recent exodus from Zimbabwe, it is very likely that the total number is considerably more than the upper figure of this range. The EU estimates are much more likely to be reliable because of the efforts made there to develop meaningful migration policies. The political and economic failures that produced brain drain from the continent largely explain why many Africans become irregular migrants. Geographical distance is also a relatively important factor in influencing irregular migration to South Africa and the EU.

Botswana is a transit point for irregular migration to South Africa. In the north, the Maghreb is the principal transit point of migrants whose destination is the EU. The major destinations of irregular migrants from the Maghreb are France, Spain, the Netherlands, Italy, Belgium and Germany, and the major sources Morocco, Tunisia and Algeria in the Maghreb, and Senegal, Nigeria and Ghana in West Africa. The passage to the EU is much more complex and financially costly than it is to southern Africa. The risks involved frequently result in injury, or even the death of the migrants.

To complement Campbell's suggestion, the notion of there being an excess of unwanted, largely unskilled, migrant workers needs to be re-examined in light of the reality in Europe. In southern Spain, for example, immigrants from Morocco work in unpleasant conditions picking vegetables; thousands of Poles do similar work in Germany; Indians pick fruits in Belgium; Russians harvest crops in Ireland; Latvian, Ukranian, and Lithuanian youths are recruited seasonally to cut, wash, and pack spring onions for the supermarket chains in Britain. These temporary migrants are vital to the local economies and authorities and locals turn a blind eye to their presence. As living conditions in Europe improve, the aspiration of Europeans, especially youths, to do only clean, sedentary, well-paid jobs is constantly on the rise. Without unskilled migrant workers who do the unglamorous jobs which indigenes are increasingly reluctant to take up, some services in rich countries could not function. The migrants help sustain jobs, not only in the dirty, dangerous and poorly paid jobs, but also in other areas. Indeed the Minister responsible for employment in Spain put it bluntly thus: 'We need people to do the jobs Spaniards no longer want to do.' (*The Economist*, 6 May 2000).

This scenario is not a preserve of the rich countries. In South Africa, for instance, despite widespread unemployment, in some areas locals will not pick fruit and vegetables, leaving these 'demeaning' jobs to migrant workers from neighbouring Lesotho.

Among the problems faced by migrant workers is the fact that undocumented immigrants are exploited and vulnerable, compelled to accept jobs irrespective of the risk, physical demands, low and irregular wages, and long working hours. Conscious of the fact that these illegal workers can neither unionise nor approach the authorities for redress, it is not uncommon for employers to lay off undocumented migrants at the end of a work period without paying them – with the threat of exposing their undocumented status, which would result in their expulsion (Human Rights Watch 1998).

Campbell is of the opinion that the economic benefits of irregular migration to destination countries are huge. Remittances to families at home help improve access to basic needs and can alleviate moderate poverty. But emigration from rural areas has adversely affected agricultural production, especially in the Maghreb.

Alice Afolayan, in Chapter 6, states that the rationale for setting up an institutional framework for the management of migrants, data and information globally – and in particular in Africa – is to promote the formulation and implementation of an effective migration policy. Migration, as a process, involves different elements of management at various stages. Since the onus for formulating policies, including migration policy, falls on the state, it is the state that must synchronise and coordinate migration policy within its overall activities for the good of the nation and of society. However, the development plans and activities of many African governments have not reflected sufficient consideration of migration factors, nor of the management system that would be needed to keep track of the dynamics of migration. Rather, migration issues have been handled as an adjunct issue in many African states, as well as in regional bodies. Also, many African government ministries, international agencies and non-governmental organisations have been working as separate units, with very few of them sharing data, information and practices on migration issues.

Using the IOM's 'Conceptual Model for Comprehensive Migration Management' as it relates to the establishment of an institutional framework for managing migration, Afolayan explains that it is the state that sets the goal for this model, which is the promotion of migration rather than its restriction. Using the expertise and knowledge of institutions which collect, collate and publish data and information for migration policy, the four main areas of migration management that the state should coordinate are migration and development, migration facilitation, migration regulation and forced migration – replacing irregular flows with orderly, regular migration and harnessing regular migration to serve the interests of all, including the governments. The state is, therefore, to oversee the diverse, cross-cutting management and activities associated with these four main aspects of the management of migration.

At national level, since most African governments have no comprehensive migration policy, holistic institutional frameworks have not been established. For instance, the Nigerian government created a draft of a National Policy on Migration in 2007 and was proposing the establishment of an Agency or Commission for managing the different migration issues. At regional level, ECOWAS, faced with the challenges of managing migration and the lack of a well-designed institutional framework, is prioritising effective management of migration as a regional phenomenon. Consequently, it has set in motion a flood of activities and institutions on regulating migration – with fewer activities and institutions directed at harnessing or facilitating migration and forced migrations. The ECOWAS coordinating unit at the national level is the individual Member State's National Task Force, whose activities are coordinated by the ECOWAS Trafficking in Persons Unit.

Also, the Joint ECCAS/ECOWAS Plan of Action against Trafficking in Persons, especially women and children in West and Central Africa (2006-2009) explicitly stipulates which different ministries, agencies and international organisations are to handle migration issue in the two regions. In all these, evidence abounds that the regional bodies are quicker in naming and allotting activities for regulating migration (trafficking in persons) than for actually facilitating migration (regular migration).

With the assistance of the International Organization for Migration (IOM), the agendas of the Migration Dialogue for Southern Africa (MIDSA) and the Migration Dialogue for Western Africa (MIDWA) also address migration management, through regional dialogue and cooperation on migration-related issues. In all, Afolayan concludes that an institutional framework for managing migration for Africa as a unit is yet to be defined. All the frameworks that exist presently are in the form of documents highlighting the premises for considering migration. These include outcomes of seminars and recommendations of ministerial meetings. Among these seminars are the Seminar on Intra-African Migration (Cairo, 1995), the Euro-Africa Ministerial Conference on Migration and Development (Rabat, 2006), and the Joint Africa-EU Declaration on Migration and Development (Tripoli, 2006).

The final chapter, by Aderanti Adepoju, on promoting managed migration through bilateral and multilateral agreements between European migrant-receiving countries and African migrant-sending countries analyses a series of bilateral and multilateral agreements set up since 2001 between African sending- and EU receiving-countries with large concentrations of immigrants.

These agreements are aimed at fostering an improved migration management mechanism through cooperation, capacity-building and dialogue between the countries concerned; promoting managed migration for employment purposes by expanding avenues for regular labour migration, and ensuring ethical recruitment of health professionals from poor countries. They aim to address aspects such as admission procedures, flows, social security, family reunification, integration policy, and return, and to prevent and combat irregular labour migration. Other agreements are aimed at fostering an improved migration management mechanism through cooperation, capacity-building and dialogue between the countries concerned, the latter in the context of the 2001 Berne Initiative. Further initiatives aim at promoting managed migration for employment purposes – for instance by expanding avenues for regular labour migration, while having regard to market needs and demographic trends in the various countries. Yet others are focused on issues such as the ethical recruitment of health professionals from poor countries.

Adepoju reviews the objectives of these bilateral agreements, how these were implemented, the lessons learnt and the best practices employed. He makes recommendations that take into account the interests and concerns of countries of origin and destination, as well as of the migrants themselves. Examples he gives are Nigeria, which is a major source of trafficked victims in women and children for sexual exploitation in Europe; Senegal, as a major country of departure for irregular migrants attempting to cross to Europe via the Canary Islands; and Mali, as a major source of irregular migrants but also as the site for the EU's pilot project on development and job creation to reduce poverty and help retain potential emigrants. Some detail is also given of the situation regarding the Maghreb region, especially Morocco.

Adepoju summarises the attitudes and actions of the EU towards migrant-sending countries in Africa in five key points. Firstly, the initial concern in Europe was with rounding up irregular migrants and victims of trafficking and deporting them from Europe back to their countries of origin. In most cases this was done without consultation with the countries of origin and often effected in inhumane conditions and in breach of the rights of the expellees. His second point is that emphasis did later shift to some form of dialogue and consultation with the sending countries, with the objective of guaranteeing the readmission at home of the irregular persons to be expelled. A part of this strategy was the tightening of border controls in what became 'fortressed Europe', and a zero tolerance of irregular migration. Third, outsourcing the responsibility for policing of borders, and halting irregular migrants from the EU to Morocco, Libya and Algeria is a strategy that is both unrealistic and unsustainable. These Maghreb countries include those with poor records of human rights which also lack the financial and logistical facilities essential for carrying out the defence of their borders against the surge of irregular immigrants from other parts of Africa and beyond. The fourth phase involves rewarding cooperating sending countries with donations of technical and operational equipment – to make 'home' more desirable, and thus contain irregular emigration from source. This 'carrot' part of the 'carrot and stick' strategy also rewards cooperating sending countries by granting only token work quotas for their nationals in receiving countries. The last refers to the most recent phase: recognising that strict control does not produce the desired results – and instead inadvertently spurs trafficking – the EU countries have proposed investing in job creation, economic growth and poverty alleviation schemes inside Africa, in order to stem the tide of irregular emigration. This strategy includes some form of 'guest worker' scheme, as well as circulatory migration that allows Africans to work in regular situations for fixed periods of time in specified sectors of labour shortage in EU countries. Mali is serving as a pilot for this strategy.

In all these phases, Adepoju notes that the receiving countries of the EU have been the prime architects of the schemes, initiating the bilateral agreements, their contents, the modalities for their implementation, and providing funds to cajole sending countries to fall in line and implement the agreements. Sending countries do not seem to have sufficiently critical inputs in the negotiations leading to the agreements – which are therefore mostly Eurocentric. Little wonder then that some of the earlier agreements have not been implemented in either the letter or the spirit of these accords.

As already mentioned in other contexts, bilateral and multilateral agreements between countries sending and receiving migrants must also address the issue of depleting Africa of its scarce skilled-manpower resources. It is important that residential laws of rich countries be made flexible, to give skilled professionals the opportunity of relocating without losing their residence rights in those countries.

African countries need to ensure that their specific interests and concerns are adequately reflected in any bilateral or multilateral migration negotiations. Issues relating to the treatment of their nationals living and working in regular situations in EU countries, the rights of irregular migrants to basic services, and the need to review the unfair trade regimes which impoverish the millions who are engaged in farming at home should assume centre stage in future migration agreements. Efforts should be made to revisit existing agreements in order to review and amend unfavourable conditions. Above all, Adepoju concludes, the embassies and missions of African countries should provide their nationals with appropriate information on the rules that guide entry, residence and work – in short, their rights and obligations when they are in receiving societies.

Overview

Migration is a factor of development; immigrants in general bring their energy, determination and enterprise and can dynamise economies, social organisation and interchange of experience. As economic and political processes evolve, the major challenge is how to channel migration movements to benefit the three key actors: the migrants themselves, origin and destination countries, and societies and families in places of origin. In that wise, we need to broaden our perspectives in dealing with migration and development issues with a focus on the three D's – demography, development and democracy.

The debate on trade regimes is of particular importance to poor countries, in the context of migration and development interrelations. The clamour by African leaders to achieve mutually beneficial trade relations is understandable: deepening poverty has frustrated recent achievements in democratic and economic reform, and efforts to improve the living conditions of their people, stimulate economic growth and generate employment opportunities have made little progress. Preferential trade between emigrant-sending poor African countries and immigrant-receiving rich countries can help reduce emigrant pressure through its indirect effects on economic activity, employment and wages. Donors should therefore use official development aid constructively to improve infrastructure for human capital and related development, and support growth policies to decrease the pressure to emigrate. Unless economic and other opportunities are created in these African countries, pressures for international migration will intensify, further stalling development.

Remittances form an important link that migrants maintain with their areas of origin at micro, meso and macro levels – as lifelines to poor family members. They are used to pay for basic services, to educate siblings and children, to set up small enterprises, and to enhance agricultural production. In view of the potential economic and social impact of remittances by migrants and migrants' associations at family, community and national levels, policies should creatively promote their effective use, and minimise transfer costs and risks. The efforts of political leaders to promote migrant remittances for domestic investment efforts should be supported.

At the level of demographics the North and the South have needs that can be seen as complementary: in rich countries ageing populations and labour shortages may accentuate the demand for workers, especially in certain areas, for instance health care, while in poor countries high population growth has resulted in an over-supply of manpower, creating a pool of emigrants of a mix of skills ready to fill vacancies in the North. The sticking point is that this scenario – which might seem, on the face of it, to be a win-win situation – may additionally drain poor countries of their professionals. Rich countries allow entry to professionals, while continuing to tighten restrictions on the immigration of unskilled workers from Africa who are willing to do the dirty, dangerous and poorly-paid jobs.

The migration of skilled professionals to promote development is a global issue, and is of concern to both poor and rich countries, albeit from opposite perspectives. Rich countries need highly-skilled professionals for knowledge-intensive economic activities, and, because of local shortages, these people must be recruited from poor and emerging market economy countries. For poor Africa, the loss of specialists in IT, and in engineering and medicine, has impacted far beyond the numbers involved. This brain drain migration process denies Africa the optimum utilisation of the skills of those now in diaspora.

A major challenge now facing African countries is twofold: how to attract qualified nationals back from the OECD countries (as well as how to utilise effectively the rare skills of those remaining) for national development. Most African transnational communities rarely sever ties with home and initiatives to identify and attract back skilled professionals and utilise their expertise for national development should be encouraged and supported by development partners and rich countries. Political leaders courting nationals to return home must also – importantly – address the push factors that spur the brain drain.

At the personal (micro) level, migrant professionals should be able to increase their skills, as well as their income and living standards and those of their families, but many face problems of diploma accreditation, and are therefore often de-skilled through lack of appropriate employment, resulting in brain waste. Remittances, no matter how large or how desperately needed, do not compensate – as has been mentioned before – for the loss of the contribution of skilled emigrants through training and the transfer of expertise to younger cohorts at home. Immigrants bring their energy, determination, fresh ideas and entrepreneurship, which are then lost to their home places.

In many developed economies, highly qualified labour for knowledge-intensive activities is being actively recruited from poor and emerging market economy countries. This battle for brains', or 'talent hunt', is propelled by the dynamics of knowledge-based economies, and accelerated by the possibilities offered by technology and the globalisation of economic activities. Rich countries may engage in direct recruitment of professionals through unfair competition, deciding how many workers to recruit and from where, and selecting the potentially best in the international market. Poor regions thus lose their 'best and brightest', producing human capital for use by the rich countries, and simultaneously losing potential for the wealth-creation needed to establish a foundation for future growth at home.

What we now need is openness and transparency in dealing with these issues. The fact is that immigrants bring benefits through their energy, determination, fresh ideas and entrepreneurship.

Migration and development policies might have a better chance of succeeding if both sides of the migratory space – the circumstances in the countries of origin and destination – were taken into account. Indeed a critical ingredient in the formulation of a coherent migration-friendly policy is an understanding of the different dynamics and underlying factors of migration at the origin and at the destination. Migration matters should nevertheless no longer be handled only bilaterally: a global approach that harmonises migration policies – supported by international organisations and governments – is required to help African countries participate effectively in, and benefit appropriately from, world trade and the global market. Poverty eradication strategies should be at the forefront of the region's development agenda, aligned with mechanisms for creating a stable macro-economic environment, favourable to growth, to generate employment opportunities and foster enterprise and self-sustaining livelihoods in the region.

The short-term solution to curtailing 'unwanted' migration at destination, hitherto anchored on strict border patrol, is unsustainable. Any long-term solution will have to emphasise economic growth and employment generation, the promotion of human rights, and security and related policy measures – all factors that generate emigration from poor countries.

Efforts by African countries to restructure their economies and open their markets to share in the global economy have been disappointing. In this context also, African countries' human and financial resource capacities need to be reinforced – to manage their demographic dynamics, generate employment and moderate migratory pressures. In fact rich countries have a moral responsibility to assist programmes for the orderly return and reintegration of migrants to their countries of origin, especially home-trained highly-skilled professionals whose expertise has been productively utilised in these rich countries. Moreover, importing skills from poor countries is a short-term solution to the acute skilled shortage problem in rich countries; in the long-term, the solution lies in improving training and educational opportunities locally.

Africa is burdened with poverty, unemployment and socio-economic insecurity, drawing more people into circular or temporary migration to a variety of destinations. The migration configuration in the region has become extremely complex: some migration that would otherwise have taken place internally is now emerging as sequential intra-regional and international migration, after replacement migration to urban areas. Traditional patterns of migration are feminising, migration destinations are diversifying, and the migration of entrepreneurs is replacing labour migration. In addition, brain circulation between countries within the region is slowly replacing brain drain migration out of the region. Women are migrating independently in search of secure jobs in rich countries, as a survival strategy to augment dwindling family incomes and are thus redefining traditional gender roles within families and societies. Trafficking in human beings is a dark side of the migration configuration.

Compensation for the brain drain in the form of projects which involve professionals going back to their countries of origin for short periods, to work, among others, in special health and education programmes need to be put on the table. Besides, ethical recruitment of highly-skilled professionals, based on multilateral agreements, is imperative – to minimise adverse consequences on the development of source countries, and to address the haemorrhaging of scarce skilled manpower resources from poor countries. Receiving countries could help recover the training and education investments of countries of origin by means of a 'brain tax', and by supporting their health systems and human resource bases. International standards and monitoring of recruitment, and an ethical recruitment code of conduct are needed, to avoid the unacceptable labour conditions currently imposed by receiving countries, at the expense of migrants' rights.

Residential rules in rich countries should be made flexible to give skilled professionals the opportunity for virtual relocation without losing their residence rights. Other necessary measures are the strengthening of linkages with diaspora communities overseas, providing infrastructure facilities and opportunities for overseas nationals to invest in their home countries, promoting the active involvement of local communities in developing and implementing reintegration programmes for returnees, and fostering possibilities for investment and entrepreneurship.

In order to provide planners, politicians and policy makers with comprehensive data on migration dynamics, cross-country collaborative research is required on a number of themes. Foremost among these is information on the interlinked factors that drive traditional and changing migratory flows – labour migration, brain drain, brain circulation in various contexts in the region. Of special policy concern is the independent migration of female professionals and its impact on gender roles, as well as on family, social and development policies. Since migration in sub-Saharan Africa is essentially intraregional, policy research must also address the causes of the region's contagious conflicts. Peace and stability are prerequisites for investment, development and employment generation, and good governance can help curtail skills flight and the exiling of the intelligentsia.

References

Adegbola, O. 1990. *Demographic effects of economic crisis in Nigeria: the brain drain component*, Spontaneous paper for UAPS Conference on the Role of Migration in African Development: Issues and Policies for the '90s, 19–24 February. Dakar: Union for African Population Studies.

Adepoju, A. 1991. South-North Migration: the African Experience, *International Migration*, 29 (2).

Adepoju, A. 1995. Emigration dynamics in Sub-Saharan Africa, *International Migration*, 33 (3, 4).

Adepoju, A. 2000. Regional integration, continuity and changing patterns of intra-regional migration in Sub-Saharan Africa. In M.A.B. Siddique (ed.) *International migration into the 21st century: Essays in honour of Reginald Appleyard*. Aldershot, UK: Edward Edgar Publishing.

Adepoju, A. 2002. Fostering free movements of persons in West Africa: Achievements, constraints and prospects for international migration, *International Migration*, 40 (2).

Adepoju, A. 2004. Trends in international migration in and from Africa. In D.S. Massey & J.E. Taylor (eds.) *International Migration Prospects and Policies in a Global Market*. Oxford: Oxford University Press.

Adepoju, A. 2005. Review of Research Data on Trafficking in Sub-Saharan Africa, *International Migration*, 43 (1, 2).

Adepoju, A. 2006. Internal and international migration within Africa. In P.D. Kok, J. Gelderblom, J. Oucho & J. van Zyl (eds.) *Migration in South and Southern Africa: Dynamics and determinants*. Cape Town: Human Sciences Research Council.

Adepoju, A. & T. Hammar (eds.). 1996. *International Migration in and from Africa: Dimension, Challenges and Prospects*. Dakar: PHRDA; Stockholm: CEIFO.

Bach, S. 2003. International migration of health workers: Labour and social issues, Sectoral Activities Programme, Working Paper 209. Geneva: International Labour Organisation.

Black, R., R. King & J. Litchfield, with S. Ammassari & R. Tiemoko. 2004. *Transnational Migration, Return and Development in West Africa*, University of Sussex, Centre for Migration Research and Poverty.

Block, A. 2005. *The Development Potential of Zimbabweans in the Diaspora: A Survey of Zimbabweans living in the UK and South Africa*. Geneva: International Organisation for Migration.

Buchan, J. 2002. *International recruitment of nurses: a United Kingdom case study*. Edinburgh: Queen Margaret University College.

Buchan, J. & D. Dovlo. 2004. *International recruitment of health workers in the UK*. London: Department for International Development, Health Systems Resource Centre.

Campbell, E.K. 2003. Attitudes of Botswana citizens towards immigrants: Signs of xenophobia?, *International Migration*, 41 (4).

Carling, J. 2002. Cape Verde: Towards the end of emigration?, *Migration Information Source*. Washington DC: Migration Policy Institute. www.migrationinformation.org.

Castle, S. & A. Diarra. 2003. *The international migration of young Malians: Tradition, necessity or rites of passage?* London: London School of Hygiene and Tropical Medicine.

Crush, J. 1999. The discourse and dimensions of irregularity in post-apartheid South Africa, *International Migration*, 37 (1).

Ghanaian Government. 2001. *Homecoming Summit*, www.homecoming.com.gh/summitpackage.html.

Heran, F. 2004. Five immigration myths, *Bulletin Mensuel d'Information de l'Institut National d'Études Démographique: Population and Societies*, No. 397, January 2004.

Horowitz, S. & D.E. Kaplan. 2001. The Jewish Exodus from the new South Africa: realities and implications, *International Migration*, 39 (3).

Human Rights Watch. 1998. *Prohibited Persons: Abuse of Undocumented Migrants, Asylum Seekers, and Refugees in South Africa.* New York: Human Rights Watch.

IMP (International Migration Policy Programme). 2002. *Activity Report: International Migration Policy Seminar for West Africa*, Dakar, Senegal, 18–21 December, 2001. Geneva: IMP.

IMP. 2003. *Migrant Remittances – country of origin experiences: Strategies, policies, challenges and concerns*, International conference on migrant remittances: Development impact and future prospects, London, 9–10 October. London: IMP.

IOM (International Organization for Migration). 2002. Managing Migration at the regional level: Strategies for regional consultation. Paper prepared for Round Table on Managing Migration at the Regional Level, 5 June. Geneva: IOM.

IOM. 2003. The Trafficking of Women and Children in the Southern African Region, Presentation of research findings (unpublished), 24 March. Pretoria: IOM.

IOM. 2004a. *Migration for Development in Africa*, General Strategy Paper, June. Geneva: IOM.

IOM. 2004b. *Towards the development of an International Agenda for Migration Management*, Berne Initiative Regional Consultations Resource Document. IOM, Migration Policy and Research Department.

Johns, D. 2001. Health and Development in South Africa: from principles to practice, *Development*, 44 (1).

Koser, K. (ed.). 2003. *New African Diasporas.* London: Routledge.

Lefko-Everett, K. 2004. Botswana's changing migration patterns, *Migration Information Source*. Washington DC: Migration Policy Institute.

Martens, J., M.M. Pieczkowiski & B. van Vuuren-Smyth. 2003. *Seduction, Sale and Slavery: Trafficking in Women and Children for Sexual Exploitation in Southern Africa.* Pretoria: International Organisation for Migration, Regional Office for Southern Africa.

Milazi, D. 1998. Migration within the context of poverty and landlessness in Southern Africa. In R. Appleyard (ed.) *Emigration Dynamics in Developing Countries, Vol. 1: Sub-Saharan Africa.* Sydney: Ashgate Publishing.

OECD (Organisation for Economic Co-operation and Development). 2004. *Trends in International Migration: SOPEMI 2003*. Paris: OECD.

Oucho, J.O. 1998. Regional integration and labour mobility in Eastern and Southern Africa. In R. Appleyard (ed.) *Emigration Dynamics in Developing Countries, Vol. 1: Sub-Saharan Africa.* Sydney: Ashgate Publishing.

Republic of South Africa. 2004. Department of Health, SA-UK Bilateral Forum Ministerial Meeting, 25 August. Cape Town. www.doh.gov.za/docs/pr/2004/pr0825.html.

Republic of South Africa. 2005. Department of Health, Seminar with the UK Health Protection Agency, 21 April. Pretoria. www.info.gov.za/speeches/2005/05042610451002/htm.

Sander, C. & S.M. Maimbo. 2003. Migrant Remittances in Africa: Reducing Obstacles to Development Contributions. Africa Region, Working Paper Series No. 64. Washington DC: World Bank.

SAMP (South Africa Migration Project). n.d. *Migration Resources: Brain Drain Resources.* SAMP, www.queensu.ca/samp/migrationresources/braindrain/.

UNICEF. 2000. *Child Trafficking in West Africa: Policy Responses.* Florence, Italy: UNICEF Innocenti Research Centre.

UNICEF. 2003. *Trafficking in human beings especially women and children in Africa,* Florence, Italy: UNICEF Innocenti Research Centre.

UKNMC (United Kingdom Nursing and Midwifery Council). 2005. *Annual Statistics 2004-2005.* London: UKNMC.

United Nations. 2003. Reversing Africa's 'brain drain': New initiatives tap skills of African expatriates, *Africa Recovery*, 17 (2).

United Nations. 2004. Mixed results for regional economic blocks, *Africa Renewal*, 18 (3).

Van Doorn, J. 2002. Globalisation, remittances and development. Paper presented at Knowledge Network Meeting, World Commission on the Social Dimension of Globalization, International Labour Organization, December 16-17, Geneva.

World Bank. 1995. Rethinking teaching capacity in African universities: Problems and prospects, *Findings, African Region*, No. 33 (May). Washington DC: World Bank.

CHAPTER TWO

Regional Economic Commissions and Intra-Regional Migration Potential in Africa: Taking Stock

Anthony Barclay

Introduction

The movement of people across national, regional and continental borders, generally referred to as human migration, is a natural global phenomenon.[1] In Africa this phenomenon has manifested itself historically as an important feature of the socio-cultural, economic and political lives of the people. Currently, migratory flows, characteristics, trends and processes are complex and diverse, with multifaceted consequences for both the migrants and their countries of origin, transit and destination. These consequences impact on the development process through opportunities for and constraints on peace, security, political advancement, socio-economic growth and human development. This situation has led to increased focus by migration authorities, specialists, researchers, politicians and other stakeholders on the dynamics of migration and development. These dynamics may be referred to as the migration-development nexus. Various initiatives are being undertaken with a view to understanding the complexity of this nexus, and exploring ways and means of capitalising on the opportunities for maximising its positive effects and minimising the negative ones.

With this background, and given the regional and global dimensions of migration, it is widely acknowledged that effective management of migration is imperative not only at the country level, but also at regional and international levels. This is primarily because the process requires a balanced and comprehensive approach that necessitates confidence-building, cooperation, consultative dialogue, substantive partnership, international support and shared responsibilities at all levels. At the regional level, regional organisations are expected to play a major role in the process.

---
1 'Migration' can also refer to movements within countries – such as rural-urban, urban-rural, urban-suburban, etc. These aspects of migration are not covered in this chapter.

From this perspective, this chapter is intended to illuminate and assess the role of regional organisations in Africa. More specifically, it aims to contribute to the sharing of information, experiences and insights, in an African regional context, on intra-regional migration. Utilising an eclectic approach, it provides an overview of the evolution of and challenges to intra-regional migration potential, and assesses the role and response of some of the regional economic organisations (RECs).[2] Several African regional organisations are considered, but particular focus is placed on the Economic Community of West African States (ECOWAS) Commission and the Southern African Development Community (SADC). The focus is placed on these two RECs because of the relative availability and accessibility of requisite information. In essence, the chapter attempts to take stock of the potential, progress and constraints of the initiatives of these regional organisations over the period since they were established more than a decade ago. It also examines the role of the African Union (AU) and the implications for the African Economic Community (AEC) as envisaged in the 1991 Abuja Treaty[3] within the context of intra-regional migration and development in Africa.

The chapter makes use of a wide range of literary sources, secondary data and professional insights. The issues covered are not exhaustive. They are also subject to limitations due to the general lack of comprehensive and up-to-date information required for rigorous migration study. Nevertheless, the data used here serves as an indication of magnitude and, as such, provides a useful basis for discussion. From this perspective, the discussion in this chapter may buttress additional research and serve as a meaningful contribution to stimulate strategic thinking. It is hoped that it will also accelerate concerted results-oriented actions towards mainstreaming migration issues into relevant development activities.

The chapter is structured in six sections. Following this introduction, Section 2 presents an historical overview of intra-regional migration in Africa, highlighting the levels, trends, characteristics, causes and other factors including the gender dimensions that define the nature of African intra-regional migration. Section 3 discusses theoretical and empirical views on the implications of and potential for development through intra-regional migration. It reviews the potential and real positive and negative impacts of migration from the perspectives of sending, transit and receiving countries. Section 4 discusses the roles and functions of some of the major RECs, particularly ECOWAS and SADC, in intra-regional migration and their achievements, constraints and opportunities. This is followed by a brief discussion of other RECs. The current treaties, protocols, positions, approaches

---

2 'REC', the acronym for 'Regional Economic Community', is used here to refer to the fourteen regional integration groupings even though only eight are recognised as Regional Economic Communities by the African Union. The term 'Regional Economic Commission' is also used here – interchangeably with 'Regional Economic Community'.

3 The Abuja Treaty is a Pan-African International Agreement signed on June 3rd 1991 in Abuja, Nigeria. It established the African Economic Community. Its modalities are to be carried out primarily through various mechanisms of coordination, harmonisation and a gradual integration of the activities of the Regional Economic Communities. It is to take place over a period of 34 years from the date of its establishment (i.e. until 2025).

and declarations of the RECs are reviewed, and their degree of implementation is assessed. Section 5 discusses the role of the AU and its implications for the AEC. Section 6 provides concluding remarks, highlighting lessons learned and possible ways forward.

Historical overview and current dynamics of intra-regional migration in Africa

Historical overview

Long before the arrival of Europeans in the fifteenth century, African kingdoms and other dynamic African social organisations existed and flourished. History reveals that several places in Africa, including the Egyptian and Nubian kingdoms, in northern Africa, the Ghana, Mali and Songhai kingdoms in western Africa, the Zulu and Great Zimbabwe kingdoms in southern Africa, the Axum and Buganda kingdoms in East Africa, among others, experienced rich dynamic interactions manifested by exchanges of goods, ideas and people through migration over a considerable period of time (MSU 2000). This included the nomadic or semi-nomadic movements over relatively long distances associated with the activities of herdsmen. Also during this time frequent conflicts between tribal groups over natural resources and the control of trade routes were associated with the regular uprooting, movement and resettlement of people (de Haas 2007). Generally then, the major motives for migration were the search for personal and political security, freedom from religious coercion, trade and commerce. Another motive was the acquisition of land, mainly for human settlement and agricultural purposes. Box 2.1 explains further aspects of the pre-colonial migration commonly known as the Bantu Migration.

Box 2.1: Pre-colonial migration (the Bantu Migration)

From the beginning of human history, people have moved, or migrated, from one location to another. People migrate for many reasons. For example, a particular area may experience large population growth that may in turn lead to a shortage of land. In this situation people with little or no access to land may decide to leave their home areas in search of new areas where land is more available. Approximately 2000 years ago, a massive migration of peoples, which continued for 1500 years, began in central Africa. This migration is sometimes called the Bantu Migration since it involved the movement of people whose indigenous language belonged to the same language family – the Congo-Niger language group.

Historians are not in agreement as to why Bantu-speaking peoples began to move away from their home areas in Central Africa in the contemporary countries of Cameroon, Congo and the Central African Republic. Some historians think that this area experienced rapid population growth at this time that resulted in a shortage of land. Other historians point to the development of centralised kingdoms: the process of bringing people under the control of a central authority resulted in the dislocation of defeated peoples, some of whom migrated in search of autonomy. Whatever the reasons for the migration, there is more information available on the impact of these migrations on East and southern Africa than for other regions.

From Central Africa these migrations took some people eastward into present-day Uganda, Kenya, and Tanzania. Other peoples moved to the south-east into present-day Zambia, Malawi, Mozambique and Zimbabwe, reaching into South Africa by the fourteenth century. Still other peoples migrated south into contemporary Gabon, Angola and Namibia.

These migrations were very important in the history of eastern, central, and southern Africa. Most of the peoples living in these regions today are descendants of these migrants or from the peoples who resulted from the integration of Bantu migrants with indigenous groups. Importantly, the migrants brought with them new skills that changed the economic, social, and political practices in their new homes. Agriculture, the skills of mining and smelting metal, and methods of forging tools and weapons from copper, bronze, and iron were first introduced by the migrants. Along with these practices, the migrants brought with them new ideas of social and political organisation that resulted in the development of many important kingdoms in East and southern Africa.

Source: MSU, 2002 (edited)

After the arrival of the Europeans, with their desire for territorial aggrandisement and their avaricious speculation through policies of colonialism[4], migration continued. It has been observed that colonialism initiated and was dependent on massive movements of people and goods within African colonies and between these colonies and Europe for several decades beginning 1885 (MSU 2002).

---

4   Between 1885 and 1914 all of Africa, except Ethiopia and Liberia, came under the colonial control of one of seven European powers: Britain, France, Portugal, Germany, Belgium, Italy and Spain.

However, the motivations for colonialism-induced migration differed. As noted in Box 2.2 below, such migration was driven mainly by the exploitation of Africa's natural resources. In general, the exploitation had significant adverse effects on the African people and the socio-economy of the regions involved. In specific reference to West Africa, which is applicable to other parts of Africa, Adepoju (2005a: 1) notes 'colonial regimes altered the motivation and composition of migration by introducing and enforcing various blends of political and economic structures, imposing tax regimes and establishing territorial boundaries.' He states, moreover, that these regimes employed various economic and recruitment policies – such as compulsory recruitment contract and forced labour legislation and agreements – to stimulate regional labour migration.

Box 2.2: Colonial era migration

Colonialism also resulted in the massive movement of people in many African colonies. Most of the movement was directly related to the exploitation of Africa's natural resources. Large numbers of people, working as labourers, were needed to produce raw materials for export. For example, the production of cotton for export from West Africa necessitated the movement of workers into areas for cotton production. Much of this labour migration took place within countries, but in southern Africa, labour migrants were recruited from neighbouring countries to work in the mines of Zambia, the Congo, and South Africa.

These movements resulted in the growth of large urban areas, but they have also had a negative impact on many rural areas where able-bodied men were forced to leave their home areas, leaving their families and communities with a shortage of labour to produce food and other goods necessary for survival. Strong evidence suggests that many regions of rural Africa suffered economically as the result of labour migration.

Source: MSU, 2002 (edited)

Current trends

During the post-colonial era, including the current period, intra-regional migration has evolved into a more dynamic occurrence, involving multiple factors that influence and characterise intra-African movements. This situation has culminated in what Konseiga (2005: 24) describes as 'a complex grid of relations and interdependence over the borders inherited from colonialism'.

The evolution of this dynamic migration began with a motive similar to that of the pre-colonial migratory movements: many people move between different African geographic areas in search of better economic opportunities and living conditions. Currently, with the varying economic status of individual African countries, people tend to move from countries with fewer opportunities to those with more opportunities, largely for employment and other income-generating activities.⁵ In countries that cause their nationals to emigrate, return and re-emigrate, the reasons for this movement include their response to changing circumstances, such as periods of economic boom, decline and recovery. Along with other factors, the changing circumstances stimulate the transformation of labour flows from mere 'labour migration' into what has been termed 'commercial migration, where people are involved with extensive cross-border trading (Adepoju 2006).⁶ Thus return migration, circular migration, labour migration and commercial migration are distinctive features of current intra-regional migration in Africa.

These movements, including inter-regional migration, are also influenced by both the facilitative and the disruptive effects of globalisation. On the one hand, the evolution of globalisation has contributed to increased availability and use of modern transportation and communication systems that influence and inform the migration process and make movements easier and faster. It has also, on the other hand, excluded an increasing number of people from more productive and meaningful economic participation – due to their lack of opportunity to benefit competitively from globalization-induced increased production of goods and services and a more equitable trading system. This exclusion, which contributes to the high incidence of poverty and other migratory 'push' factors, is believed to have intensified emigration.⁷

Generally, people move due to both involuntary and voluntary changes in their circumstances. Involuntary movements are largely due to forced circumstances such as to escape from civil wars, other violent political upheavals, political and ethnic persecution and human rights violations as well as severe artificial environmental degradation and natural disasters. People who move in such circumstances are generally referred to as refugees. Other involuntary movements are manifested through human trafficking, primarily of women and children.

Voluntary movements may be characterised as the willing decision of people to move in search for better professional opportunities, family wellbeing, better working and living environments, and higher income. People who migrate under such circumstances include some of the most educationally qualified – experienced and skilled professionals who can more readily afford the transportation cost and more easily acquire legal travelling documents. While

---

5   For a more detailed account of these movements, see Adepoju, 2005a; Konseiga, 2005.

6   According to Adepoju (2006: 5) there is a general trend away from mere labour migration of unskilled persons towards the commercial migration of entrepreneurs who are self-employed, especially in the informal sector.

7   Manolo Abella, Chief of the ILO Migration Branch, observed that, while globalisation has liberalised trade, 'it has not had a positive impact on a lot of people nor on a large number of countries.' He further notes that there are only thirteen developing countries worldwide that have managed to successfully integrate the global market for manufactured products: 'The rest of the developing world is still stuck in the traditional schemes of crop and national resource export whose markets have been declining over the past two decades' (Abella, 2001).

many of such migrants go to Europe, the United States and other parts of the world, including, more recently, the Gulf States, there are many others who migrate within the region. These are generally referred to as 'regular migrants'. A sub-category of this group includes those who voluntarily migrate as transit migrants to other sub-regions of Africa en route to areas outside of Africa. Many of these transit migrants are youths tempted by perceived opportunities or inveigled with false promises. Most migrants in this sub-category cannot easily afford regular transport costs or acquire legal travel documents – even for travel between African sub-regions. They usually risk travelling without legal documents and, in many cases, with the aid of smugglers, at a cost many cannot easily afford. Such voluntary migrants are generally referred to as 'irregular migrants'. There are also others who deliberately overstay the time permitted by their visa permits. Thus, while their initial movement classifies them as regular migrants, their subsequent overstay puts them in the category of being irregular during the period in which their stay remains illegal.

Thus, overall, intra-African migration, and migration in general, is propelled by a variety of factors. These factors include the quest for personal security, professional advancement, increased income through hired labour, trade and commerce, and better living conditions. The primary motives for migrating represent, in addition to other reasons, an important socio-economic livelihood quest[8] and a coping strategy to deal with natural and artificial disasters, including the consequences of failed leadership, national policies and the negative aspects of globalisation.

Current dynamics: level, scope, characteristics and causes of intra-regional migration in Africa

According to the United Nations Department of Economic and Social Affairs (UNDESA 2006), the global migrant stock was estimated at about 190.1 million, of which Africa accounted for about 17.1 million (about 9%) in 2005. The data indicates a generally increasing trend in African migrant stock from 9.1 million in 1960 to 17.1 million in 2005, peaking at 17.9 million in 1995. However, as a percentage of population, African migrant stock decreased from 3.2 per cent of the population to 1.9 per cent over the period 1960–2005 (Table 2.1). This decrease can be attributed to population growth being more rapid than the increase in migration.

---

8 Globalisation contributes significantly to the 'push' and 'pull' factors that constitute some of the root causes of labour migration – such as increasing income disparities between more developed and less developed countries. This may be attributed to the fact that the integration of world markets has not been manifested in a more balanced and equitable movement of capital and investment to all regions, nor to an increase in the share of trade to the less developed countries. This in turn leads to employment and other income-generating opportunities in less developed countries being limited relative to those in more developed ones.

Table 2.1: Total African migrant stock, 1960–2005

Indicators	1960	1965	1970	1975	1980	1985	1990	1995	2000	2005
International migrants: estimated mid-year total (millions)	9.13	9.44	9.94	11.01	14.10	14.43	16.35	17.94	16.50	17.07
Population at mid-year (millions)	0.28	0.32	0.36	0.42	0.48	0.55	0.64	0.72	0.81	0.91
International migrants as percentage of population	3.2	3.0	2.7	2.7	2.9	2.6	2.6	2.5	2.0	1.9

Source: UNDESA, 2006

On a regional basis, in 2005, the migrant stock was the highest in Western Africa with a total number of 7.5 million constituting 2.9 per cent of the population. Eastern Africa was second with 4.5 million migrants, constituting 1.6 per cent of the population (Table 2.2).

Table 2.2: Africa: sub-regional estimated migrant stock and refugees, 2005

Africa and sub-regions	Total population (1000s)	Migrant stock		Number of refugees (1000s)	Net migration (average annual)	
		Number (1000s)	Percentage of population		Number (1000s)	Rate per 1000 pop.
	2005	2005		2004	2000–2005	
Africa (whole)	905 936	17 069	1.9	3 023	–455	–0.5
Eastern Africa	287 707	4 516	1.6	1 515	–41	–0.2
Middle Africa	109 641	1 791	1.6	639	6	0.1
Northern Africa	190 895	1 838	1.0	415	–294	–1.6
Southern Africa	54 055	1 381	2.6	46	–1	0.0
Western Africa	263 636	7 543	2.9	407	–125	–0.5

Source: UNDESA, 2006

Table 2.3: Africa: regional percentages of migrants who were refugees in 2005

Region	Number of migrants (1000s)	Number of refugees (1000s)	Percentage of migrants who were refugees in 2005
Africa (whole)	17 069	3 023	18
Eastern Africa	4 516	1 515	34
Middle Africa	1 791	639	36
Northern Africa	1 838	415	23
Southern Africa	1 381	46	3
Western Africa	7 543	407	5

A major component of the migrant stock is the refugee population. As illustrated in Table 2.4 and Figure 2.1, refugee numbers increased from about 79 000 in 1960 to just over 3 million in 2005. The highest number of refugees recorded during this period was about 6.4 million, in 1995. Between 1995 and 2005 there was a significant decline from 6.4 million to 3 million. According to a report of the United Nations Commission on Human Rights (UNCHR 2008), the general decline observed globally can be attributed to a decrease in the number of armed conflicts and several large scale repatriations. The report further asserts that despite the decline, many of those who remain in exile live without any immediate prospect of a durable solution to their plight.

Table 2.4: Estimated number of refugees at mid-year, 1960–2005 (thousands)

1960	1965	1970	1975	1980	1985	1990	1995	2000	2005
79	541	989	1300	3578	3531	5350	6363	3575	3025

Source: UNDESA, 2006; UNCHR, 2008

Figure 2.1: Estimated number of refugees at mid-year, 1960–2005

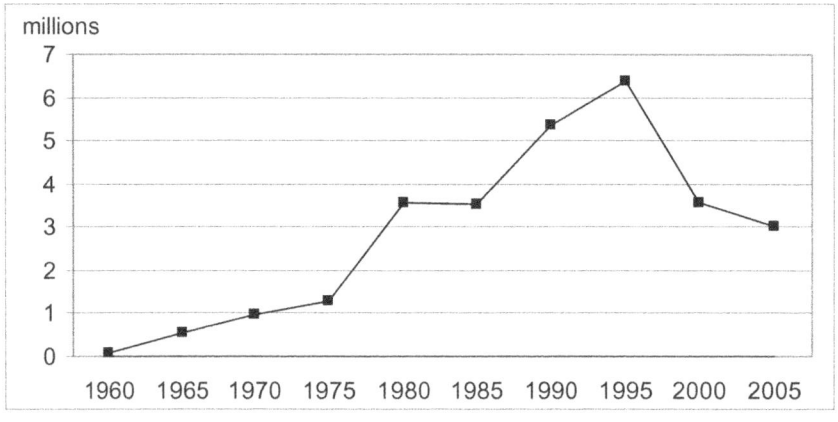

Source: UNDESA, 2006; UNCHR, 2008

On a regional basis (Tables 2.2 and 2.3), in 2005 eastern Africa accounted for 1.5 million refugees, followed by middle (Central) Africa with 639 000, northern Africa with 415 000, and western Africa with 407 000. At that time, southern Africa had the least number of refugees, 46 000. Crisp (2006) ascribes the relatively small number of refugees in the southern Africa region in 2005 to the resolution of long-standing conflicts in such countries as Angola, Mozambique, Namibia and South Africa between the late 1980s and early 2000s. In the other regions, he contends, the refugee situation, while declining, has developed in relatively more recent years.[9] A notable recent alteration in these figures has, however,

---

[9] This is particularly with reference to the following countries: Côte d'Ivoire, Guinea, Guinea-Bissau, Liberia and Sierra Leone in Western Africa; Eritrea, Burundi, Ethiopia, Kenya, Rwanda, Somalia, Equatorial Guinea and Uganda in Eastern Africa; Sudan in Northern Africa and DRC, Congo Brazzaville, Central African Republic and Chad in Middle Africa.

been caused by the economic and political situation in Zimbabwe. Anecdotal evidence suggests that there are currently about a million Zimbabweans in South Africa, and that as many as 1000 may be moving daily in Zambia.

Female migration

Another aspect of the dynamics of African regional migration is the significant increase in women migrants since 1960. As seen in Table 2.5 and Figure 2.2, the growth in the number of women migrants displays an upward trend from about 3.8 million in 1960 to 8.1 million in 2005. This is attributed to the changing role of women in fulfilling their own economic needs, rather than simply depending on their spouses or moving to join their spouses. (Adepoju 2004; IOM 2003). According to Adepoju (2004), there is anecdotal evidence that there are increased numbers of African professional women, such as doctors and nurses, now engaged in international migration without the company of their spouses or other male relations[10]. He further notes that 'women in West Africa have historically been involved in cross-border migration; they now dominate the informal commercial sector, which is less affected by economic crisis than the wage sector where most male migrants work' (Adepoju 2006: 5).

Table 2.5: African female migration 1960–2005 (thousands)

1960	1965	1970	1975	1980	1985	1990	1995	2000	2005
3859	3992	4241	4739	6217	6410	7505	8357	7785	8092

Source: UNDESA, 2006

---

10 This is particularly with reference to the following countries: Côte d'Ivoire, Guinea, Guinea-Bissau, Liberia and Sierra Leone in Western Africa; Eritrea, Burundi, Ethiopia, Kenya, Rwanda, Somalia, Equatorial Guinea and Uganda in Eastern Africa; Sudan in Northern Africa and DRC, Congo Brazzaville, Central African Republic and Chad in Middle Africa.

Figure 2.2: African female migration 1960–2005

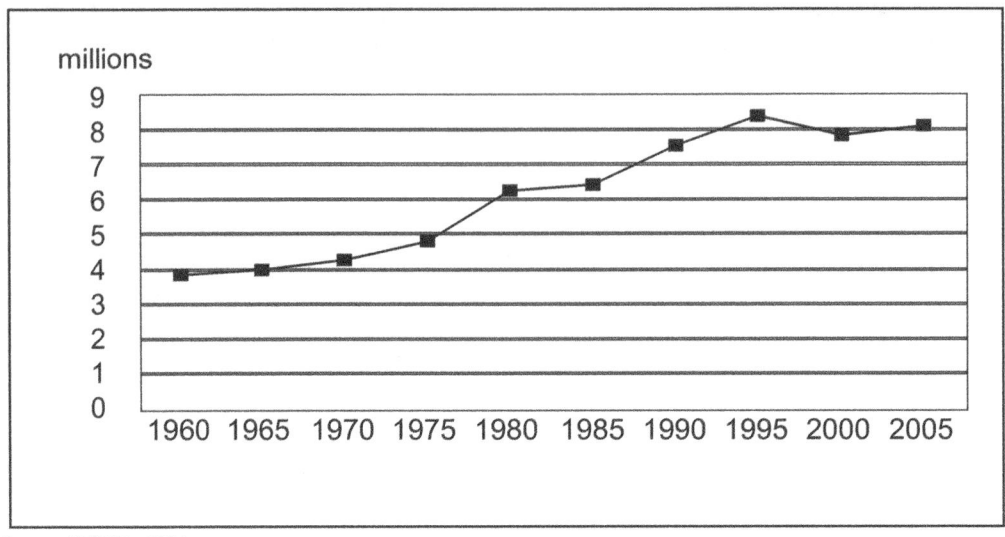

Source: UNDESA, 2006

At the regional level, in 2005 western Africa had the highest number of female migrants (3.7 million), constituting about 21.6 per cent of total African migrants (17.1 million) and 41.4 per cent of total female migrants. This was followed by eastern Africa, middle Africa, northern Africa and southern Africa (Table 2.6 and Figure 2.3).

Table 2.6: Estimated migrant stock, Africa and sub-region, by gender, 2005

	Africa (whole)	Western	Southern	Northern	Middle	Eastern
Female	8 091 923	3 694 522	585 121	801 190	828 907	2 182 183
Male	8 976 958	3 848 570	795 777	1 036 386	962 176	2 334 049

Source: UNDESA, 2006

Figure 2.3: Estimated migrant stock, Africa and sub-region (by gender) 2005

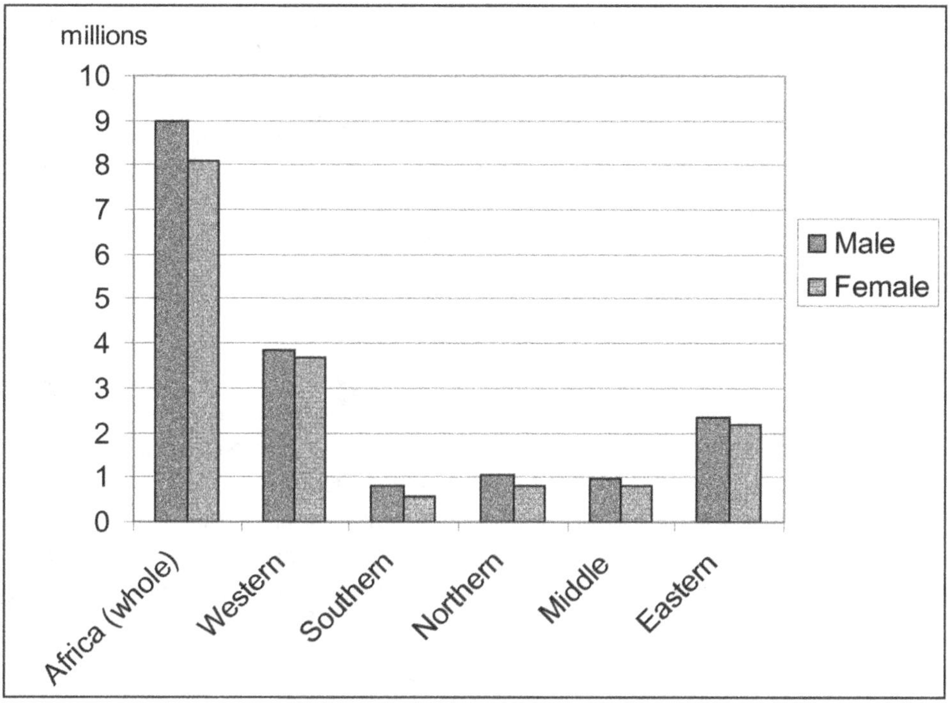

[Bar chart showing migrant stock in millions by gender across African regions:
- Africa (whole): Male ~9.0, Female ~8.1
- Western: Male ~3.8, Female ~3.7
- Southern: Male ~0.8, Female ~0.6
- Northern: Male ~1.0, Female ~0.8
- Middle: Male ~0.9, Female ~0.8
- Eastern: Male ~2.3, Female ~2.2]

Source: UNDESA, 2006

Youth migration

While data is sketchy, general observation suggests that another dynamic aspect of African migration is the youth's component. This changing age-composition of the migrant population is likely to be caused mainly by forced migration – as evinced by the number of children in refugee camps. It is also manifested by transit migrants, a number of whom are of adolescent and youthful ages. Projections for the region indicate that the total West African population is expected to reach about 430 million by 2020 (UNOWA 2005). According to Lauzon (2005) this demographic growth trend will be embodied by a predominance of youths seeking employment. This situation would most likely lead to heightened migratory movements.

HIV/AIDS

Another emerging characteristic of migration in Africa is the high incidence of HIV/AIDS (Human Immuno-deficiency Virus/Acquired Immune Deficiency Syndrome). Anecdotal evidence suggests that this disease has impacted significantly on intra-regional migration. The problem is believed to be most severe in the southern Africa sub-region. Crush, Williams & Peberdy (2005: 1) contend that 'not only is the rapid diffusion of the epidemic inexplicable without reference to human mobility, but new forms of migration are emerging in response.' Given the HIV/AIDS-migration linkage, these authors assert that the epidemic will increasingly become an important factor influencing migration and mobility in Africa. This observation is buttressed by the close correlation observed between migration and vulnerability to being infected with HIV, as noted in Box 2.3.

Box 2.3: Migration and the spread of HIV/AIDS

> As stated in the 2004 UNAIDS report, 'human mobility has always been a major driving force in epidemics of infectious diseases'. Similarly to other health issues, the links between mobility and HIV/AIDS are generally related to the conditions and structure of the migration process. Studies have shown that migration correlates with a higher vulnerability to being infected with HIV. However staying in one's country of origin does not necessarily reduce one's risk of infection. In many cases men migrate to find a better living and return with the disease. The situation of family members left behind can be further aggravated when migrant partners do not send money, leaving only sex work as a recourse for survival.

Source: Usher 2005: 12 (edited)

Having described the magnitude, characteristics and scope of intra-regional migration in Africa, it may now be useful for this discussion to indicate succinctly the more direct causes of migration. Generally, the causes of migration, intra-regionally and inter-regionally, may be attributed to several conceptual 'pull' and 'push' factors. These factors can be classified into four categories: economic and demographic; political; social and cultural; and environmental (see Table 2.7). However, it is important to note that in some cases people migrate due to a combination of reasons and circumstances. These may include economic and non-economic factors as well as forced and voluntary circumstances. In some cases the lines among both the causes and the circumstances are not clearly discernible. Box 2.4 briefly elaborates on the reasons for migration and the difficulties in making such distinctions.

Table 2.7: Causes of migration

Classification	Push Factors	Pull Factors
Economic and demographic	Human poverty Unemployment Low wages High fertility rates Lack of basic health and education (accessibility, affordability and quality)	Possibilities for employment and other income-generating activities Better standards of living Perceived opportunities for personal and professional growth
Political	Conflict Insecurity Violence Poor governance Corruption and human rights abuses	Personal safety, security and political freedom
Social and cultural	Discrimination on the basis of ethnicity, religion, gender or caste	Family reunion Freedom from ethnic/social discrimination
Environmental	Harvest failure Resource depletion Natural and man-made disasters	Less incidence of environmental degradation (natural and artificial) Better management of and facilities for environmental disasters

Sources: UK House of Commons, 2004: 18; author's input

Box 2.4: Migration: distinguishing the reasons and circumstances

> Distinctions are often drawn between types of migrants (voluntary or forced), between their motivations for moving (economic and non-economic) and between push and pull factors in motivating migration. Voluntary migrants choose to move; forced migrants do not. Economic migrants move to gain access to resources or to improve their employment opportunities, whereas non-economic migrants move to escape persecution. Migrants responding to push factors are leaving places where life is a struggle, migrants responding to pull factors are moving to places where they think they might prosper.
>
> Making distinctions between migrants and their motives is necessary in order to ensure that refugees fleeing political persecution are afforded protection and asylum. But people who move have multiple motives and the places from which they move have multiple problems – such as a lack of economic opportunities and political instability – linked to a common thread of poor governance. Forced migrants may retain some choice as to where they flee; voluntary migrants may be escaping depths of poverty and insecurity which give little room for choice. Economic migrants may be fleeing persecution as well as poverty. Policy-makers may seek clarity, but the line between voluntary and forced and economic and non-economic migrants is frequently blurred

Source: UK House of Commons, 2004: 19 (edited)

It should also be noted that while push and pull factors are important in explaining the causes of African migration, they cannot be said to constitute a unified theory of migration. As noted by the United Nations Economic Commission for Africa, the complex interaction between varying perceptions of push and pull factors, individual decision-making processes, and different migration destinations, make it very difficult to create such a theory (ECA 2006a: 9). The ECA further indicates that, although a large proportion of migration is clearly related to the quest for economic betterment, economic disparities are not enough to explain all facets of international movements. It argues that factors such as the perceptions of the situation in the receiving country as well as policies and legislation that facilitate or complicate movements may play a very important role in shaping migratory flows (ECA 2006a).

It is nevertheless true to say that most countries in sub-Saharan Africa, particularly during the period from 1981 to the early 2000s, have had critical levels of poverty. According to Bhorat (2005: 3), and based on the work of Chen and Ravallion (2004), the highest level of regional poverty is to be found in sub-Saharan Africa where, during the period from 1981 to 2001, close to half of the region's population was classified as 'poor' (Chen & Ravallion 2004). Also over this period, as other researchers correctly observe, the region experienced major civil wars, other social upheavals, inter-state violent conflicts, deteriorating governance, regime collapses and state disintegrations. This situation, and its attending ill-effects, impacted on migration flows (Adekanye 1998; Adepoju 2006). For example, brain drain is widely acknowledged as adversely affecting virtually every sector of the socio-economy and public and private organisations as well as institutions of higher learning (Barclay 2002).

In recent years however, many countries in the sub-Saharan region have experienced improvements in economic indicators. The International Labour Organization (ILO 2007) notes that inflation is down to historic lows, most exchange rates distortions have been eliminated, and fiscal deficits are contracting. In addition, in a number of countries the crisis situation is evolving towards peace, security and improved governance. Furthermore, it is being increasingly recognised that migration does have a real and potential positive impact on development through the economic, political and social contributions of migrants.

However, these gains, with a few exceptions, are not yet significantly reflected in stable GDP growth rates or even in stable GDP per capita, or in better labour market conditions and employment opportunities (ILO 2007). Similarly, while there has been some progress in education, health, infrastructure and agriculture productivity, the situation is still not at a level required and desired for sustainable development. According to the United Nations 2006 Human Development Report, most African countries still fall in the 'low human development' category. Poverty and unemployment therefore remain a major challenge, and reasons to migrate are expected to persist. Nevertheless, given the increasing focus on the positive aspects of migration, it is expected that opportunities with potential to impact positively on development – such as the transfer of financial, human and social capital – will continue to evolve.

This discussion of the historical evolution and contemporary dynamics of the migration phenomenon has been an attempt to facilitate the reader's understanding of the context and background that shape the complexity and multi-dimensions of African intra-regional migration. It is from this perspective that the migration-development nexus is now considered, with regard to the potentials and implications for development of various regional organisations in Africa.

Theoretical and empirical overview of intra-regional migration and development

Many theoretical and practical views on migration and development suggest that there are close inter-linkages between the two (Fassmann, Kohlbacher, Reeger & Sievers 2005). However, explicitly defining this relationship in a general context has been difficult. The basic argument is that migration is influenced by development, and, in turn, impacts on it. The inter-linkages, as noted in the previous section, are complex and multi-dimensional. Moreover, they can be either positive or negative in the context of development, with the potential to support or constrain the development process, depending on the specific circumstances.

From the positive perspective, in the context of countries of origin, migration can be instrumental in alleviating some of the problems of unemployment, and can provide other benefits emanating from the diaspora. These potential benefits are the inflow of remittances to meet humanitarian and investment needs, which may be called 'economic remittance'. They also include contributions such as sources of ideas, behaviours, identities and social capital, which Levitt (1996) refers to as 'social remittance'. Migrants also transfer knowledge and technical skills, referred to as 'technological remittance' (Sriskandarajah 2005), as well as political support, identities and practices, referred to as 'political remittance' (Golding 2004).

Economic remittances can provide to the countries of origin injections of resources that enable them to reduce the trade gap, increase foreign currency reserves and finance poverty reduction programmes such as health, education, skills training and micro-finance schemes, and so on. Economic remittance can also contribute towards increasing employment and other legal income-generating opportunities, as well as easing unemployment and underemployment (Todaro 1976). Social remittance, technological remittance and political remittance could lend support to teaching and research, practical consultancy and the provision of medical and other services, as well as productive participation in the political process.

For the negative perspective, migration may inhibit the development of countries of origin through the 'brain drain' phenomenon that adversely affects human capital through the depletion of the highly skilled. Migration may also cause general labour depletion, rural exodus, social inequalities and reduced service delivery capacity as well as engendering over-dependency on remittance. Moreover, economic remittances do not necessarily yield a positive developmental impact as they may be used for non-essential consumption rather than investment purposes. In addition, it is said that a large flow of remittance could generate spiralling inflation (Ammassari & Black 2001).

For the countries of destination, and in some cases also for transit countries, the potential positive benefits include the mitigation of labour shortages, enrichment of human capital, and the innovation and wealth creation that result from migrant entrepreneurial activities (IOM 2006). The influx of foreign agricultural workers, entrepreneurs, medical professionals, teachers and other skilled or semi-skilled workers into some African countries through intra-regional migration is one of the many instances where countries of destination and transit can benefit. (In the transit situation, this would refer specifically to cases in which migrants stay for protracted periods before departing to their final intended country of destination.)

As regards negative aspects: in destination countries and in some transit countries, the adverse impact of migration includes the potential undermining of local wages, loss of jobs to migrants, and deterioration in working conditions. According to the AU (2006a: 3-4), migration 'can have serious negative consequences for states and migrants' well-being, including potential destabilizing effects on national and regional security and jeopardizing inter-state relations, [as well as][11] tensions between host communities and migrants, and [may] give rise to xenophobia, discrimination and other social pathologies'. Another potential negative effect is the escalation of the cost of providing public benefits and services. These factors have real and potential negative consequences for socio-economic human development, peace and stability.

With the current perspectives on the potential and real impact of migration being both positive and negative, and with the contradictory results of many research studies on the impact of migration on development, one cannot easily draw general conclusions with validity for every situation. One of the reasons given for the difficulty is the weaknesses of the theoretical base for understanding the migration-development nexus (Massey et al 1993). The difficulty may also be attributed to the dynamic and complex processes that characterise both migration and development, which vary across time and space and can be considered from very different perspectives, including short-term and long-term (Ammassari & Black 2001). IOM (2006: 3) also indicates that 'while at the global level evidence shows that migration has a net positive impact, its impact on

---

11 Parenthesis inserted by author.

development in individual countries and communities depends on the political, social, legal, and economic environment in which migration takes place and on the characteristics, resources and behavior of individual migrants.' Box 2.5 indicates some of the major factors that can affect the potential of migration for increasing development.

In considering the overall migration phenomenon and its linkages with development, one thing that is certain is that migration in general, and intra-regional migration in particular, is very likely to continue. Moreover, migration does undoubtedly have both positive and negative impacts on development – despite the difficulties in generalising the context in which these impacts are manifested. As such, it is implicit that effective migration management is necessary, just as the development process itself requires effective management.

It must also be noted that the perceived potential benefits cannot be realised, neither can the perceived potential negative impact be avoided, without timely and relevant policies on intervention, and adequate institutional capacity to implement these policies in a sustainable way. It is further implicit that formulating evidence-based policies requires better statistical data and other reliable information than are currently available, as well as rigorous analytical policy-oriented research. From a regional context, in addition to the above factors, such policy formulation implies the need for political commitment, a sufficiently common position, harmonisation of policies, and shared responsibility among all member states intra-regionally and among countries inter-regionally. Considering globalisation and the inherent inter-continental migratory movements, international cooperation and partnership are also imperative. Implicitly, they should be promoted and supported at the national, regional and international levels.

Box 2.5: **Factors affecting the potential of migration for development**

a) Number of returnees, in absolute and relative terms;

b) Concentration of returnees in time: when migrant returns are concentrated in a shorter time span, the critical mass exists that is needed to bring about change;

c) Duration of absence: when absence is too short, not enough may be learned to transfer anything meaningful; when it is too long, migrants may become too detached from home or too old to translate new ideas into practice;

d) Social class of the migrants: skilled elite migrants seem more likely to assume the role of agents of change than unskilled labour migrants;

e) Motives for return: the more return migrants have responded to pull factors in their home countries, the greater the chance for innovation; the more they have reacted to push-factors in the country of emigration, the less the chance for innovation;

f) Degree of difference between the country of emigration and the country of immigration: if this is too great, the skills and experiences that migrants acquire abroad may not be useful back home;

g) Nature of the acquired skills: the more general the training received abroad, the greater the chances of creating innovation on return; the more specific the training, the less transferable in the home setting;

h) Organisation of return: the better the return is planned and organised, the greater the chance for constructive change on return;

i) Political relationship between the countries of emigration and return: the definition of progress in the home country may influence the returnees' impacts.

Source: Adapted from Ammassari & Black, 2001 (edited)

Initiatives for intra-regional migration of the African regional economic commissions: achievements, constraints and opportunities

General observations

African Regional Economic Community organisations are to be the building blocks for regional integration in Africa. This integration ultimately covers not only political, trade, macroeconomic and market issues, but also sectoral issues such as transportation, electricity, agriculture, health, water, gender, and other regional public goods and services. Also covered are migration, governance, peace and security. This is implied in the evolution of the historical popular call for 'Pan-Africanism'[12] and more specifically, as currently stipulated in the Abuja Treaty of June 1991.

It is widely believed that the benefits of regional integration include gains from new trade opportunities, larger markets, increased competition and the facilitation of larger investments. Regional integration can also contribute towards making governments commit to reforms, increasing bargaining power and enhancing cooperation (ECA 2004). This assertion is based on the premise that countries in the region may be able to achieve a higher level of development more expeditiously through results-based institutional collective actions and enhanced cooperation than through the separate efforts of individual countries (Barclay 2006). However, as the Economic Commission for Africa states:

> Regional integration can commit governments to reforms, increase bargaining power, enhance cooperation, and improve security. But these benefits are neither automatic nor necessarily large. Regional integration arrangements must be viewed as means to improve welfare in participating countries – not as ends in themselves (ECA 2004: 11).

Improving welfare in the participating countries necessitates policy coherence, to ensure that the implementation of policies in one area does not adversely affect those in other areas.

Currently, there are about fourteen African inter-governmental organisations working on regional integration issues. The AU recognises eight of these as 'Regional Economic Communities', in accordance with Decision Number 1 of the Banjul Summit of June–July 2006[13] (ECA 2007). Table 2.8 shows the RECs

---

12 Pan-Africanism may be defined as an ideology that embraces the concept that all people of African ancestry are connected – both those in the African Diaspora and those who are still resident on the African continent – and that they should consciously work together for their mutual benefit through political and socio-economic development.

13 The Banjul Summit refers to the 7th African Union Summit held in Banjul, the Gambia, from 25 June to 2 July 2006, on the theme 'Rationalisation of the Regional Economic Communities and Regional Integration'.

recognised by the AU, and those that are not. It is important to note, however, that the other RECs – including the West African Economic and Monetary Union (UEMOA) and the Central African Economic and Monetary Community (CEMAC) – operate in virtually the same way as the AU-recognised RECs, 'as they are all devoted to promoting economic cooperation and integration among their member countries' (ECA 2007: 1).

While the RECs in general have made some significant achievements in their focal areas for integration (Box 2.6), they are still faced with significant challenges. These challenges are caused by several deficiencies. According to ECA (2006) some of the main deficiencies are:

- too much overlap in REC membership;
- duplication of programmes;
- little translation of REC goals into national plans and budgets;
- poor implementation of agreed programmes;
- lingering obstacles to the movement of people across borders, mainly with respect to the right of establishment for citizens of concerned RECs;
- weak legislative processes for integration;
- poor fulfilment of financial obligations to the RECs;
- almost no popular participation;
- little continental coordination.

These deficiencies, particularly the 'overlapping of memberships, mandates, objectives, protocols and functions, create unhealthy multiplication and duplication of efforts and misuse of the continent's scarce resources – making these regional groupings very inefficient' (ECA 2006b: xiii). The ECA further notes that while these organisations have initiated processes to improve their operational efficiency and have their work harmonised and coordinated, success has been limited. This suggests that much more needs to be done.

With regard to migration, despite its importance having been underscored for regional development, only a few of the RECs actually deal with it as an area of specific policy issue or programme activity, especially regarding the free movement of people. Even in most of the cases where the issues are enshrined in the objectives and protocol, implementation has been a major problem. Nevertheless, some RECs have made more progress than others. Perspectives of the experiences and outlooks of these RECs are discussed in the sub-sections below.

Table 2.8: African regional economic organisations

RECs recognised by the AU	RECs not recognised by the AU
UMA – Arab Maghreb Union	CEPGL – Economic Community of Great Lakes countries
EAC – East African Community	SACU – Southern African Customs Union
ECOWAS – Economic Community of West African States	MRU – Mano River Union[1]
SADC – Southern Africa Development Community	UEMOA – West African Economic and Monetary Union
CENSAD – Community of Sahel-Saharan States	CEMAC – Central African Economic and Monetary Community
IGAD – Inter-Governmental Authority on Development[2]	IOC – Indian Ocean Commission
COMESA – Common Market for Eastern and Southern Africa	
ECCAS – Economic Community of Central African States	

Source: ECA, 2007

---

1. Liberia, Sierra Leone and Guinea
2. Djibouti, Ethiopia, Kenya, Somalia, Sudan and Uganda

Box 2.6: Successes in regional integration

Although progress in African integration has been mixed, some strides have been made in trade, transport, communication, energy, knowledge sharing, free movement of people, and peace and security.

In trade, the West African Monetary Union, the Central African Economic and Monetary Community and the Southern Africa Customs Union are already customs unions, and other Regional Economic Communities are establishing free trade areas. All are implementing transport programmes that remove non-physical barriers to trade in order to strengthen transit facilitation, harmonise customs, and improve overall trade efficiencies. The Common Market for Eastern and Southern Africa (COMESA) has agreed axle load limits and road transit charges for its members, and has introduced a regional customs guarantee and third party motor insurance schemes. The Economic Community of West African States (ECOWAS) and the Southern African Development Community (SADC) have also introduced comprehensive transport facilitation programmes.

To minimise energy costs, Regional Economic Communities are using regional hydropower to share energy costs across countries. SADC has been a pioneer, with twelve members, creating the Southern Africa Power Pool in August 1995. In ECOWAS, the connections between Benin and Nigeria, and between Benin, Côte d'Ivoire, Ghana and Togo are the most important links of the West African Power Pool.

The global revolution in telecommunication technology and the growing commercialisation and privatisation of national services have boosted inter-country connectivity in communication. Some Regional Economic Communities – for example the Arab Maghreb Union, COMESSA, ECOWAS and SADC – are more connected than others.

As regards knowledge sharing, successful cooperation exists in early warning systems, agricultural research and capacity building. SADC is served by the Southern African Centre for Cooperation in Agricultural Research and Training, and organisations such as the International Institute for Tropical Agriculture and the International Water Management Institute are helping Regional Economic Communities exchange information on best practices.

On free movement of people, ECOWAS has introduced the ECOWAS passport, a giant step towards eliminating barriers to the cross-border movement of citizens, and indeed towards promoting a common identity among ECOWAS citizens. The East African Community has also introduced a common passport to facilitate cross-border movement of its members' nationals within the community.

Source: ECA, 2006a (edited)

Intra-regional migration: the case of ECOWAS

Through a consultative process, ECOWAS was established as a regional organisation by a treaty signed in Lagos, Nigeria in May 1975. Its current membership comprises fifteen countries.[14] The ultimate aim of ECOWAS is to raise the standard of living of its people, increase and maintain economic stability, and contribute to the progress and development of Africa through closer regional cooperation. In 1993, the ECOWAS Treaty was revised to reflect emerging realities in the process of regional integration. Its revised vision, as stated in the ECOWAS 2008/2009 draft Capacity Building Plan, reflecting the 1993 Treaty and its expanded role as the focal point for NEPAD programmes in the West African region, is as follows:

> To create a borderless region in which the people have access to and are able to harness its enormous resources through the creation of opportunities for sustainable production and environment; a space in which the people transact business and live in dignity and peace under the rule of law and good governance; a zone that is an integral part of the African continental space, within the context of a global village where all human beings live with shared values of mutual respect, mutual solidarity and equitable exchange. (ECOWAS 2008a)

In pursuit of this vision, ECOWAS established a framework for regional development based on the following main pillars: (i) peace, security, stability, good governance and capacity building; (ii) infrastructural facilities; (iii) trade and related factors; (iv) free movements of people; (v) monetary and financial policies and other harmonised or coordinated socio-economic policies, including education, health, agriculture, transportation, industry, gender, environment, youth, sports, and culture as well as other social affairs relevant to regional development. This framework is translated into protocols, policies, programmes and activities by the decisions of the ECOWAS governance organs and institutions[15], based upon the directions from member states through the relevant authorities as stipulated in the Treaty. Box 2.7 provides the full text of the ECOWAS aims and objectives.

---

14 Currently Benin, Burkina Faso, Cape Verde, Côte d'Ivoire, Gambia, Ghana, Guinea, Guinea-Bissau, Liberia, Mali, Niger, Nigeria, Senegal, Sierra Leone and Togo.

15 The main organs and institutions include: the Authority of Heads of State and Government, The Council of Ministers, the Economic and Social Council, the Community Court of Justice, the Commission Community Parliament, the ECOWAS Bank for Investment and Development, the West African Monetary Agency, and the West African Health Organisation. The ECOWAS President heads the Commission and serves as the Chief Executive Officer of the Community. There is also a Vice-President, as well as seven commissioners and a Financial Controller, and several departments, divisions and other sub-units, with varied inter-linked functions and responsibilities.

Box 2.7: Aims and objectives of ECOWAS

1. The aims of the Community are to promote cooperation and integration, leading to the establishment of an economic union in West Africa in order to raise the living standards of its peoples, and to maintain and enhance economic stability, foster relations among Member States and contribute to the progress and development of the African Continent.

2. In order to achieve the aims set out in the paragraph above, and in accordance with the relevant provisions of this Treaty, the Community shall, by stages, ensure:

   a) the harmonisation and coordination of national policies and the promotion of integration programmes, projects and activities, particularly in food, agriculture and natural resources, industry, transport and communications, energy, trade, money and finance, taxation, economic reform policies, human resources, education, information, culture, science, technology, services, health, tourism, legal matters;

   b) the harmonisation and coordination of policies for the protection of the environment;

   c) the promotion of the establishment of joint production enterprises;

   d) the establishment of a common market through

   - the liberalisation of trade by the abolition, among Member States, of customs duties levied on imports and exports, and the abolition, among Member States, of non-tariff barriers in order to establish a free trade area at the Community level;

   - the adoption of a common external tariff and a common trade policy vis-à-vis third countries;

   - the removal, between Member States, of obstacles to the free movement of persons, goods, service and capital, and to the right of residence and establishment;

   e) the establishment of an economic union through the adoption of common policies in the economic, financial, social and cultural sectors, and the creation of a monetary union;

   f) the promotion of joint ventures by private sector enterprises and other economic operators, in particular through the adoption of a regional agreement on cross-border investments;

   g) the adoption of measures for the integration of the private sectors, particularly the creation of an enabling environment to promote small- and medium-scale enterprises;

> h) the establishment of an enabling legal environment;
>
> i) the harmonisation of national investment codes, leading to the adoption of a single Community investment code;
>
> j) the harmonisation of standards and measures;
>
> k) the promotion of balanced development of the region, paying attention to the special problems the promotion of each Member State, particularly those of land-locked and small island Member States;
>
> l) the encouragement and strengthening of relations and the promotion of the flow of information, particularly among rural populations, women and youth organisations, and socio-professional organisations such as associations of the media, business men and women, workers, and trade unions;
>
> m) the adoption of a Community population policy which takes into account the need for a balance between demographic factors and socioeconomic development;
>
> n) the establishment of a fund for cooperation, compensation and development; and
>
> o) any other activity that Member States may decide to undertake jointly with a view to attaining Community objectives.

Source: ECOWAS, 1993 (edited)

In the specific context of intra-regional migration, one of the aims and objectives of ECOWAS, as stated in its Treaty under point 2(d), is 'the removal between Member States, of obstacles to the free movement of persons, goods, services and capital, and to the right of residence and establishment' (ECOWAS 1993: 5). It is within this context and is the *raison d'être* for the ECOWAS Protocol on the Free Movements of Persons, Rights of Residence and Establishment. The major highlight of this protocol is the stipulation that all citizens of member states have the right to enter, reside in and establish in the territory of other member states. These rights of entry, residence and establishment are to be operationalised by progressively abolishing all obstacles to the free movement of persons and to the right of residence and establishment.

This is to be done in three phases (ECOWAS 1999):

Phase I: Right of Entry and Abolition of Visa [Protocol A/P1/5/79];
Phase II: Right of Residence [Supplementary Protocol A/SP1/7/85]; and
Phase III: Right of Establishment [Supplementary Protocol A/SP2/5/90].

To facilitate implementation of the protocol, it called on member states to strengthen their relevant administrative institutions and to ensure the harmonisation of techniques and methods of actions.

As indicated in an ECOWAS Memorandum (2008b), Phase I of the protocol was signed in Dakar in May 1979, and ratified by member states on 8 April 1980, thereby entering into force. This allows a citizen from a member state, who has valid travel documents and an international health certificate, to enter the territory of other member states without a visa, through official entry points, for a period not exceeding ninety days. If there is cause to stay for more than ninety days, then a citizen would have to request permission for an extension of stay from the appropriate authority in the host member state. The protocol further states that member states reserve the right to refuse entry permission to any Community citizen who falls within the category of inadmissible immigrant in terms of the laws of the country concerned.

Phase II (Right of Residence) was signed in Abuja on 1 July 1986, and ratified on 12 May 1989. This gives a citizen from a member state the right to reside in another member state, as long as they have a valid residence card or a permit issued by the host member state in accordance with the latter's rules and regulations (ECOWAS 1999; 2008b).

Phase III (Right of Establishment) was signed in Banjul on 29 May 1990 and ratified on 19 May 1992. This allows a Community citizen to settle or establish in another member state and to have access to and engage in economic activities, including the management of enterprises, under the same conditions as defined by the laws of the host member state for its own nationals (ECOWAS 1999; 2008b).

In the context of irregular or clandestine migration, the protocol stipulates that 'measures shall be taken to guarantee that illegal immigrants enjoy and exercise their fundamental human rights. The fundamental human rights of expelled immigrants or of the immigrant subject to such a measure by virtue of the laws and regulations of the host member state, as well as the benefits accruing from his employment, shall be respected. Any expulsion orders shall be enforced in a humane manner without injury to the person, rights or properties of the immigrant' (ECOWAS 1999: 17).

At the more global level, in January 2008 ECOWAS defined its regional Common Approach on Migration. Besides the Protocol and the Common Approach, ECOWAS has undertaken several other measures. These include the introduction of the ECOWAS travel certificate and the ECOWAS passport, the establishment of national committees to monitor ECOWAS programmes on free movement of persons and vehicles, and the introduction of the Brown Card Motor Vehicle Insurance Scheme. These measures are discussed in the next section.

Assessment of ECOWAS initiatives for intra-regional migration: constraints, achievements and challenges

Overall, the ECOWAS Protocols on the Free Movement of Persons and on Right of Residence and Establishment are consistent with its objectives for regional integration and development. The above-mentioned Common Approach on Migration implicitly defines areas in which the migration-development nexus may be more potentially positive than negative to the countries of origin, the countries of transit and destination and to the migrants themselves, at the regional and international levels. The other measures mentioned above (travel certificates, passport, monitoring mechanisms, vehicle insurance schemes, etc.) have also been instrumental in the facilitation of intra-regional migration. However, it is important to note that the consistency of the protocols and the potential of the Common Approach can be most substantively meaningful when implementation of the relevant policies, plans and related measures are efficiently, effectively and sustainably executed.

Unfortunately, implementation has been problematic due to several constraints and impediments over the years. These constraints and impediments include glaring violations of the provisions of the protocol by some member states. Examples of these violations are the erection of non-tariff barriers and other checkpoints and toll gates along borders and interstate regional highways, and harassment and extortions at some border points. Violations also include the expulsion of non-national citizens (citizens from other member states) from member states experiencing periods of socio-economic and political stress, including the fear of these non-nationals influencing the outcome of national elections.[16] Other violations are the enactment or retention of regulations that effectively restrict non-nationals from engaging in selected economic activities (ECOWAS 2005; Adepoju 2005a, 2005b). In addition, the immigration authorities of some member states do not adhere to allowing an initial 90-day stay of non-national citizens from other member states, as stipulated in the protocol. Further constraints include the lack of effective human and other resource capacity at the national level to effectively implement and coordinate the activities required to carry out ECOWAS decisions. The weaknesses of statistical and information systems, limited relevant policy-oriented research, and the ineffective application of follow-up mechanisms are also areas of concern. In addition, operational mechanisms, including supporting technologies, have been either lacking or ineffective. Moreover, many Community citizens have not been well informed of the provisions of the protocol and their rights, thus increasing their vulnerability to extortion and other forms of corrupt practices by some of the border immigration and security authorities. It also appears that awareness

---

16 See Adepoju, 2005a for more detail on violations of protocol, especially the specific member states that have violated the treaty or introduced measures with such potential.

of the Brown Card Motor Vehicle Insurance Scheme is limited and thus many people seem not to be utilising it.

At the regional institutional level some of these constraints are attributed to limitations in the initial ECOWAS establishment, in the inter-governmentalism mode of regional integration. In this approach, the executive arm of ECOWAS has, in most cases, virtually no independent power of enforcement to ensure that member states abide by the decisions they have agreed to. In such situations, and based on the principle of subsidiarity where the implementation of decisions is primarily the prerogative of member states, the role of ECOWAS is to facilitate, coordinate, monitor and provide appropriate advice, based on expert analysis and recommendations from member states (Barclay 2006). Another limitation is the constraints posed by institutional internal inefficiency – for instance inadequate capacity. As observed in a recent study (ACBF 2008) ECOWAS lacks adequate human capacity, infrastructural facilities and administrative and financial support systems to run its programme or implement its growing mandate effectively.

Another area of concern that has severely affected the implementation of the Protocol is the proliferation of civil wars, intra-state internecine socio-economic upheavals, and violent inter-state border disputes that have been an unwholesome characteristic in the region over the last two decades. Although the situation is improving significantly, there remain lingering adverse consequences that constitute major challenges for the migration-development nexus and development in general.

Despite the constraints discussed above, the situation should not be seen as all doom and gloom. ECOWAS is making accelerated progress in facilitating the intra-regional migration process. To date, despite implementation limitations, the ECOWAS Protocol on the Free Movements of Persons, Rights of Residence and Establishment has been instrumental in expediting the intra-regional migration process. The ECOWAS travel certificate has entered into circulation in Burkina Faso, the Gambia, Ghana, Guinea, Niger, Nigeria, Sierra Leone and a few other states. The ECOWAS passport is in use in Benin, Senegal, Guinea, Liberia, Niger and Nigeria, while other ECOWAS countries are initiating or considering production. These documents facilitate and simplify the formalities for cross-border movement; ECOWAS citizens holding a travel certificate or an ECOWAS passport are exempted from filling out immigration and emigration forms in ECOWAS member states. However the exemption from filling out forms is not being fully adhered to in all member states. Consequently, some community citizens experience an unnecessary waste of time at borders. It appears that some member states are not fully aware of this provision.

To minimise other shortcomings at the borders, ECOWAS has established and operationalised pilot Monitoring Units at the borders of Nigeria, Benin, Togo, Ghana, Burkina Faso, Mali and Guinea (ECOWAS 2007). As reported in its 2007 Annual Report, ECOWAS is also in the process of 'mobilizing the private sector and civil society for their involvement and ownership of the implementation of the Protocol' (ECOWAS 2007: 62). ECOWAS has, in addition, embarked on a 'Cross Border Initiatives Programme (ECOWAS 2007). This programme supports and legalises on-going non-criminal traditional social and economic interactions over current national borders. It also aims to enhance organised cooperation through which actions are planned and implemented by private and public local actors from two or more countries in cross-border areas. The objective of the Cross Border Initiative is to promote the free circulation of persons, goods and services. It is intended to contribute to development by improving the living conditions of cross border populations (who are often marginalised), promoting peace, and supporting inter-communal living with the view to ultimately enhancing regional cooperation and integration.[17] There are currently four Cross Border Programmes: (i) Sikasso–Bobo Dioulasso (Mali–Burkina Faso); (ii) Sénégambie méridionale (The Gambia–Senegal–Guinea-Bissau); (iii) Kano–Katsina–Marad ('K²M') (Nigeria–Niger); and (iv) Karakoro Basin (Mali–Mauritania). Box 2.8 provides a brief description of these areas and indicates the potential for cross-border cooperation, integration and development.

---

17 See Memorandum of ECOWAS Meeting of Foreign Affairs Ministers: 'Cross Border' Concept or Local Integration; Accra, 18 January 2005, www.oecd.org/dataoecd/39/34/38444782.pdf and Memorandum of ECOWAS Meeting of Foreign Affairs Ministers: 'Cross Border Initiatives Programme; Ouagadougou, 18–19 December 2006, www.oecd.org/dataoecd/39/32/38444821.pdf.

Box 2.8: ECOWAS cross-border programmes – description and potential

(ii) Sénégambie méridionale (The Gambia–Senegal–Guinea-Bissau) Straddling continental and oceanic influences, this geographic area lies between the Senegalo-Mauritanian and Futa Djallon land formations, with various populations having been attracted to these 'river countries of the south'. Colonisation established political borders that divided the area into three linguistic groups and different administrative systems. Recent trends in migration reflect the contrasts in the region between the rich economic potential and the existing situation, exacerbated by political tensions. Today there are few links between the economies of the three constituent parts of Sénégambie méridionale, despite their complementarities in terms of production systems and shared natural resources. If one were to attempt to measure the interconnections between the land, its inhabitants and their activities in this southern river region, one would have to assert that there is great potential for cross-border integration.

(iii) Kano–Katsina–Maradi 'K²M' (Nigeria–Niger) This 'Haussa country' extends over 83 000 square kilometres, astride Nigeria and Niger, and includes more than 50 million inhabitants. The towns of Maradi (in Niger) and Katsina-Kano (in Nigeria) constitute one of the oldest development corridors in West Africa, for centuries open to the Gulf of Guinea, North Africa and the Middle East. The dense urban network organised around the built-up area of Kano illustrates the Niger economy's polarisation by Nigeria all along the 1500 kilometre border. Favourable to industrialisation, the development of this area relies on the cultural homogeneity of the Haussa people. Commerical trade is robust, with cattle from Niger, cereal and manufactured products from Nigeria, and even products re-exported towards Nigeria through Cotonou, and the border hub of Malanville-Gaya.

(iv) Karakoro basin (Mali–Mauritania) The Karakoro basin, the 'great lake' in Soninké, has it source in the foothills south of Assaba and flows into the Senegal River at Guidimakha (in Mauritania). Along 150 kilometres – three-quarters of its length – the wadi constitutes a natural border between Mauritania and Mali. The basin extends over 25 000 square kilometres, with 250 000 inhabitants. Situated in the pre-Sahelian zone, its high rainfall is favourable to agro-pastoralism. Streaked with numerous watercourses, the area is difficult to move around during the rainy season, notwithstanding the constant human mobility (of Fulas, Soninkés and Maures) which has always characterised this area. Economic trade across the three borders (including Senegal) is centred on cattle, and agricultural and manufactured products. These dynamics have been intensified by the decentralisation and consultation processes underway on the joint management of the Karakoro basin.

Source: OECD (edited)

To extend its influence at the international level, ECOWAS authorities have adopted the ECOWAS Common Approach on Migration, mentioned earlier. The overarching intent of this 'Common Approach' is to enhance the management of migration through the development of a harmonised system and through a comprehensive balanced approach, to be used as a basis upon which member states would develop, strengthen, implement and coordinate migration policies and programmes. This Common Approach may serve as a precursor to the development of an ECOWAS migration policy, although this is not specifically mentioned in the document.

Anecdotal evidence suggests that the implementation of the ECOWAS Protocol has promoted intra-regional migration, buttressed by developments such as regional programmes in the areas of market and monetary integration, transport facilitation, increased political cooperation, security, democracy, good governance and conflict management.[18] These regional programmes are contributing to the creation of an enabling environment that is impacting positively on intra-regional migration. Among other things, the activities of the programmes are geared towards the establishment of an ECOWAS single currency, the convergence and harmonisation of customs codes and domestic tax legislation, and trade expansion – as well as achieving political stability, peace and security in the region. From this perspective and within the context of the protocol stipulations, citizens of member states are able to pursue business interests and educational advancement, seek employment and visit or reunite with family in the region. The protocol also contributes to the flow of resources such as remittance to family members, as well as of capital and skills to support development and socio-economic livelihood in the migrants' home countries. While some of these activities were admittedly already in existence through national legislation and inter-state arrangements, they are now being facilitated through established regional mechanisms, common understanding and shared responsibility.

In terms of addressing the problems of its institutional internal efficiency, ECOWAS has initiated a results-based change-management process. The process includes the transformation of the ECOWAS Secretariat into a Commission with increased powers, and the creation and staffing of a new department directly responsible for the intra-regional free movement of persons (Department of the Free Movement of Persons). It has also embarked on a robust capacity-building programme that is gradually gaining momentum with the support of its development partners.[19]

Despite the progress achieved and the important actions being taken, there are still a number of challenges facing ECOWAS in directly promoting intra-regional migration. Besides the issues that relate to the deficiencies of the RECs

---

18 These programmes refer to the ECOWAS Monetary Cooperation Programme, the Application of the ECOWAS Common External Tariffs, the Harmonization of the Community Customs Code and Customs Valuation, the ECOWAS Regional Road Transport and Transit Facilitation Programme, the ECOWAS Mechanism for Conflict Prevention, Management and Resolution, Peace Keeping and Security, and the ECOWAS Protocol on Democracy and Good Governance (ECOWAS, 2007: 55–81).

19 This programme covers, among other things, new recruitment, training, networking mechanisms, equipment, documentation and institutional support to priority areas of focus, including the service departments and new organisational departments/units directly linked to its identified priorities for 2008/2009 (ECOWAS, 2006: 120; 2007: 111–114).

in general – as mentioned at the beginning of section 4 of this chapter – there are other critical issues. Among them is the development of solid mechanisms to ensure that the relevant aspects of the ECOWAS Protocol and the Common Approach are integrated into the legal statutes, operational programmes and development action plans of member states. Critical challenging issues also include the development of a dynamic information management system and a statistical and policy-relevant research capacity, as well as the creation of more robust national public awareness systems to inform people about the protocol and the Common Approach on Migration. This needs to be done at both regional and national levels. In addition, particular attention should be given to the strengthening of migration management in general and cross-border management in particular. This would necessitate targeted training and the provision of supporting equipment and supplies for migration officials at both levels, to develop the expertise and the implementation and monitoring skills required for executing migration protocols, plans, legislation and administrative regulations.

At the national level the challenges are also significant. They involve the streamlining of institutions dealing specifically with migration and the strengthening of their capacity to manage the migration process effectively. Other challenges are issues associated with creating awareness of the migration-development nexus so as to disentangle the dynamic interactions relating to the freedom to migrate, the varied positive and negative consequences of migration, and the imperative for effective migration management. Negative issues that must be dealt with should include brain drain, human trafficking, smuggling, and inhumane exploitation of labour migrants – including women and children. Another negative issue is the increased probability of a higher incidence of HIV/AIDS and other communicable diseases due to the increased movement of people. Positive aspects should include the enhancement of social, economic, technological and political remittances for personal advancement and national development.

Overall, with generally improving political and socio-economic development trends at national levels, as well as from a regional peace and security perspective, there is reason for optimism that ECOWAS will become progressively responsive to the challenges of intra-regional migration. The degree and rapidity of success will ultimately be determined by the extent to which there is sustained commitment, cooperation and support from all stakeholders, including development partners.

Intra-regional migration: the case of SADC

The origin of the Southern African Development Community (SADC) was in a consultative process that led to the establishment of the Southern African Development Coordination Conference (SADCC) in 1980. In 1992 SADCC was transformed into SADC by a Declaration and Treaty signed in Windhoek, Namibia. Its membership currently comprises fifteen countries[20]. Its vision is stated as follows:

> The SADC vision is one of a common future, a future in a regional community that will ensure economic well-being, improvement of the standards of living and quality of life, freedom and social justice, and peace and security for the peoples of Southern Africa. This shared vision is anchored on the common values and principles and the historical and cultural affinities that exist between the peoples of Southern Africa (SADC 2006).

The 'ultimate objective' of SADC as a Regional Economic Community is 'to build a Region in which there will be a high degree of harmonisation and rationalisation to enable the pooling of resources to achieve collective self-reliance in order to improve the living standards of the people of the region' (SADC 2006). These objectives, as stated in Article 5 of the SADC Treaty, were later amended to underscore the need to ensure that poverty alleviation is addressed in all SADC activities and programmes, with the ultimate objective of eradicating it. Similarly, HIV/AIDS, which is regarded as a major threat to the attainment of the overarching objectives, is also prioritised. Box 2.9 provides the full text of SADC's current objectives in the amended Treaty.

Box 2.9: Objectives of the SADC

The objectives of SADC shall be to:

a. promote sustainable and equitable economic growth and socio-economic development that will ensure poverty alleviation with the ultimate objective of its eradication, enhance the standard and quality of life of the people of southern Africa and support the socially disadvantaged through regional integration;

b. promote common political values, systems and other shared values which are transmitted through institutions which are democratic, legitimate and effective;

c. consolidate, defend and maintain democracy, peace, security and stability;

---

20 Angola, Botswana, Democratic Republic of the Congo, Lesotho, Madagascar, Malawi, Mauritius, Mozambique, Namibia, Seychelles, South Africa, Swaziland, Tanzania, Zambia and Zimbabwe.

d. develop policies aimed at the progressive elimination of obstacles to the free movement of capital and labour, goods and services, and of the people of the region generally, among member states;

e. promote the development of human resources;

f. promote the development, transfer and mastery of technology;

g. improve economic management and performance through regional cooperation;

h. promote the coordination and harmonisation of the international relations of Member States;

i. secure international understanding, cooperation and support, and mobilise the inflow of public and private resources into the region; and

j. develop such other activities as Member States may decide in furtherance of the objective of this Treaty.

k. mainstream gender in the process of community- and nation-building.

In order to achieve the objectives set out in paragraph 1 of this article SADC shall:

a. harmonise political and socio-economic policies and plans of Member States;

b. encourage the people of the Region and their institutions to take initiatives to develop economic, social and cultural ties across the Region, and to participate fully in the implementation of the programmes and projects of SADC;

c. create appropriate institutions and mechanisms for the mobilisation of requisite resources for the implementation of programmes and operations of SADC and its institutions;

d. develop policies aimed at the progressive elimination of obstacles to the free movement of capital and labour, goods and services, and of the people of the region generally, among member states;

e. promote the development of human resources;

f. promote the development, transfer and mastery of technology;

g. improve economic management and performance through regional cooperation;

h. promote the coordination and harmonisation of the international relations of Member States;

Source: SADC, 2008 (edited)

Under the SADC Programme of Action, several protocols have been developed and signed in the areas of shared water course systems, energy, combating illicit drug trafficking, transport, communication and meteorology, trade, education and training, mining, immunities and privileges, health, wildlife conservation and law enforcement, tribunal and legal affairs, and others. Most of these protocols have been ratified and are at various stages of implementation.

With specific regard to migration, the evolution of the SADC response to the issue of the free movement of people took a major step following a meeting on the subject in Harare in 1993. After another meeting in Swaziland 1994, the decision to draft a Protocol on the Free Movement of People was taken by the authorities, and in 1996 a draft document was produced. This document, 'Draft Protocol on the Free Movement of Persons in the Southern African Development Community', was, however, not approved, due to the objections of some member states on the grounds that it was virtually an 'open border policy' that did not consider its potentially negative consequences (Oucho & Crush 2001).[21]

After several revisions the document was approved in 2005 under a revised nomenclature as the 'Protocol on the Facilitation of Movement of Persons in SADC'. It was signed by six member states (Williams & Carr 2006). The protocol is to come into effect when at least nine member states sign and ratify it. At the time of writing it would appear, from the SADC website, that this has not yet happened.

In the official communiqué following the signing of the Facilitation of Movement of Persons in SADC protocol, it was stated that this protocol is viewed as a means of giving effect to the SADC Treaty calling for the progressive elimination of obstacles to the free movement of capital and labour, goods and services, and of the people of the region generally (Williams 2006). Moreover, some of the other protocols (Trade, Transport, Education and Training, among others) recognised the need for increased economic cooperation, and specifically for increased intra-regional movement of people, capital and goods (Williams & Carr 2006).

Assessment of SADC initiatives for intra-regional migration: constraints, achievements, and challenges

The SADC Protocol on the Facilitation of Movement of Persons is, in general terms, consistent with the treaty that established SADC but is less ambitious in its time frame and content than previous draft protocols on free movement (Solomon 1997). However, as already mentioned, the Protocol on the Facilitation of Movement of Persons appeared not yet to have come into effect at the time of writing. In 2006, at its meeting in Lesotho, the Council of Ministers, the second highest decision-making body within SADC, while calling for the exemption of

---

21 As noted by Williams and Carr (2006: 6), these member states were South Africa, Botswana and Namibia.

visa requirements as a priority, noted that full implementation of the Facilitation of Movement Protocol may take some time, because a lot of decisions would have to be made in relation to infrastructure, services and procedural policies (Ngwawi 2006). Solomon (1997: 3) also observes that regional integration and the free movement of people in the SADC context are fraught with obstacles. He attributes the existence of some of these obstacles to the uneven economic development in the region, and the inability of some member states to effectively police their borders, which he contends 'could prove to be the Achilles' heel for the integration process and the free movement of people'.

Given that this protocol has not come into effect, it can be said that it is significant only as an important instrument with the potential to ease the free movement of persons within the region. This potential, when realised, would in turn facilitate regional integration and its attendant positive effects and its capacity to minimise the negative ones. As Black et al (2006: 101) note, the protocol 'would have major positive implications for the poor of the region, freeing up obstacles to cross-border movement and the search for a livelihood through migration'. The significance of the implications for the poor should however be regarded with caution. This is particularly true when one considers the observation of Williams and Carr that:

> in terms of content much of the Protocol merely affirms what is already happening in the region based on either the domestic legislation of SADC member states and/or bi-lateral and multi-lateral agreements that have been signed between member states. In this sense the Protocol does not represent any radical departure from the status quo, but rather elevates to a regional level, what is already a reality in the region. This is not to undermine the importance of having such a Protocol, but to underscore the fact that in policy and legislative terms, we are unlikely to see anything substantially different in the short to medium term. Perhaps the biggest and most visible impact that the Protocol will have once it comes into effect would be in terms of the logistical mechanisms it puts in place. (Williams & Carr 2006: 10)

In the current context, intra-regional migration and migration in general are governed largely by national migration policies and bilateral agreements. As Williams and Carr observe, while progress is being made towards free trade – the free movement of capital and goods – 'the free movement of persons continues to be balanced against the political and economic interest of individual member states' (2006: 3). These authors believe that the situation is unlikely to change unless two conditions are met: 'a greater degree of economic parity… between Member States' and the conceptualising, designing and implementing of 'a regional regime involving all SADC Member States, that promotes the achievement of greater economic parity' (Williams & Carr 2006: 4).

As already mentioned, there have been calls for the exemption of visa requirements among member states to be a priority action while member states prepare for the implementation of the Facilitation of Movement Protocol. This action, it is argued, would increase intra-SADC tourism and general trade growth. Some SADC member states – including Mozambique, South Africa and Swaziland – have in fact already eliminated visa requirements for citizens from another member state. It is also reported that the introduction of the UNIVISA system[22] is being pursued, with a view to implementation before the 2010 FIFA World Cup that will be hosted by South Africa. This move is intended primarily to facilitate the smooth movement of soccer teams and their supporters from outside the region (Ngwawi 2006). Crush and Williams (2005: 28) contend, however, that the UNIVISA system would 'allow for more freedom of movement for people from outside the region than for southern Africans themselves'.

Besides the Protocol on the Facilitation of Movement of Persons, SADC does have a mechanism that facilitates the free movement of persons, but this is only in the context of education and training. This is provided for in the Protocol on Education and Training. As stipulated in Article 7 section A.6 of this protocol:

> Member State agree to facilitate movement of students and staff from the Region for purposes of study, research, teaching and any other pursuits relating to education and training. To this end, Member States agree to work towards the gradual relaxation and eventual elimination of immigration formalities that hinder *free student and staff mobility.* (Italics added by author.)

From the above discussion it could be argued that, even though the Protocol on the Facilitation of Movement of Persons has not come into effect, there seems to be a favourable stance toward a gradual approach to the free movement of people. While limited progress is being made using this approach, it is mainly at the bilateral level and for the education sector.

Another consideration for strategic thinking is the preponderance of political and economic interests of SADC individual member states and their negative implications. This is especially true in terms of the disparities, alluded to earlier, at the level of socio-economic development, which some member states believe would be disadvantageous to their political, social and economic development. Achieving a closer degree of socio-economic development parity poses tremendous challenges since it appears to be a major condition for the promotion of intra-regional migration along the lines of the free movement of people. Moreover, even when the protocol is signed and ratified, some member states would be faced with significant constraints in implementing it. As Williams and Carr (2006) correctly observe, putting the required mechanisms into place for

---

22 The UNIVISA system would allow visitors from outside the region to use one visa to travel around the region.

the implementation of the protocol would be beyond the immediate capacity of some member states. Nevertheless, these and other actions – including on-going poverty reduction, and achieving closer socio-economic parity among member states – must be sustained as an imperative. Moreover, programmes should be institutionalised in an attempt to change the mindset of people with xenophobic and/or criminal tendencies. Capacity building and institutional reforms, already initiated, should also be sustained.

Overall, the challenges facing SADC do not necessarily constitute a reason for pessimism. They can be minimised through enhanced regional consultative processes, and this initiative is already in progress. The International Organization for Migration (IOM), the Southern African Migration Project (SAMP) and other organisations set up the Migration Dialogue for Southern Africa (MIDSA) in 2001. MIDSA serves as a medium through which consultations between member states are facilitated for the purpose of identifying areas of common interest and raising awareness and capacity among member states. It has already held some consultations with a view to harmonising the immigration legislations of member states. The general opinion seems to be that incremental steps towards a multilateral, harmonised approach to promoting intra-regional migration are more likely to succeed than comprehensive multilateral protocols (Crush & Williams 2005). The protocol was nevertheless expected to come into force in 2008 (Shaw 2007). (At the time of writing, information available to the author could not confirm this.) The ultimate success of the MIDSA initiative, the poverty reduction programmes and other regional initiatives that contribute to the realisation of the positive aspects of intra-regional migration would necessarily depend on the level of shared understanding, commitment, collaboration and responsibility of all stakeholders. When it comes into force, the expected effective implementation of the Protocol on the Facilitation of Movement of People, with the inclusion of other guaranteed rights granted at the multilateral level, rather than merely through bilateral arrangements, would go a long way in promoting, intra-regional migration in southern Africa.

Intra-regional migration: the case of other Regional Economic Communities

As already noted, besides ECOWAS and SADC, there are several other Regional Economic Communities (RECs) in Africa (see Table 2.8). They have multiple specific objectives, but most of them, including ECOWAS and SADC, were established initially in response to the economic stagnation of individual countries that resulted from small markets and weak production structures. These conditions were aggravated by political instability and widespread conflicts (ECA 2006b). The ultimate aim of most RECs is regional development, manifested in poverty reduction and improved human development. Poverty reduction and improved human development would enable people to live longer and more productive lives, have a reasonable standard of living and personal security, and acquire knowledge and skills in an enabling environment. People would also have the opportunity to participate in and benefit from the development process (UNDP 1990).

The development potential of intra-regional migration is generally acknowledged, but, as already mentioned, not many of the RECs deal with it as a specific area of policy-relevance to development. While it is reported that citizens of COMESA and EAC now lawfully enjoy visa-free entry to their respective member states, the extent of the manifestation of this freedom of movement could not be determined by the author at the time of writing nor were results available of any evaluation of its implementation. In many cases the free movement of people across borders is included in the protocols and / or objectives of the various RECs (see Box 2.10), but its realisation is proceeding at a slow pace or not at all. One minister in the East African Community is quoted as saying: 'free movement is not actually as free as we claim. It is free in inverted commas'.[23] This may be attributed to real and perceived obstacles in the implementation of these measures. Thus it may be argued that, due to national concerns and practical constraints, support for intra-regional migration is more rhetorical than substantive, at least from a short- to medium-term perspective. Currently, the intra-regional movement of member state citizens in most of these RECs is restricted and/or pursued through bilateral rather than multilateral arrangements outside of the domains of the RECs.

The challenge to moving away from the status quo in these RECs is enormous. Even setting aside the general deficiencies of Regional Economic Communities outlined in the beginning of section 4, concerted action needs to be taken at both regional and national levels to address specifically the constraints to effective intra-regional migration. Very briefly, these actions would include increasing human development and poverty reduction efforts so as to make migration a matter of calculated choice rather than a matter of desperate necessity. In addition, migration policies must be developed and harmonised, and buttressed by putting in place migration-focused statistical and research apparatus, as well as capacity-building programmes and advocacy, awareness and monitoring mechanisms. Financial and other support for the Cross Border Initiative in western Africa, as well as similar programmes in eastern and southern Africa and the Indian Ocean regions, should be encouraged.

Overall, the process requires more dialogue, cooperation, capacity, political will and financial support at all levels. At the national level particularly, political will needs to be galvanised. At the regional level, from an institutional perspective, capacity-building, appropriate research, and the strengthening of management information systems and monitoring structures all need to be seriously addressed.

---

23 Quoted in *The Citizen*, 7 July 2008 (http://allafrica.com/stories/200807070891.html).

Box 2.10: RECs that include freedom of movement and other migrant rights in their protocols and/or objectives

UMA (Union of the Arab Maghreb)

Article 2 of the Treaty of the Union of the Arab Maghreb (UMA), adopted on 17 February 1989, states that this institution aims to achieve, progressively, free movement of persons, services, goods and capital. To this end, the UMA promotes the circulation of persons and goods as a vehicle for the edification of a united Maghreb region. In this perspective, various conventions and agreements have been signed under the auspices of this union in areas such as trade, customs, social security and law.

ECCAS (Economic Community of Central African States)

The Economic Community of Central African States has a Protocol on Freedom of Movement and Rights of Establishment of Nationals of Member States within the Economic Community of Central African States.

CEN-SAD (Community of Sahel-Saharan States)

The objectives of the Community of Sahel-Saharan States include the elimination of all obstacles impeding the unity of its member states through adopting measures that would guarantee the following: a) facilitating the free movement of individuals and capital, and meeting the interests of member state citizens; b) freedom of residence, work, ownership and economic activity; c) freedom of movement of national goods, merchandise and services; d) encouragement of foreign trade through drawing up and implementing an investment policy for member states; e) the enhancement and improvement of land, air and sea transportation and telecommunications among member states, through the implementation of joint projects; f) the consent of community member states to give the citizens of member states the same rights and privileges as provided for in the constitution of each member state.

COMESA (Common Market for Eastern and Southern Africa)

In the Common Market for Eastern and Southern Africa (COMESA) intra-regional migration is addressed in its objectives for trade promotion, stated specifically as: Improving the administration of transport and communications to ease the movement of goods, services and people between the member countries; and creating an enabling environment and legal framework to encourage the growth of the private sector, the establishment of a secure investment environment, and the adoption of common sets of standards. Member states citizens now enjoy visa-free entry within COMESA.

> **EAC (East African Community)**
>
> The East African Community's bid to create a single East African market entails, among other things, easing travel restrictions, harmonising tariffs, increasing cooperation between security forces, and improving communications. The EAC has also introduced a common passport, to facilitate cross-border movement of member nationals within the community.
>
> **IGAD (Intergovernmental Authority on Development)**
>
> The objectives of the Intergovernmental Authority on Development include harmonising policies with regard to trade, customs, transport, communications, agriculture, and natural resources, and promoting free movement of goods, services, and people within the region; and creating an enabling environment for foreign, cross-border and domestic trade and investment.
>
> **WAEMU (West African Economic and Monetary Union)**
>
> West African Economic and Monetary Union Articles 91 and 92 provide for the drawing up of regulations or directives in order to organise free movement and the right of establishment, and to foster the effective enforcement of these rights. A draft regulation to this effect has been prepared, but no information regarding its implementation was available to the author at the time of writing.
>
> **CEMAC (Economic and Monetary Community of Central Africa)**
>
> The Economic and Monetary Community of Central Africa declaration of 25 June 2008 calls for the implementation of a principle of free movement of citizens and goods. Following its meeting in Chad in 2007, an agreement was reached that would bring into use by January 2010 a single passport for all m ember countries, to facilitate the free movement of people and goods within the sub-region.

Source: ECA (http://allafrica.com/stories/200806271088.html) (edited)

The role of the African Union and its implications for the African Economic Community

In 2002, the Organisation of African Unity (OAU) was transformed into the African Union. The OAU Charter and the Constitutive Act through which mechanism the transformation was actualised defined regional integration as one of the foundations of African Unity (ECA 2004). Among the objectives of the African Union is the coordination and harmonising of policies between the existing Regional Economic Communities, with a view, among other things, to accelerating the process of integration in the continent. In essence, the role of the AU is to provide the necessary continental policy guidance and framework, and thereby serve as the primary institutional anchor of regional integration by streamlining the process across all regions in the continent (ECA 2006a). This is to be done while also addressing the multifaceted internal socio-economic and political problems facing the countries of the continent. In many cases, these problems are exacerbated by the adverse impact of environmental degradation, world trade patterns and terrorism – all of which compound the challenges faced by the African Union.

In the areas of intra-regional migration and migration in general, while it is recognised that migration management rests mainly with member states, the RECs should directly support and expedite migration processes through relevant instruments and mechanisms. This would include providing organisational leadership in promoting regional cooperation, and encouraging and supporting collaboration with other relevant national and international organisations that deal with issues related to the migration-development nexus. It further includes promoting the AU agenda that prioritises the realisation of the aims of the AEC. Among its activities and functions, the AU is expected to build consensus on key migration-development nexus issues, and support the process by promoting the effective and efficient implementation of the regional instruments.

In general the AU is further expected to promote global awareness of its needs for intra-regional migration and demonstrate a commitment to achieving them. In this regard, the AU needs to lend support to ensuring increased policy and operational coherence among the RECs. This would require the collaborative efforts of the AU and the RECs, to institutionalise mechanisms for rationalisation and coordination, in order to enhance the goal-focus orientation and efficiency of the RECs. It would also require functional frameworks, set up to serve as a common source of reference in the development of strategic migration-development nexus policies and action plans. These rationalisation and coordination mechanisms and functional frameworks would be instrumental in minimising the overlapping and duplication of the functions and roles of the RECs, as well as ensuring coherence and synergy in their policies and operations.

Within the scope of its mandate, the AU has undertaken several initiatives in support of intra-regional migration. Among these is the preparation and adoption of the African Common Position on Migration and Development through a collaborative framework with other stakeholders (AU 2006b). This recommends a series of comprehensive actions to be executed at national, regional and international levels. The document is designed to serve as a common source of reference in the development of migration policy strategies at national and regional levels. The AU has also prepared and adopted other instruments in the areas of transportation, communication and macroeconomics, among others. Furthermore, through AU initiatives, some RECs have already commenced the above-mentioned rationalisation process.[24]

Besides the common position on migration and other related integration issues,

---

24 During its Assembly Meeting in Banjul in July 2006, the AU took a decision not to recognise any new RECs (Mkwezalamba & Chinyama 2007).

the AU needs to more vigilantly promote cooperation among the RECs. With the overlapping membership, mandates, objectives, protocols and programmes that characterise the RECs, on-going efforts to monitor and rationalise them should be strongly supported. Also important is the need for the AU to consolidate its gains by strengthening its capacity to coordinate the functions of the RECs, and for it to address collaboratively any lingering constraints and emerging development challenges. From lessons learned, the implementation of the protocols, conventions, declarations, agreements, policies and programmes constitutes a major hurdle. Through results-focused dialogues and consultations, innovative means should be explored to overcome this hurdle – with the participation of the diaspora, other categories of migrants, civil society, the private sector and other stakeholders in developing and implementing relevant policies and programmes. In addition, the gradual adoption and application of appropriate supra-nationality principles should be explored for concerted action.

In consideration of the above, there are a number of implications for the AEC. In the 1991 Treaty which established the AEC, it is indicated that its aim is to integrate economic and non-economic sectors, uphold democratic principles and foster new social and cultural values. An explicit objective is to integrate productive capacities and infrastructural facilities in Africa, leading to a more sustainable and autonomous development path (ECA 2006a). Developing and implementing appropriate policies would therefore be critical to the functioning of the AEC. This implies the imperative for policy coherence, which would be pivotal in the process. Evolving from a situation in which there was a proliferation of different mandates and policies to a situation in which such mandates and policies would be virtually uniform, implies a change in the management process which the AEC would be expected to sustain. This suggests that the AEC would require significant latitude of supranationality, with the requisite enforcement mechanisms to ensure compliance with relevant policies and implementation modalities.

Policy coherence would be particularly critical in this regard, since the migration-development nexus involves migration characteristics, patterns and trends that influence and are influenced by other development issues. These issues include employment, urbanisation, infrastructure, trade, and other sectoral and macroeconomic factors, as well the gender dimensions of these issues. In such circumstances, policies on one issue may impact upon the likelihood of policies on some other issue achieving their objectives. The effects of these circumstances are also applicable at the member state level, where policies pursued by one state may impact on the likely success of those of another (UK 2004). It would therefore be incumbent upon the AEC to ensure that intra-regional migration policies, and migration policies in general, do not undermine the objectives and expected benefits of other policies. For this to be realised, the AEC must ensure that policies are evidence-based. Evidence-based policies require the availability of statistical and other information, based on rigorous policy-oriented research.

In addition to policy issues, matters of supranationality and capacity, to handle implementation should be given careful consideration.

Conclusion

Many African countries appear to support the virtues of African integration. The benefits to be derived from integration would contribute significantly to the achievement of robust pro-poor economic growth and sustainable human development of the African continent. This view is predicated on the potential for strengthening its collective capacity and the productive value of its vast and lucrative natural resources. The RECs are to be the building blocks of an integration process that would culminate in a fully functioning African Economic Community (AEC).

In the AEC, economic, monetary, fiscal, and social policies would be harmonised and the factors of production would be exchanged freely within an effectively managed structure. The process would be facilitated by good governance, trade facilitation, improved transportation and global communication interconnectivity. It would – ideally – be unencumbered by ethnic rivalry, ideological differences or other socio-economic and political vices likely to result in insecurity and prolonged violent conflicts. The realisation of this ideal cannot be achieved in the short run but sustained signs of encouraging progress can be expected. While some advances have been made by the RECs, the results have been mixed, and, in some cases, not consistent and sustainable. Much more has to be done to realise the potential of the AEC, especially if the fast-tracking of the process – as called for at the AU Summit in January 2007 – is to succeed.

The idea of intra-regional migration has been endorsed by most RECs: it is considered a critical measure among the priority actions aimed at bringing the AEC into effective operation. As discussed, most of the RECs treaties and protocols advocate the freedom of movement of people, and certain guarantees for residence and establishment, including access to and management of other factors of production. Nevertheless, from the author's review of available information and existing activities, it would appear that these instruments have either not been effectively brought into force, or that the implementation of the programmes and mechanisms needed for their full and successful functioning is fraught with difficulties.

Admittedly, some RECs have made more progress than others in the promotion of intra-regional migration. This progress notwithstanding, there are still significant on-going challenges. From experience and lessons learned, one must expect that many of these challenges have been – and are likely to continue to be – conditioned by political fluctuations, socio-economic circumstantial pressures and mistrust by some governments of other member state governments. Other constraints observed are due to human, financial and other capacity inadequacies, as well as because of the lack of enforcement mechanisms to ensure compliance with agreed decisions. Furthermore, the general problems of multiple memberships, inadequate translation of REC goals into national plans and budgets, general laxity in programme implementation and ineffective continental coordination exacerbate the problems of intra-regional migration.

As a way forward, it must be recognised that the prospects are not as bleak as sometimes portrayed. First, it is encouraging to note that on the national level, despite some political and economic setbacks in a few countries as well as lingering constraints in governance and socio-economic challenges in a number of others, there is a general positive trend. In most countries there is a gradual and ongoing consolidation of peace and democracy, greater political inclusiveness, an expanded voice of the people, public sector accountability and significant economic management reforms (Mkwezalamba & Chinyama 2007; ECA 2006a). Second, progress is also being made at the regional level, albeit slowly and sometimes with fluctuations due to historical political and socio-economic setbacks and inadequate capacity for greater collaboration among and within countries and regions (ECA 2006b). An important consideration however is that there is a heightened awareness in Africa, at the highest level, of the critical need for enhanced intra-regional migration as a pre-requisite for the realisation of the aims of the AEC. Concerted efforts should be made to accelerate the integration process by consolidating achievements and steadfastly addressing both lingering and emerging constraints.

From this context, several actions should be undertaken. Among them are the following: (a) increase support for and the use of gender-sensitive and results-oriented regional consultative processes on intra-regional migration; (b) strengthen internal and external efforts to reinforce and sustain human, financial, technical, legal and institutional capacities; (c) develop, and institutionalise, a robust knowledge-management and statistical information system on migration in general and intra-regional migration in particular; (d) provide regular support for African migration-development nexus and related policy-oriented research; (e) intensify and widely promote public awareness campaigns about current and emerging migration issues relevant to evidence-based information on the advantages and disadvantages of migrating, as well as about the rights and responsibilities of migrants; (f) institutionalise and strengthen legal measures to deter criminal cross-border activities, including the trafficking and smuggling of humans and of illicit drugs; (g) institutionalise measures to eliminate xenophobic and negative exploitative tendencies directed at labour migrants; (h) increase resource-mobilisation efforts, and ensure adequate results-based and accountability-based absorptive capacity of the RECs; (i) continuously develop and nurture partnerships and networks with civil society, other non-state actors, the private sector, other continental organisations, and the international community; (j) continue to vigilantly pursue poverty alleviation and human development goals.

These suggested measures are necessarily brief and general. Strengthening intra-regional migration management in Africa requires much more in-depth research and analysis of the opportunities for and challenges of the situation from a short, medium and long term perspective. Expanding on the insights and general suggestions provided in this chapter may contribute to such perspectives.

CHAPTER TWO Regional Econnomic Commissions and Intra-Regional Migration Potential in Africa: Taking Stock

References

Abella, Manolo. 2001. Speech to the 82nd Session of the IOM Council. November. Geneva, 27–29. Cited in IMP 2000.

ACBF (African Capacity Building Foundation). 2008. *A Survey of the Capacity Needs of Africa's Regional Economic Communities*. USA: Lynne Reinner Publishers.

Adekanye, J. Bayo. 1998. Conflicts, Loss of State Capacities and Migration in Contemporary Africa. In Reginald Appleyard (ed.) *Emigration Dynamics in Developing Countries Vol.1 Sub-Saharan Africa*. Aldershot: Asgate Publishing.

Adepoju, Aderanti. 2004. *Changing Configurations of Migration in Africa*. Migration Information Source, MPI. www.migrationinformation.org/Feature/display.cfm?ID=251 (accessed June 2008).

Adepoju, Aderanti. 2005a. Creating a Borderless West Africa: Constraints and Prospects for Intra-Regional Migration. unesdoc.unesco.org/images/0013/001391/139142e.pdf (accessed June 2006).

Adepoju, Aderanti. 2005b. *Migration in West Africa*. Paper presented at the Policy Analysis and Research Programme of the Global Commission on International Migration. Lagos, Nigeria. www.gcim.org/attachements/RS8.pdf.

Adepoju, Aderanti. 2006. *Recent Trends in International Migration in and from Africa*. Background paper for the Centro Studi Politica Internazionale and Society for International Development (CeSPI–SID) Project on Development and Sustainable Management of Migration Flows from Africa. Rome: CeSPi–SID.

AU (African Union). 2006a. *The Migration Policy Framework for Africa*. Addis Ababa: AU Executive Council.

AU. 2006b. *The African Common Position on Migration*. AU Executive Council, Banjul, The Gambia.

Ammassari, Savina & Richard Black. 2001. *Harnessing the Potential of Migration and Return to Promote Development*. IOM Research Series No. 5 Geneva: International Organization for Migration.

Barclay, Anthony. 2002. The Political Economy of Brain Drain at Institutions of Higher Learning in Conflict Countries: the case of the University of Liberia. *African Issues*, XXX (1).

Barclay, Anthony. 2006. Regional Cooperation, Migration Management and Development: A Perspective of ECOWAS Experience and Outlook. Unpublished paper presented at CREA International Seminar, Abidjan, Côte d'Ivoire. Abidjan: Centre de Researche et Formation sur l'Etat en Afrique (CREA).

Bhorat, Haroon. 2005. *Poverty, Inequality and Labour Markets in Africa: A Descriptive Overview*. DPRU Working Paper 05/92. Cape Town: Development Policy Research Unit, University of Cape Town.

Black, Richard, Jonathan Crush, Sally Peberdy, Savina Ammassari, Lyndsay M. Hiker, et al. 2006. *Migration and Development in Africa: An Overview.* African Migration and Development Series No. 1. South Africa: SAMP and IDASA; UK: Development Research Centre on Migration Globalisation and Poverty, University of Sussex.

Chen, S. & M. Ravallion. 2004. *Measuring Pro-Poor Growth.* Washington DC: World Bank.

Crisp, Jeff. 2006. *Forced Displacement in Africa: dimensions, difficulties and policy directions.* UNHCR Research Paper No. 126. Rome, Italy: UNHCR.

Crush, Jonathan & Vincent Williams. 2005. *International Migration and Development: dynamics and challenges in South and southern Africa.* Paper prepared for United Nations Expert Group Meeting on International Migration and Development. New York: UNDESA.

Crush, Jonathan, Vincent Williams & Sally Peberdy. 2005. *Migration in Southern Africa.* Paper prepared for the Policy Analysis and Research Programme of the Global Commission on International Migration.

De Haas, Hein. 2007. *North African Migration Systems: evolution, transformation and development linkages.* IMI Working Paper no. 6. Oxford: International Migration Institute, University of Oxford.

ECA (United Nations Economic Commission for Africa). 2004. *Assessing Regional Integration in Africa, I.* Addis Ababa: ECA.

ECA. 2006a. *Assessing Regional Integration in Africa, II.* Addis Ababa: ECA.

ECA. 2006b. *International Migration and Development: implications for Africa.* Addis Ababa: ECA.

ECA. 2007. Highlights. *One Africa.* 1 (1). http://www.uneca.org/integration/numero1/highlights01.asp.

ECOWAS (Economic Community of West African States). 1993. *ECOWAS Revised Treaty.* Abuja: ECOWAS.

ECOWAS. 1999. *An ECOWAS Compendium on Free Movement, Right of Residence and Establishment.* Abuja: ECOWAS.

ECOWAS. 2005. *ECOWAS Annual Report 2005.* Abuja: ECOWAS.

ECOWAS. 2006. *ECOWAS Annual Report 2006.* Abuja: ECOWAS.

ECOWAS. 2007. *ECOWAS Annual Report 2007.* Abuja: ECOWAS.

ECOWAS. 2008a. *ECOWAS 2008/2009 Capacity Building Plan.* Abuja: ECOWAS.

ECOWAS. 2008b. *Memorandum on the Status of Ratification of the ECOWAS Revised Treaty, Protocols and Conventions as at May 2008.* Abuja: ECOWAS.

Fassmann, H., J. Kohlbacher, U. Reeger & W. Sievers. (2005). *International migration and its regulation,* State of the Art Report Cluster A1. Amsterdam: IMISCOE.

Golding, L. 2004. Family and Collective Remittances to Mexico: a multi-dimensional typology. *Development and Change,* 35 (4).

ILO (International Labour Organization). 2007. *Global Employment Trends Brief.* January. Geneva: ILO.

IMP (International Migration Policy Programme). 2000. *Global and Regional Migration Policies: recent developments towards strengthening international cooperation on migration.*

Paper presented at IMP regional meetings with senior government officials. Geneva: IMP.

IOM (International Organization for Migration). 2003. *The Migration-Development Nexus: evidence and policy options*. Geneva: IOM.

IOM. 2006. *International Migration and Development: perspectives and experience of the international organization for migration*. Geneva: IOM.

Konseiga, Adama. 2005. New Patterns of Migration in West Africa. *Stichproben. Weiner Zeitschrift für kritische Afrikastudieni*, 8.

Lauzon, Norman. 2005. Food Security over the Medium and Long-Term in the Sahel and West Africa. Statement by Norman Lauzon. Paris: OECD. Cited in UNOWA, 2005.

Levitt, P. 1996. *Social Remittances: a conceptual tool for understanding migration and development*, Working Paper Series, No. 96. Cambridge MA: Harvard University.

Massey, D.S., J. Arango, G. Hugo, A. Kouaouci, A. Pellegrino & E. Taylor. 1993. Theories of International Migration: a review and appraisal. *Population and Development Review*, 19 (3) 431–466.

Mkwezalamba, Maxwell M. & Emanuel J. Chinyama, 2007. Implementation of Africa's Integration and Development Agenda: challenges and prospects. *African Integration Review*, 1 (1).

MSU (Michigan State University). 2002. *Exploring Africa*. www.exploringafrica.matrix.msu.edu/students/curriculum/m6/activity5.php (accessed June 2008).

Ngwawi, Joseph, 2006. SADC Eyes Further Visa Exemptions as Region Targets Cross-Border Movement of People. *Southern Africa News Features*, No. 66, August. Harare: Southern African Research and Documentation Centre. http://www.sardc.net/editorial/NewsFeature/06660806.htm (accessed July 2008).

OECD. n.d. *Sahel and West Africa Club: Cross-border pilot operations*. www.oecd.org/document/48/0,3343,en_38233741_38246954_38480624_1_1_1_1,00.html (accessed July 2008).

Oucho, John & Jonathan Crush. 2001.Contra Free Movement: South Africa and SADC migration protocols. *Africa Today* 48 (3) 139–158. Cited in Williams & Carr, 2006.

SADC (Southern African Development Community). 1997. *Protocol on Education and Training*. http://www.ub.bw/ip/document/1997_SADC_protocol.pdf (accessed July 2008).

SADC. 2005. *Draft Protocol on the Facilitation of Movement of Persons*. Pretoria: SADC.

SADC. 2006. *SADC History, Evolution and Current Status*. Pretoria: SADC. http://www.sadc.int/about_sadc/history.php (accessed June 2008).

Shaw, William. 2007. *Migration in Africa: a review of the economic literature on international migration in ten countries*. Development Prospects Group. Washington DC: World Bank.

Solomon, Hussien. 1997. *Towards the Free Movement of People in Southern Africa?* Institute for Security Studies, Human Security Project, Occasional Paper No. 18, March. http://www.iss.co.za/Pubs/PAPERS/18/Paper18.html (accessed July 2008).

Sriskandarajah, Dhananjayan. 2005. Migration and Development: options for managing mutual impacts. Unpublished paper presented at the Sixth Global Development Network Conference, Dakar, Senegal.

Todaro, Michael P. 1976. *International Migration in Developing Countries: A Review of Theory.* Geneva: ILO.

UK House of Commons International Committee. 2004. *Migration and Development: how to make migration work for poverty reduction.* Sixth Report of Session 2003–2004. London: House of Commons.

UNOWA (United Nations Office for West Africa). 2005. *Youth Unemployment and Regional Insecurity in West Africa.* Dakar, Senegal: UNOWA. http://www.un.org/unowa/unowa/studies/yunemp-v2-en.pdf (updated version; accessed January 2009).

UNAIDS (Joint United Nations Programme on HIV/AIDS). 2004. *Report on the Global Aids Epidemic.* Geneva: UNAIDS.

UNDESA (United Nations Department of Economic and Social Affairs). 2006. *Trends in Total Migrant Stock: the 2005 revision.* UNDESA Population Division. http://esa.un.org/migration (accessed June 2008).

UNDP (United Nations Development Programme). 1990. *Human Development Report.* New York: Oxford University Press.

UNDP. 2006. *Human Development Report.* New York: Palgrave Macmillan.

UNHCR (United Nations High Commissioner for Refugees). 2008. *The State of the World's Refugees: human displacement in the new millennium.* http://www.unhcr.org/static/publ/sowr2006/toceng.htm (accessed June 2008).

Usher, Erica. 2005. *The Millennium Development Goals and Migration.* Paper prepared for the IOM. Geneva: International Organization for Migration.

Williams, Vincent. 2006. *Regional Identity, Citizenship and the Free Movement of Persons in the Southern African Development Community.* Centre for Policy Studies: CPS Policy Studies Bulletin, 1 (8).

Williams, Vincent & Lizzie Carr. 2006. *The Draft Protocol on the Facilitation of Movement of Persons in SADC: Implications for State Parties,* SAMP Migration Policy Brief No. 18. Cape Town: Southern African Migration Project.

CHAPTER THREE A

African Skilled Labour Migration: Dimensions and Impact*

Ben hadj Abdellatif

Introduction

At a time when we are confronted with globalisation that is becoming increasingly common in the world, and when massive brain drain from the South is happening concomitantly with the ageing of manpower in the north, the issue of manpower mobility and the need for its effective management – for the identification of urgent and relevant responses – cannot be overemphasised.

This chapter is a discourse on the phenomenon commonly labelled 'brain drain', and on the movement of qualified manpower from one country to another. I will focus on the causes and scope of the phenomenon, and on the policy options that are available to African governments, as well as to countries of destination, for effective management of the international migration of skilled African professionals to developed countries. The international migration of skilled workers is itself symptomatic of the deep-rooted problems confronting African countries and affecting development at a global level.

I will also examine the impact of south-to-north migrations on the economic development of Africa as a whole. International migrations have both positive and negative impacts on countries of departure as well as on countries of destination. This chapter is an attempt, using recent statistics, to assess the net effect on the countries of departure under consideration. The first part of the chapter defines the scope of skilled labour migration from Africa to industrialised countries. It is followed by a presentation of the impact of south-to-north migrations on the economic development of certain African countries. The chapter ends with a short case study of the situation in Tunisia, followed by some concluding recommendations.

* Translated from original French text

Defining the issue

First, taking France as an example, until the year 1870 the terms 'immigration' and 'migrants' were virtually non-existent in legal and sociological terminologies; the long-used term 'stranger' had no clear legal connotation.

The first legal definition of the term 'migrant' was contained in an international convention, the Rome Convention of 1924, that reads thus: 'An immigrant is any stranger who comes to a country for employment, and with the manifest or veiled intention to settle permanently; a labourer is any stranger who comes with the sole intention to settle for a short period.'

Presently, the High Commission for Integration (in France) defines an immigrant as a person who was born abroad, and came to France in that capacity (i.e. as a foreigner), with the aim of long-term settlement. An immigrant could therefore be a French citizen who has acquired French nationality after entry into France through the process of naturalisation, or through marriage, or through lineage. Conversely, a foreigner born in France is not considered an immigrant but remains a foreigner.

While a generally accepted definition of 'migration' is unclear, that of 'skilled labour' is even more complex. This issue arose in South Africa some decades ago, during the apartheid era. Professional nomenclature does not state clearly the meaning of 'skilled', nor is it easier to define 'experience', though some analysts use educational level to determine this qualification.

Figures showing the number of migrants moving from one country to another, especially unskilled migrants, have never been clearly stated. Even if the statistical data were 'perfect', this question could never have a single answer. The number of migrants varies depending on who is considered to be a migrant, and on who is taking a census of migrants. Not only are there no universal definitions of who is a migrant, but, even with the same definition, figures differ, depending on whether these are enumerated in their place of origin or in the place of destination. Statistical data are far from being perfect, and migratory data are particularly reputed to be poorly managed. Censuses carried out since the 1990s in OECD countries[1] – reflecting the origin and qualification of foreign migrants – have, however, to some extent made up for this weakness.

It is a known fact that migration figures released by countries of origin, even where available, give only a partial, and hardly accurate, representation of trans-border movements. Migrant populations can be determined only through immigration data produced, reliably, by the host country. Some studies have indeed been carried out to determine in greater detail the brain drain situation in the world, particularly from developing countries to industrialised ones. In one

---

1 The OECD countries are Australia, Austria, Belgium, Canada, Czech Republic, Denmark, Finland, France, Germany, Greece, Hungary, Iceland, Ireland, Italy, Japan, Korea, Luxembourg, Mexico, Netherlands, New Zealand, Norway, Poland, Portugal, Slovak Republic, Spain, Sweden, Switzerland, Turkey, United Kingdom, United States.

of the first studies in this area, Carrington and Detragiache (1998) used census figures collected in the USA in the 1990s to define the magnitude of skilled labour migration from developing countries to the USA in particular, and also to OECD countries in general.

Till very recently, the number of African migrants residing in OECD countries was not clearly defined, and data on international migration produced by international organisations such as Eurostat and the UN is only rough, showing no details. It thus provides very incomplete and disjointed information on the countries of origin, and on the qualification and other particulars of migrants. The lack of availability and reliability of data therefore constitutes the greatest obstacle confronting any researcher in international migration.

The scope of international migration

In 2005, the world global population of migrants stood at 191 million. Africa's share in this figure was around 17 million, up from just over 16 million in 1990. Africa has 22 million refugees and displaced persons. The net migration rate is −0.2 per 1000. This appears to be a modest figure if one considers the fact that the largest migratory flow is intra-regional – between countries on the continent (United Nations 2005). Due to the incomplete nature of these data, this estimate does not reflect the actual migratory flow, thus limiting analysis of the migratory phenomenon.

Developing countries accounted for somewhat over 40 per cent of the migration population over the 1990 to 2005 time period; Europe and Asia were by far the main regions of destination, each with a share of around 30 per cent, as can be seen in Table 3.1.

Table 3.1: International migration trends

Regions of destination	Millions		Variations 1990–2005		Percentage of whole	
	1990	2005	Millions	%	1990	2005
Global figure	154.8	190.6	35.8	23.1	100	100
Developed countries	82.4	115.4	33.0	40.0	53	61
Developing countries	72.4	75.2	2.8	3.9	47	39
Asia	49.8	53.3	3.5	7.0	32	28
Europe	49.4	64.1	14.7	29.8	32	34
North America	27.6	44.5	16.9	61.2	18	23
Africa	16.4	17.1	0.7	4.3	11	9
Latin America and Caribbean	7.0	6.6	−0.4	−5.7	5	3
Oceania	4.8	5.0	0.2	4.2	3	3

Source: IOM, 2005

Generally, the immigration ratio in European countries is relatively low compared to the total population, and to the population of other foreigners. According to the OECD (2003: 12), in the year 2000, 5.4 million foreigners were living within the European economic space (excluding Greece) and the net immigration ratio was 2.5 persons per 1000 (meaning that nearly 1½ million people entered that region).

Table 3.2 shows the size of sub-Saharan Africa south-to-north migration, in relative and absolute values in the year 2000.

Table 3.2: Sub-Saharan Africa south-to-north migration, 2000

Africa region	Migrants recorded in OECD countries (absolute values)	Migrants recorded in OECD countries (percentages)
Central Africa	775 972	14.6
Western Africa	1 718 539	32.4
Eastern Africa	2 427 357	45.9
Southern Africa	366 043	6.9

Source: Docquier & Marfouk 2004

These figures reveal that in 2000 the estimated total number of sub-Saharan African migrants in OECD countries was 5 287 911 persons. As shown in Table 3.2, East Africa accounts for nearly half of these (46%), and West Africa for another third (32%). These two regions alone thus provide almost 80 per cent of sub-Saharan African migrants in the countries of the North, with central and southern Africa together making up only about 22 per cent.

Other estimations indicate that sub-Saharan Africa south-to-north migrations constitute only a marginal phenomenon. Indeed, Africans living in the North represented less than 1 per cent of the total African population in the year 2000, as against 1.5 per cent for migrants from South America, 3 per cent for North America, 11 per cent for Central America and 14 per cent for the Caribbean. Looked at it another way, for every 1000 persons in sub-Saharan Africa, only about 8 migrate to the OECD countries, as against 139 from the Caribbean, 110 from Central America, 32 from Central Asia, 30 from North Africa, 17 from South East Asia, 15 from South America and 5 from East or Central Asia (Docquier & Marfouk 2004). It is clear from then that sub-Saharan Africa is one of the regions with the lowest migratory flows to industrialised countries.

Migration to France is mainly from Africa: from the Maghreb and sub-Saharan Africa. Out of the approximately 210 thousand new immigrants recorded in 2004 (INSEE n.d.), more than 100 thousand – nearly half – came from Africa, well over 64 thousand from Europe, close to 30 thousand from Asia, and over 15 thousand from America and Oceania. Despite these figures, it should be noted that out of the 16 million sub-Saharan Africans living outside their countries of origin, only 1 out of more than 30 live in France. The remaining 830 000 persons, representing 17 per cent of migrants, or 1.3 per cent of the total population, come from other parts of the world – mainly from Asia. The share of Asia, including Turkey, in the migrant population in France is 14 per cent, as against 12.7 per cent in 1999, and only 3.6 per cent in 1975 (Docquier & Marfouk 2004).

Table 3.3: Migrations from Maghreb to main European countries, 1997 (thousands)

Country	Morocco	%	Algeria	%	Tunisia	%	Total Maghreb	Total foreign
France (1991)	573	15.9	614	17.1	206	5.7	1393	3597
Netherlands	136	20.0	1.1	0.2	1.5	0.2	139	678
Belgium	133	14.7	9	1.0	5	0.5	147	903
Italy	134	10.6	0		49	3.9	183	1241
Germany	84	1.1	18	0.2	25	0.3	127	7366
Spain	111	18.2	0		0		111	610
Total (millions)	1168		642		287		2097	14 395

Source: SOPEMI-OCDE (1999)

Generally, Africans in diaspora were spread as indicated in Table 3.4.

Table 3.4: African diaspora in European and North American countries

Country of interest	Africans in diaspora	Year of most recent data
France	1 652 400	1999
Italy	411 492	2000
United Kingdom	373 000	2000
Germany	300 611	2000
Spain	261 385	2001
Netherlands	149 764	2000
Belgium	143 745	2001
Portugal	89 516	2000
Sweden	25 651	2001
USA	36 700	1999
Canada	229 300	1996

Source: IOM, 2003

Education and migration

The educational level of migrants has been rising over the past decades: about a quarter of migrants now hold certificates from higher institutions, which is four times the figure for 1982. In 2003, 11 per cent of students registered in France were foreign; between 1998 and 2003 this figure increased at a yearly rate of 12 per cent. According to the French National Institute for Statistics and Economic Studies (INSEE 2003), nearly 50 per cent of foreign students registered in French universities came from francophone Africa, a quarter of whom were natives of Morocco and Algeria.

In 2000/2001, there were 22 679 African students reading for a Bachelors degree in the USA, and 9 833 doing post-graduate studies (Open Doors 2001: Table 2). However, when compared to the numbers of students from the rest of the world, African students in the USA, Europe, Asia and Oceania represent a very low proportion of the population of international students in those regions (see Table 3.5). Furthermore, since the events of 9.11.2001, restrictions imposed by Europe and USA have made the acquisition of visas by foreign students even more difficult.

Table 3.5 Ratios of African students in selected countries

Country	Percentage
United Kingdom	18
Germany	13
France	11
Australia	8
Other	11

Foreign education is the biggest reason for skilled migration; indeed, there are very few students who return to their countries of origin. The reasons for this are discussed later in this chapter.

African skilled labour migration

The expatriation of highly-skilled African manpower had been happening since the 1960s, when African countries embarked upon an unprecedented educational development programme (Fadayomi 1996). Uganda represented the most striking case, with a very large and rapid increase in highly qualified persons (Adepoju 2004); highly educated persons and experts were forced to migrate to Kenya, South Africa, Botswana, Europe and North America. For similar reasons, qualified people from Somalia, Ethiopia and Zambia left in large numbers to work in other parts of Africa.

Among the factors that trigger migration are lack of job satisfaction, lack of productivity incentives and the deterioration of the socio-economic and political environment. In Kenya for example, university graduates often must wait up to three years before getting employment. The situation has worsened, and unemployed graduates are moving in large numbers to countries in southern Africa, with Botswana having recently become a country of destination in this region.

Gabon, a small but rich country, often has to resort to labour contracts for migrants to make up for its local manpower deficit. Most of these workers come from Mali, Equatorial Guinea, Nigeria, Senegal, Benin, Cameroon and Togo. In recent years, thousands of migrants from Burundi, Rwanda, and the Democratic Republic of Congo have also entered Gabon illegally, in search of jobs. Prevailing conflicts and political instability in their home countries have forced these people to migrate to Gabon in search of security and a better life. However, the issue of unemployment has become a source of concern in this country – where the unemployment rate has reached 20 per cent – and consequently the government has decided to adapt employment to local needs.

Female migration

A largely unconnected phenomenon is female migration. Female migrations are not confined to national territories: highly skilled women from Nigeria, Ghana, and to some extent, Tanzania, presently move out of their region of origin, often leaving their husbands to take care of the children back home. Nurses and female doctors were recruited from Nigeria to work in Saudi Arabia; some went to work for a short period in USA, taking advantage of the generous remunerations to build up savings in anticipation of economic hard times awaiting them back home. Other women migrate with their children, and further their studies in the USA and the UK, because the educational system in Nigeria has virtually collapsed. A World Bank study shows that, as a result of the economic crisis ravaging the continent, 23 000 qualified university graduates leave Africa each year to look for better working conditions. The study estimates that about 12 000 Nigerian university graduates are working in the USA (World Bank 1995). The most striking impacts of the economic stagnation on African universities include the reduction of the higher education budget, low levels of academic remuneration, the reduction of research grants and recurrent student unrest.

Sub-Saharan African migrant qualifications in OECD countries

For a long while, the migration of skilled labour has been an issue of concern to development experts, as it deprives countries of origin of the most skilled members of the active population, whose contribution to development is most crucial. The original theoretising publications by Romer (1986, 1987) and Lucas (1988) clarified the argument about the endogenous growth model. In their models, the income gaps between countries are explained by the increasing external productivity associated with the accumulation of human capital and knowledge. In such a context, 'brain drain' can have only a negative impact on the long-term growth of the countries of supply.

According to Stalker (1994), sub-Saharan Africa is one of the regions most affected by brain drain – it was estimated that between 1960 and 1987 sub-Saharan Africa lost 30 per cent of its skilled manpower. More recently, another researcher, Ammasari (2005, citing Pang et al. 2002), stated that about 23 000 skilled workers leave Africa each year. (These estimates should however be considered with some caution, given the difficulty in measuring this phenomenon.)

Regarding professional qualifications, the trend points to a rapid increase:

from 40 per cent of 'technical, engineering and management' migrant manpower recorded in 1995, the figure rose to 59 per cent in 1998. The data also reveal a great disparity in skills levels from different countries of departure: 94 per cent of migrants coming from the USA are skilled, about 70 per cent from China, and 1 per cent from sub-Saharan Africa.

Estimates of global migration ratio, considering the level of education, from Africa to OECD countries reveal that brain drain is a serious issue in the region as can be seen from Table 3.6.

Table 3.6 South-North emigration rates, by country and education level in sub-Saharan Africa in 2000

Country	Level of education (percentages)			
	Primary	Secondary	Tertiary	Aggregate
Central Africa				
Angola	2.1	3.4	25.6	2.7
Burundi	0.1	2.0	19.9	0.3
Cameroon	0.2	1.4	14.6	0.7
Central African Rep	0.1	0.5	4.7	0.2
Chad	0.0	0.8	6.9	0.1
Republic of Congo	1.4	2.1	19.1	2.6
DRC	0.1	0.5	7.9	0.3
Equatorial Guinea	2.9	6.4	34.1	4.1
Gabon	0.3	1.1	19.3	0.8
Rwanda	0.0	2.1	19	0.2
São Tomé	4.0	9.6	35.6	5.6
West Africa				
Benin	0.1	0.5	7.5	0.3
Burkina Faso	0.1	0.4	3.3	0.2
Cape Verde	14.7	60.9	69.1	23.5
Côte d'Ivoire	0.3	1.8	7.8	0.6
Gambia	1.7	7.8	64.7	0.6
Ghana	0.7	2.2	42.9	1.9
Guinea	0.3	0.4	11.1	0.5
Guinea Bissau	1.3	9.3	29.4	1.8
Liberia	0.4	7.4	37.4	2.6
Mali	0.6	1.7	11.5	0.7
Mauritania	1.0	3.9	23.1	1.4
Niger	0.0	0.5	6.1	0.1
Nigeria	0.1	3.7	36.1	0.4
Senegal	1.7	5.9	24.1	2.6
Sierra Leone	0.3	5.3	41	1.4
Togo	0.5	2.3	13.6	1.0
East Africa				
Comores	1.9	2.6	14.5	2.2

CHAPTER THREE A African Skilled Labour Migration: Dimensions and Impact*

Country	Level of education (percentages)			
	Primary	Secondary	Tertiary	Aggregate
Djibouti	0.2	1.3	17.8	0.5
Eritrea	0.6	12.8	45.8	2.3
Ethiopia	0.1	2.8	17	0.5
Kenya	0.1	0.9	26.3	0.7
Madagascar	0.1	1.8	36	0.2
Mauritius	5.3	5.0	48	7.2
Mozambique	0.5	5.8	42	0.9
Seychelles	9.7	10.0	58.6	14.6
Somalia	9.7	10.0	58.6	14.6
Tanzania	0.1	1.0	15.8	0.3
Uganda	0.1	1.2	21.6	0.5
Southern Africa				
Botswana	0.1	0.8	2.1	0.3
Malawi	0.0	0.8	9.4	0.1
Mozambique	0.5	5.8	42	0.9
Namibia	0.1	0.2	3.4	0.3
South Africa	0.4	0.5	5.4	1.0
Swaziland	0.2	0.2	5.8	0.5
Zambia	0.1	0.3	10	0.3
Zimbabwe	0.2	0.7	7.6	0.8

Source: Docquier & Marfouk, 2004

All sub-Saharan African countries are confronted with the issue of brain drain. It was observed that a sample of 74 per cent African countries had a migration ratio of at least 10 per cent in the year 2000. In East Africa, Seychelles and Somalia are the most affected countries, followed by Mauritius.

Some statistics on brain drain from Africa

According to the figures in a 2003 US National Science Foundation report, 55 300 science and engineering graduates living in USA came from Egypt and Nigeria, and these included about 6 000 holders of PhDs.[2] The Homeland Security Department report for 2002 gives an immigration figure of 7847 'specialist workers' and 381 'extraordinary-skilled' workers.[3] Respective percentages for the countries of origin of these two categories of immigrants were: South Africa 49 and 44, Nigeria 10 and 4, Egypt 9 and 12, Kenya 7 and 4, Morocco 5 and 4, and Ghana 4 and 6. A report by WHO (2003) indicates that only 30 per cent of the 1200 doctors trained in Zimbabwe in the 1990s were still practising in the country in 2001, and the 1992 UNDP report stated that Ghana lost 60 per cent of the medical doctors who trained there in the 1980s.

2 See also http://www.nsf.gov/statistics/infbrief/nsf05317/.
3 See also http://www.dhs.gov/ximgtn/.

Causes of the exodus of skilled labour

There seem to be many factors behind the increase of sub-Saharan African brain drain, but two are singled out here as the most significant, namely the size of the country and the conflict situation.

As regards size: small countries are more affected by the migration of skilled manpower within their region. This is the case for Gabon, Equatorial Guinea and São Tomé & Principe in Central Africa, and for Eritrea and Seychelles in East Africa. Another reason for this situation is the fact that entry requirements into OECD countries are less stringent for citizens of those countries.

Countries that experienced armed conflicts also seem, not surprisingly, to be particularly exposed to significant migration of skilled labour. Such countries are Angola, Burundi, Republic of Congo and Rwanda in Central Africa; Liberia and Sierra Leone in West Africa; and Eritrea, Mozambique and Somalia in Eastern Africa. Indeed, OECD countries tend to relax entry requirements for skilled citizens of countries in states of conflict. This has been the prevailing situation in recent years, in addition to measures adopted to curb the immigration of unskilled or less skilled labour.

In 1994, Zimmermann made a distinction between factors that 'push' people to leave their country of origin, and 'pull factors' that attract people to new countries. For the first category, one can mention the unfavourable conditions at home; these include inadequate educational facilities, low living standards, technological limitations, mismatch of training and employment, uncertain future, political malaise, an absence of realistic manpower development policies and a lack of economic stability (Chang, 1999).

Political factors influencing skilled migration

When a skilled person opts for migration there may be many factors that influence this decision. This section deals with the most important factors influencing the choices made by skilled migrants.

European policy: migration, public opinion and civil society

Migration was a topic that caught the attention of European Union parliamentarians during the session at the end of 2004, and during the debate on the 2005 budget. The following areas were considered:

- the social and economic situation of the youth; their integration into the local society;
- specific conditions of women and the migrant family; cultural and social
- adaptation to the host country;

- necessary steps to enhance the participation of migrants in the development process;
- the prospects for organised migration.

Civil society, working with human rights organisations, has focused attention on the protection of migrants' rights. In various documents the labour unions have openly expressed the view that labour migration and migration for better opportunities in life are fundamental human experiences that many people have gone through. They added that, in their opinion, migration also represents a factor of shared progress and cultural enrichment that has played a prime role in bringing peoples together and fostering cooperation. The unions condemn clandestine migration which is promoted by trafficking networks and is often patronised by employers. They consider that the issue should not be viewed only from a security standpoint, but rather from that of the need for proper management of migratory flows, combating illicit labour, creating investment opportunities and providing professional training in the countries supplying the migrant labour.

The unions have also called for the introduction of measures to control all forms of discrimination, and for the extension of rights provided for in the European Social Charter to persons coming from outside the Community.

Policies adopted by some European countries

Different EU states have adopted different legislations for dealing with migration into their countries. A few are given here as examples.

The British government initiated a Highly Skilled Migrant Status Programme in 2002 that allows highly qualified workers to come into the United Kingdom without a prior offer of job. This was replaced in 2008 by the Tier 12345 scheme, a five-tier points-based immigration service. Various qualifications apply, for example Tier 3, which pertains to temporary low-skilled work, is for people from countries with which a returns arrangement with the UK is in place. The UK has also introduced a new pilot project allowing multinational corporations to process the issuance of work permits for its migrant in-house staff.

Ireland has a policy for a fast-track processing of work permits for highly-qualified professionals. Germany has adopted a Green Card System. Germany, France and Norway have introduced rules that allow foreign students to stay back at the end of their study programme and obtain a work permit on the basis of their qualification.

Denmark amended its immigration rules to attract more skilled manpower; spouses are now automatically covered by the request made by the original applicant. The Netherlands introduced fiscal incentives to attract highly-qualified workers in 1995. Foreigners who start work in the Netherlands can enjoy 30 per cent tax exemption, provided there is no indigene to fill the post occupied by the migrant worker (Expatax 2007).

Maghreb immigration rules copied from the European Union. The attitude of Maghreb countries towards migration and asylum started changing when, following the outcome of the European Council Meeting held in Seville in June 2002, some EU member states decided to integrate migration management issues into the frameworks guiding their relations with foreign countries. The need to preserve good relations with the European Union and its members is, however, not sufficient justification for the position held by Maghreb countries on the issues of migration and asylum. Indeed, these countries considered the adoption of policies designed to manage and control the entry and stay of foreigners as methods of protecting vital national interests. Similarly, it should be noted that the Maghreb countries have been more involved in this issue through various consultative processes on migration management.

The organisation of Maghreb inter-ministerial meetings – in Tunis in October 2002, in Rabat in October 2003, and in Algiers in September 2004 – as a follow-up of the '5+5 Dialogue' on migration in the western Mediterranean was very symbolic. These consultations took place in an atmosphere characterised by greater security concerns and increased control of international movement.

The regular involvement of Maghreb representatives in these consultations is important for a number of reasons. It is meant to increase the credibility of their countries in international negotiations on migration; determine the advantages and disadvantages of migration with respect to their countries; present the financial and development support that their countries expect from an enlarged Europe; and confer to the countries of destination the position of strategic partners in the fight against illegal migration and in the strengthening of control measures over EU external borders.

Pull factors

From an economic viewpoint, particularly that of skilled workers, the basic motivation for migration remains net financial gain. There are at least two potential economic pull factors – advantages to migration – for those in the labour market. The first one is simply income. A medical doctor in Kenya earns about US $250 per month. If he or she migrates to South Africa, the UK or the USA, his or her income can be as much as ten times higher. Table 3.7 gives a comparison between the richest and poorest regions.

The second advantage has to do with employment availability. People move with a view to enhancing their income on the labour market; migration therefore results from the search for employment. People move to increase their chances of getting a job; migration is intrinsically linked to the search for employment. In most African countries, highly qualified science and technology graduates find it difficult to secure employment. The economic growth rate is low – even negative in some cases. In the case of Zimbabwe, the unemployment rate is currently 70 per cent for the adult population. In such economic contexts, it is difficult for qualified people to stay back, even if they cannot immediately find a job in the destination country.

The most compelling 'pull' reasons for the international migration of skilled and unskilled labour are thus likely to be higher income and better employment prospects.

Table 3.7: Per capita GDP in 2000

Countries / Group	Per capita GDP (US dollars) per annum
OECD high income countries	27 820
European Monetary Union	23 540
Middle income countries	4650
Low income countries	2010
Least developed countries (United Nations classification)	1220

Source: World Bank 2002, as cited in Dzvimbo 2003

In industrialised countries the demand for highly-skilled manpower is underpinned by the expansion of technology-driven industries. Enhanced social services, which constitute an important pool of manpower, particularly in the technological sector, are assuming an increasingly significant role on the national and international labour markets for IT specialists and S&T experts (Lopez-Bassols 2002).

Contrary to numerous statements on the shortage of IT experts, an OECD study produced a mitigated view, claiming that there was a disparity between the skills provided and those currently needed – rather than there being a global shortage of skilled manpower (Rogers 2000).

Push factors

I present here a brief listing of the main 'push' factors influencing skilled migration from sub-Saharan Africa and the Maghreb (IOM 2003). They take the form of unsatisfactory socio-economic conditions and general hardships endured by the populations of most African countries. They are: unemployment, leading to increased burdens to be borne by the few employed members of a family; depreciation of real income, currency devaluation and a rise in the cost of living; stringent employment conditions, as found in such countries as Zambia, Sierra Leone, Somalia, Liberia and the Democratic Republic of Congo; professional segregation of the intellectuals in African institutions as a result of lack of resources to improve African universities; ethnic discrimination in appointments and staff management, against the background of a diminishing 'national cake', and the battle by the elite to rise in the public and private sectors; corruption; employers' discrimination in their acceptance of qualifications, for example mistrust of certificates obtained in the former socialist countries; and competition with expatriate workers, given the fact that more and more Africans are migrating to other regions within Africa.

The impact of migration movement on development

Current theory suggests that migration has at least three positive impacts on the development of the country of origin: firstly it eases the pressure on the labour market; secondly it supports the balance of payments and development financing, and lastly it promotes knowledge development, as migrants return to their countries to contribute to development work.

The effect of migration on unemployment

As just mentioned, international migration can have a positive impact on employment – easing pressures on the labour market and by promoting the knowledge and skills development of returning nationals. This is, however not a large effect, except in regions that record high migratory movements.

As regards the Maghreb region, surveys carried out in Morocco have revealed that the ratio of unemployed among those who migrate is only moderate – in 2000 this was 7 to 13 percent in rural areas and 19 per cent in urban areas. It should be noted, however, that the unemployment rate of migrants to urban areas seems to be increasing, going from 17 per cent before 1960 to nearly 24 per cent in the mid-1970s, and topping 40 per cent in the 1990s, which was higher than the average overall unemployment rate in the cities.

There is another dimension to this issue: if migration were to be the solution to the increasingly pervasive unemployment in the Maghreb, it would have to be very much greater in extent, and thus out of proportion with the size of the population as a whole.

The economic impact of returning migrants

Despite the generally inadequate availability of data, specific surveys have been carried out in some countries, among them Egypt, Tunisia and Morocco. These surveys have given clear and positive results, as they demonstrated that returning migrants will have acquired knowledge and experience in their host countries. On their return these migrants are able to become entrepreneurs, often investing in development projects by creating small and medium enterprises. Working abroad seems to provide an opportunity to develop human resources, particularly for migrants with a good educational background.

About 50 per cent of educated migrants have benefited from their working experience abroad (in practical experience and projects) as against 33 per cent who had average education, and 22 per cent with low education. The benefits derived from migration are also linked to the duration of the stay abroad: the longer the period the greater the usefulness.

A study carried out in Egypt in the 1990s revealed that 10 per cent of returning migrants had become entrepreneurs (investing in economic projects) as against 46 per cent who invested in building houses. As well as depending on the duration of the stay abroad, the likelihood of a returning migrant becoming an entrepreneur depends, to a slight extent, on the monetary saving made. The longer the stay abroad and the greater the income brought home, and thus the greater the likelihood of becoming an entrepreneur – as is demonstrated in Table 3.8.

Table 3.8: Relationship between length of stay abroad and probability of becoming an entrepreneur

Number of years abroad	Amount saved (£ Egypt)	Probability of becoming an entrepreneur (%)
1	6 000	27
2	10 000	32
3	30 000	36

Source: Wahba 2003.

Although the businesses established by migrants are usually only medium-sized, (fewer than five staff), they are, in general, better managed than those run by local entrepreneurs, and are very dynamic in terms of job creation and in giving support to economic activities in the service sector (42%) and in the industrial sector (28%).

In most developing countries the lack of trained and competent staff is still considered a hindrance to economic development. However the issue of manpower development and employment can be better understood in the context of the socio-economic activities that have taken place in each country since independence. The nature, scope and complexity of these issues varies, depending, among other things, on the political upheavals that these countries might have experienced. It is essential for countries to assess their own specific situations, especially those related to problems of labour and manpower, with a view to finding solutions in more appropriate and realistic ways.

Case study: the contribution of skilled manpower to development in Tunisia

I now present a case study which demonstrates details of some of the points mentioned above.

New dimensions of migration in Tunisia

Since the year 2007, a new French immigration policy, based on selective migration, has led to a change in the profile of Tunisian migrants, for whom certificates have become the critical key to access. After an official visit by President Nicholas Sarkozy, Tunisia was expected to be the first Maghreb country to sign a common migration management agreement with France (*La Presse*, 13 July 2008). The agreement was designed within a holistic framework, based on three inseparable components: management of legal migration; the fight against illegal migration; and joint development programmes.

Under this policy, special dispensations are provided for Tunisian students, over 9000 of whom registered in France for the 2007–2008 academic year. These include the possibility of taking up employment without prior authorisation. There is also a 'young professionals' programme offering people aged 18 to 35 years an opportunity to work in France for 18 months in order to acquire professional experience. Also, highly skilled persons will be given a 'competent and talented person' card, valid for three years and renewable once. Five hundred such cards would be granted to Tunisians every year, as against an average of a hundred cards for sub-Saharan African countries.

The contribution of foreign-based Tunisian nationals

The French government's increasing interest in highly-skilled Tunisians can be seen through their being invited to be actively involved in the consolidation of efforts made in the areas of higher education, scientific and technological research, and public health and medical research. Various partnership arrangements are then offered to members of this highly-qualified foreign manpower base, to bring them home to carry out missions of varying durations, as well as to come and invest in the high-tech and technical sectors.

Statistics on projects initiated by foreign-based Tunisians are found mainly in the organised private sector, but their contribution to the informal sector should not be underestimated, particularly in the areas of trade, transport and services where they are very dynamic. Overall, however, the impact of their investments on the economic base has not been very significant, though it has brought an improvement in the living conditions of their families, including emigrant members.

As in other countries, Tunisian migrant investment in real estate has not only brought about an improvement in the quality of life of the immediate beneficiaries, but it has also injected some dynamism into local economies – which has had a multiplier effect on job creation in the building industry. This has led to the establishment of small enterprises such as building companies, building materials shops, and carpentry and ironmongery businesses – as well as generating other direct and indirect jobs.

Agriculture has also benefited from fund transfer by migrants, leading to the expansion of farmed acreages and the modernisation of production methods on family farms. As regards the impact on regional investments, new projects and the urbanisation of previously deprived areas have promoted economic growth and the opening-up of remote areas. But there is nevertheless a concern that the lack of hospitable facilities in remote rural areas might divert these investments to more developed areas.

Some statistics on investment projects
Effective monitoring of Tunisian migrant practices shows that these migrants do not necessarily resort to institutional channels to start and implement development projects. Nevertheless the Tunisian government's Industry Promotion Agency (API) and Agricultural Investment Promotion Agency (APIA) have specialised departments to provide assistance to migrant investors. These departments also provide statistical updates on the contribution of Tunisian immigrants to business promotion (API n.d.).

Among the data provided by API[4] were details of 6636 projects approved for immigrants during the decade from 1991 to 2001, theoretically representing a fund mobilisation of about €150 million which could create over 27 000 jobs. The breakdown of these projects was 570 in agriculture (9%), 1575 in industry (24%) and 4491 in the service sector (67%) – thus a very significant concentration of projects were in the service sector. The API survey shows a significant geographical concentration of these projects in two coastal areas of the country – industrial projects in the North-East, and agricultural and service industries in the East-central.

The investments approved in agriculture were made in three sub-sectors: miscellaneous agricultural activities (intensive livestock development, commercial farm holdings, tree cultivation); agriculture-related services (purchase of agricultural equipment for leasing), and fisheries and aquaculture projects. The results of the survey indicate that the projects in the service sector were often marginal ones, but that they covered a wide variety of activities – hotels, restaurants and leisure places, transport, coffee shops, dry cleaning, petrol stations, gymnasiums and small computer centres.

There was, however, a low ratio of project implementation in all types of projects. According to the specialised monitoring agencies this has been hardly more than a third of the projects approved. The abovementioned survey confirms this assertion. Out of the 2111 projects proposed, only 749 were actually implemented. The survey revealed that implementation ratios varied according to the sectors concerned: 47 per cent of projects approved in the agriculture sector were implemented, 64 per cent of the projects in industry, and 25 per cent

---

4   See http://www.tunisianindustry.nat.tn/en/home.asp.

in the service sector. Thus, although the service sector represented two-thirds of approved projects, it showed the lowest implementation ratio. Part of the reason for this might be the fact – also brought out by this study – that many migrants declared projects to the investment agencies only in order to take advantage of the substantial tax relief promised for project utility vehicles.

The monitoring of projects promoted by Tunisians from abroad has highlighted the fact they mobilised only 3 per cent of total foreign fund transfers during the period 1995–2001 (API n.d.). These investments look even more modest when compared to investments made by the private sector under the country's 9th Development Plan (1997–2001) because they represent only 1 per cent of total private investments

In the area of employment, the contribution of migrant projects to employment generation during the period under consideration was just over 2 per cent of the jobs created.

Recommendations

Since it is observed that, in all countries, migration management is being geared toward stabilisation and development, it would be appropriate to make the following suggestions as to what could be done:
- organise advisory programmes and activities targeting different categories of migrants: workers, women, children of migrants, businessmen, science experts, and so on;
- draw up and implement programmes within a strategy aimed at strengthening the sense of belonging to the country of origin;
- provide conditions for better participation of migrants in local, regional and national economic development endeavours taking place in their country of origin.

In addition to these is the recommendation and to mainstream the migration issue into bilateral and multilateral cooperation frameworks it is necessary to consider:
- the protection of economic and social rights of migrants, and the promotion of the right to family reunion;
- the implementation of programmes aimed at facilitating a better integration of migrants into their host communities;
- cultural and human exchanges as essential components of dialogue and cooperation.

Fruitful dialogue between countries

For many decades, employment, unemployment and under-employment have underpinned the core issues of policy options of countries. Although no government has openly advocated emigration as a solution to unemployment, yet it must be seen as a way of reducing the pressure on the employment market by transferring excess labour abroad. Any migration projects would require certain conditions. I mention three of these: firstly the development of a free-trade zone in line with signed partnership agreements taking the movement of persons into consideration; second, the implementation in the host country of effective measures to check institutions that condone undeclared labour, and, lastly, the adoption of voluntarism and appropriate policies to prevent and control illegal employment and human trafficking networks – a critical factor in irregular migration toward European countries.

The issue of migration should be viewed – at least in part – in terms of the mobility of skilled human resources. It is therefore right to seek a better consultation between member states of the EU and Africa, and also promote legal migration and visa flexibility. The management of migratory flows between Africa and Europe should first be included into a partnership framework aimed at alleviating poverty and promoting sustainable development. The quest to meet the Millennium Development Goals, the implementation of the Cotonou Agreement, the partnership strategy that Europe has adopted on Africa must, among other things, be the basis for any Europe-Africa partnership. Sustainable development, capacity-building in the food, health and medical sectors, access to education and vocational training would contribute to local development and, consequently address the root causes of migration. Development aid could also be transferred through good management of the migratory process.

Data collection

Migration data can be, and is often, collected by institutions in the host country (statistical offices, ministries of internal affairs, and some other agencies), but this is rarely done by the relevant institutions in the countries of origin (consulate offices). The establishment of data banks on the emigration of nationals constitutes a critical component in the effective use of African professionals in activities related to African development.

Regarding statistical data collection, it is necessary to establish or strengthen statistical commissions that are charged with the compilation, standardisation and harmonisation of data processing, statistical systems and policies. The adoption of a common national survey methodology could generate useful information on the cross-border movement of populations.

In the past, the contribution of professionals living abroad has been difficult to determine given the inadequate information available. However, modern information technology tools such as e-mails and the internet could facilitate the identification and location of professionals any time this is necessary.

Conclusion

Labour migration is a global phenomenon affecting both skilled and unskilled persons in search of greener pastures. The difficulties encountered in attempts made in many parts of the world to regularise the status of migrant workers and to protect their rights can be in part explained by the ready availability of a migrant population which constitutes a pool of low-cost labour that can easily be used in such sectors as agriculture, construction and other industries of host countries.

It is hoped that the foregoing discussion and recommendations will contribute to the enhancement of equality and to poverty alleviation in a globalised world.

References

API. (Industry Promotion Agency). n.d. Tunisian Industry Portal. http://www.tunisieindustrie.nat.tn/en/doc.asp?mcat=13&mrub=98.

Adepoju, A. 2004. Trends in international migration in and from Africa. In D.S. Massey, & J.E. Taylor (eds.), *International Migration Prospects and Policies in a Global Market*. Oxford: Oxford University Press.

Ammassari, Savina. 2005. Migration and Development: New Strategic Outlooks and Practical Ways Forward The Cases of Angola and Zambia. Prepared for IOM. Geneva: IOM.

Carrington, William & Enrica Detragiache. 1998. *How Big is the Brain Drain?* IMF Working Papers 98/102, International Monetary Fund.

Chang, Howard F. 1999. *Migration as International Trade: The Economic Gains from the Liberalized Movement of Labor*. Stanford Law School, John M. Olin Program in Law and Economics Working Paper No. 166; and Univ. of Pennsylvania Law School, ILE Working Paper No. 278. http://ssrn.com/abstract=184868 (accessed 23 June 2009).

Docquier F. & A. Marfouk. 2004. *Measuring The International Mobility of Skilled workers*, Policy research working paper no. 3382. Washington DC: World Bank.

Dzvimbo, Kuzvinetsa Peter. 2003. *The International Migration of Skilled Human Capital from Developing Countries*. Case study prepared for a World Bank/ HDNED Regional Training Conference on Improving Tertiary Education in Sub-Saharan Africa. September 23–25, Accra. http://siteresources.worldbank.org/INTAFRREGTOPTEIA/Resources/peter_dzvimbo.pdf

Expatax. 2007. http://www.expatax.nl/tax_plan_2007.htm (accessed 23 June 2009).

Fadayomi, T.O. 1996. Brain Drain and Brain Gain in Africa: Dimensions and Consequences. In A. Adepoju & T. Hammar, *International Migration in and from Africa: Dimensions, Challenges and Prospects*. Dakar: PHRDA; Stockholm: CEIFO.

INSEE (L'Institut national de la statistique et des études économiques[5]). 2003. http://www.insee.fr/en/insee-statistique-publique/default.asp?page=colloques/citygroup/citygroup-2003-meeting.htm

INSEE. n.d. The population census: results of surveys since 2004. http://www.insee.fr/en/bases-de-donnees/default.asp?page=recensements.htm

IOM (International Organization for Migration). 2003. *World Migration Report*. Geneva: IOM.

IOM. 2005. *World Migration Report*. Geneva: IOM.

Lopez-Bassols, Vladimir. 2002. *ICT Skills and Employment*. Paris: Organization for Economic Cooperation and Development.

Lucas, Robert E., Jr. 1988. On the Mechanics of Economic Development. *Journal of Monetary Economics* 22, 3–42.

---

5 National Institute for Statistics and Economic Studies.

OECD (Organisation for Economic Co-Operation and Development). 2003. *Annual Report*. Paris: Public Affairs Division, OECD.

OECD. 2004. *Trends in International Migration: Annual Report 2004 Edition*. Paris: OECD.

Open Doors. 2001. *Data Tables/By Country and Level/Foreign Students by Academic Level and Place of Origin*. http://opendoors.iienetwork.org/file_depot/ 0-10000000/0-10000/3390/folder/14677/OD2001ByCountryand+Level.htm (accessed 23 June 2009).

Pang, Tikki, Mary Ann Lansang & Andy Haines. 2002. Brain drain and health professionals. A global problem needs global solutions, *British Medical Journal*, Editorial, 324: 499–500.

Rogers, A. 2000. Literacy in the Information Age: final report of the International Adult Literacy Survey, *International Review of Education*, 46 (5) 467–473.

Romer, P.M. 1986. Increasing Returns and Long-Run Growth, *Journal of Political Economy*, 94 (5) 1002–1037.

Romer, P.M. 1987. Growth Based on Increasing Returns Due to Specialization, *American Economic Review*, 77: 56–62.

SOPEMI-OCDE. 1999. Panorama des statistiques de l'OCDE 1999. Paris: OCDE.

Stalker, Peter. 1994. *The work of strangers : a survey of international labour migration*. Geneva: International Labour Organization.

UNDP. 1992. http://hdr.undp.org/en/reports/global/hdr1992/ (accessed 23 June 2009).

Wahba, Jackline. 2003. *Does International Migration Matter? Arab migration in a globalized world*. Paper presented at a regional conference on Arab migration organized by the International Organization for Migration and the League of Arab States, September 2003, Cairo.

WHO (World Health Organization). 2003. *Migration of Health Personnel: A Challenge for Health Systems in Africa*, Brazzaville: WHO.

World Bank. 1995. Trends in Developing Economies. Washington DC: World Bank. http://www.ciesin.org/IC/wbank/tde-home.html (accessed 23 June 2009).

CHAPTER THREE B

Emigration of Skilled Professionals from Africa: Dimensions and Consequences

T O Fadayomi

Introduction

In a world where goods and services are expected to flow freely on account of global economic integration and competitive markets, the movement of people and their skills is still a sticky issue. The big surge in international flows of goods and capital has not been matched by an equivalent flow of migrants in the post-World War II era. Until World War I, few legislative or political barriers impeded the process of international migration. After World War II immigration became acceptable and possible only if it was in the interests of the receiving state, while the interests of the sending country was seen as secondary (Özden & Schiff 2006; Livi-Bacci 1997). However, public interest in the rapid transition from colonial economies to industrialised independent economies in the countries of emigration right after political independence started to generate concern about the emigration of skilled professionals.

Interests in both immigrant and emigrant countries span social, economic, political and strategic considerations. In immigrant countries, while there is a realistic need to supplement dwindling domestic labour supply in critical and other skills with those of foreigners, the costs of immigration include the perceived threat to cultural identity and migrants' competition for the same jobs as natives, especially for some semi-skilled jobs. With the September 2001 terrorist attacks in United States, the concern for security has come to the fore. In emigrant countries, the opportunity cost of emigration in terms of the loss of human capital – a scarce factor, critical for development – is usually counted against gains of another scarce factor: financial resources in the form of remittances. While a convergence is yet to evolve on the various perspectives of the major stakeholders on the emigration of skilled professionals, some of the affected nations have created bilateral agreements to facilitate, conditionally, the migration of workers with specific types of skills. Other countries, especially emigrant countries, have not been able to enforce any effective regulatory measures on migration; and some of them have thus accepted the inevitability of migration under the existing global conditions and have created institutions to enhance the development impact of migrant remittances and social capital.

What follows is an elaboration of the dimensions of emigration of skilled African professionals, with a discussion of the theoretical perspectives on international migration as applied to skilled workers, the political economy of the emigration of skilled professionals from Africa in terms of push and pull factors, and the magnitude and patterns of emigration from the time of political independence up till the present. The consequences are then discussed in terms of the impact of the emigration of skilled African professionals on higher education, capacity building, technology transfer, the attainment of the millennium development goals (MDGs), and remittances and development. The chapter concludes by considering ways to enhance the development impact of skilled emigrants in Africa – by gauging the effectiveness of previous attempts at reversing the emigration of skills from Africa, and by re-examining the experiences of other developing or transitional countries with regard to the emigration of skilled professionals.

The dimensions of the emigration of skilled African professionals

Theoretically, the outflow of skilled Africans to countries of the North hinges, in most cases, on the difference between actual wages at the origin of the migrants and the expected wages at destination, adjusted for migration 'costs' such as restrictive policies in the immigrant countries, transportation costs from origin to destination, time and ease of adjustment to the social and political environment of the immigrant countries etc. (Özden & Schiff 2006; United Nations 1997). While this theoretical perspective may be applied to the emigration of semi-skilled and unskilled Africans to European countries with whom they had colonial ties (Britain, France, Portugal, Spain etc.), to the United States, and to oil-rich countries in the middle East, it is also applicable to intra-African voluntary migration of skilled workers to destination countries such as Ivory Coast, Nigeria in the 1970s and early 1980s, and South Africa after the dismantling of apartheid in the 1990s.

Apart from the wage and migration cost effects, the literature points to current demographic trends in the countries of the North, and developing countries such as Africa, as being a crucial factor in the South to North 'emigration of skills'. The labour force in many countries of the North is expected to peak around 2010 and decline by around 5 per cent in the each of the subsequent two decades, accompanied by rapid increases in dependency ratios[1], resulting from

---

[1] A measure of the portion of a population who are dependents (too young or too old to work). It is the ratio of the number of people not of working age (the dependent part) to the number who are of working age (the economically active part).

ageing. Conversely, the labour force in many African countries is expanding because of the onset of fertility transition[2], resulting in declines in dependency ratios. This imbalance is likely to reduce the restrictive policies in countries of the North, encourage the liberalisation of immigration policies, and generate a strong demand for workers from developing countries (Schiff & Özden 2007). It is also argued in the literature that the emigration of skilled professionals from developing to developed countries will tend to raise the expected benefit to individual migrants from education and training. It will also induce additional investment in education, engendering an increase in the average level of education and in the skills of emigrants. However, this form of 'brain gain' may not bring higher wages to migrants at their places of destination. Skilled immigrants may earn less than nationals of the country of destination even if their skills are equal to, or even superior to, those of the nationals of the host country, thus experiencing 'brain waste' due to discrimination or excessive restrictions to entry in various professions controlled by nationals (Lucas 2005; Ellerman 2005).

While the aforementioned theoretical perspectives are useful – based as they are on the relative prosperity of emigrants at destination – they do not disentangle the total picture of the political economy of the emigration of skilled Africans whose migration decisions are influenced largely by a combination of family, social, economic and political circumstances (Fadayomi 1994; 1996). Many writers have focused on the conditions at the places of origin of skilled African emigrants as being the major factors of migration-push (Akokpari 2006; Danso 1995; Jumare 1997). Apart from the personal characteristics which distinguish emigrants from other members of their society, the emigration of highly-skilled persons from African countries has generally been influenced by the nature of the post-colonial economies of most African countries since the emergence of political independence.

After independence, a reliance on primary commodities, the unimpressive growth of import-substitution industrialisation in post-independence states in Africa, and generally unfavourable terms of trade led to slow growth in formal employment, an underdeveloped private sector and an escalating growth in inflation. Added to this economic situation was the drive for self-sufficiency in high level manpower supply, leading to a rapid increase in educational facilities and the award of scholarships for foreign acquisition of skills. Thus the outcome, right from the second decade of political independence, has been a relatively large number of graduates out of tune with employment opportunities. The access to graduate schools and other fields of specialisation in developed countries has often led to over-specialisation, which in turn reduces migrant professionals' ability to secure challenging jobs upon their return.

Another important push factor in the emigration of professionals from

---

2 Downward trend in fertility rates.

Africa was the autocratic and military-style regimes pervasive across Africa prior to the democratisation wave of the early 1990s. It played no small role in inducing the emigration of political opponents who were constantly threatened with arrests and detention. The victims of such repression and persecution included academics and professionals who, lacking propitious environments for intellectual and professional activities at home, emigrated – sometimes to other African countries which were relatively more prosperous, but more often to their former metropolitan countries and other destinations beyond the continent.

At the same time as African professionals were facing repressive regimes and abuses of human rights, especially in the 1980s, the educational system in most African countries had begun a process of decay, mainly due to IMF structural adjustment policies, which encouraged further curtailment of public sector employment and de-industrialisation. These policies discouraged investment in education and health, and encouraged the retrenchment of professionals in the civil service along with the devaluation of salaries and benefits. Included also was the premature retrenchment of academics and the disintegration of infrastructure in universities, for example through obsolete laboratories and teaching equipment, and in overcrowded classrooms. According to the United Nations Development Programme (UNDP) and the International Organization for Migration (IOM), Nigeria, for instance, lost thousands of highly specialised personnel to the developed world between 1985 and 1990.

Making these factors more effective in pushing the emigration of skilled Africans are the immigration laws in major destination countries such as the USA, Canada, the UK and many European countries, which have been selective in attracting skilled professionals. Besides, the expansion of international academic contacts – through an increasing number of students being sent to study in developed countries, exchange programmes and the large number of foreign teachers working temporarily in African countries – has been favourable to the emigration of skills.

Magnitude and patterns of the emigration of skilled professionals from Africa

There is a lack of adequate statistics on the international movement of highly-skilled persons. Statistics on the magnitude, levels and trends of this type of migration are not commonly available, partly because migrants are generally not classified with sufficient detail of occupation and educational attainment (United Nations 1997). Only estimates are therefore available of the numbers of international migrants – defined as persons who take up residence or remain for an extended stay in a foreign country, either voluntarily or by being forced (IOM 2000). However, the magnitude and patterns of emigration of skills from Africa can be discussed effectively by grouping them under the following periods:

from pre-independence to early years of independence (late 1960s), the 1970s, and the 1980s till the present.

Prior to political independence, Africa's contribution to total global emigration was insignificant. In fact most post-colonial African nations depended on their metropolitan countries for critical high-level manpower. While this situation created a drive for the rapid expansion of existing colonial educational infrastructures to meet domestic manpower requirements, post-colonial governments still encouraged students to acquire skills overseas to supplement the domestic output of such skills. The issue of brain drain from these countries began to arise in the late 1960s as many students either remained abroad or returned there after a brief stay in the home country. The dominant migration paths used to be from francophone Africa to France, from anglophone Africa to Britain and the USA, from Zaire to Belgium, and from the former Portuguese colonies (lusophone Africa) to Portugal. Usually the direction of skilled African emigration at that time was thus towards the metropolitan countries, where most of their 'foreign' skills were acquired. According to the United Nations Economic Commission for Africa (UNECA) and the IOM, an estimate of 27 000 skilled Africans left the continent for industrialised countries between 1960 and 1975 (UNDPI various; Adepoju 1991).

The early years of political independence in the majority of African countries in the 1960s witnessed an impressive rate of economic growth (due to a combination of improved prices for their primary commodities and the positive short-run impact of the import-substitution industrialisation strategy adopted). But in the mid-1970s, most African economies started sagging as a result of a general decline in world trade for primary commodities and the upsurge in the price of energy. The ensuing economic situation resulted in inflation, a curtailment of public sector employment, a downward trend in real wages and income, and falling standards in social infrastructures. Major sub-Saharan African oil-producing countries like Nigeria and Gabon witnessed an economic boom, as did Ivory Coast, which had a large agricultural surplus at the time. These countries became alternative destinations for some of the skilled migrants who would otherwise have headed for metropolitan countries. Nationals of Gambia, Sierra Leone, Liberia and Ghana with high-level skills in engineering, applied science, medicine etc. migrated to Nigeria from home countries where the impact of inflation and recession and, in some cases, political conflicts had been considerable. Highly trained migrants came to Ivory Coast from Senegal, Mali, Burkina Faso and Guinea (Fadayomi 1996). An estimate of 40 000 skilled Africans emigrated between 1975 and 1984 (UNDPI various). USA immigration statistics record, for the period of 1974 to 1985, that sub-Saharan African emigration to the USA stood at 0.7 percent of total figures in 1974, rose to 1.0 percent in 1977, 1.7 percent in 1983 and 2 percent in 1985, a trebling over a ten-year period.

The emigration of highly-skilled Africans, which started with an up-swing in the 1970s, intensified from the 1980s. Economies that were on the decline in the

1970s had worsened in the 1980s and 1990s. The state of depressed economies in Africa has been attributed to domestic inflation, arising from adverse economic policies, unrestrained and unproductive government expenditure, a weak industrial base, declining or only slowly growing agricultural production, worsening terms of trade, and trade deficits leading to huge external debts. These factors impacted on the population, especially in the period of IMF-imposed economic adjustment programmes in the form of large-scale retrenchment from the public service – which normally absorbs the largest proportion of employees in the formal sector. Rapid rates of inflation have shrunk formerly inadequate wages to the extent that salary earners often must moonlight in order to make ends meet. In some cases, salaries have been reduced to enable governments to maintain a minimum level of public employment for the provision of meagre social services.

Until the advent of democracy, with popular participation and good governance, towards the end of last century, political instability in many African states was another factor in the emigration of Africa's critical skills. The unstable political situation in many African countries engendered a politics of repression and persecution, with muzzling of the press, and intimidation targeted at students, workers and intellectuals. In several parts of Africa, political parties are largely ethnically based. While each ethnic group strove to gain political power, minority groups were often persecuted and their leaders forced to flee for safety. High level professionals caught in this web of politics, either as activists or minority intellectuals, might be forced to flee – either to other African countries or to the developed western countries.

We cannot underestimate the role which the international mass media might have played, indirectly, in the decision-making processes of high level migration from Africa to developed countries. This, in conjunction with the increasing traffic of tourists from Europe and North America to Africa, could have spurred many people to migrate to these countries where they expected that their economic aspirations would be met, and where they had personal contacts with people who had migrated earlier and might even have become citizens.

Thus, politico-economic conditions in the 1980s and 1990s were quite favourable to further emigration. A substantial number of highly-skilled people joined the stream of migration from countries where economies had collapsed. Nigeria and Zimbabwe, which used to be havens for African migrants, joined the flow of migrant-suppliers as their economies declined – with Nigerians streaming to the Gulf States in the mid-1980s. The apartheid 'homelands' of pre-democracy South Africa were a most attractive destination for all types of migrants from other southern African states, and since 1970s highly qualified and experienced workers in trades and professions that are in decline in their home countries have been migrating there from Zimbabwe, Zambia, Senegal, Ghana, Uganda, etc. While South Africa has attracted immigrants at an increasing tempo since the advent of majority rule, it has also driven out some of its own citizens, mainly white professionals who have emigrated to Australia, New Zealand, the UK and the US. By 1997, just three years into black majority rule, South Africa was estimated to have lost 11 225 'brains' in various professions. However, the influx of immigrants, estimated in 2006 at 6 million, has greatly outstripped the number emigrating (Akokpari 2006).

In spite of the increasing immigration restrictions in developed Western countries since the 1980s, African skilled professionals gained access to these nations, in some cases, through special quota measures. Under incessant economic pressure and in intolerable working conditions, professionals from Africa have generally, though not exclusively, found their former metropolises to be preferred destinations due to old historical ties, shared linguistic similarities and ease of assimilation. Other major destinations are European countries outside the metropolis areas, such as Germany, Italy etc, as well as North America and the oil-rich countries of the Middle East. While the precise figures on this pattern of emigration from Africa to developed Western countries and other continents are not available, the Economic Commission for Africa and the IOM estimated that at least 20 000 skilled Africans have left the continent each year since 1990 (UNDPI 2003). In the fifteen years from 1989 to 2004, 15.5 million immigrants from 231 nations received permanent resident status in the United States, including 675 665 immigrants from 57 countries listed in the African region. However, only one African nation, Nigeria, figures among the top thirty sending nations, with African immigrants constituting 4.4 percent of all immigrants (Hewitt 2006).

Given the critical role of universities in the sustainable development of African countries with respect to human capital development, research and technological innovations, we need to reflect on the emigration of university-based professionals: teachers, administrators and researchers, as well as medical and allied professions that are essential for the improvement of the health status of the African population.

Brain drain from African universities and health-care institutions

Without doubt, the emigration of African skills since the 1980s has made a noticeable dent on the different spheres of economic activities where critical skills are needed for Africa's development. The health and education sectors are often the hardest hit, leaving home governments with the onerous task of either replacing lost skills or grappling with massive declines in the quality of service delivery in the affected sectors. A 1995 World Bank study noted that some 23 000 qualified academic staff were emigrating from Africa each year in search of better working conditions. It is estimated that about 10 000 Nigerian academics were employed in USA at the time (World Bank 1995).

Many findings have been reported on the parlous state of African universities right from the 1980s (Oni 2000; Edokat 2000; Sako 2002; Getahun 2002; Manuh et al 2002). In Nigeria, for example, it was observed that the university continued to suffer from brain drain since 1980s, especially in the critical fields of medicine, pharmacy, computer science and engineering. Many good students who probably would have enrolled for graduate courses in these fields of study, to promote technological capability in Nigeria, had no teachers to guide their studies (Oni 2000). From the 1990s, in most other African countries, the decline in teachers in critical disciplines and the lack of ability to recruit or train new ones for succession can be traced to the drastic reduction in the salaries of university teachers. In Cameroon, university teachers lost between 35 and 42 per cent of their salaries (in nominal terms) in 1993. Added to the devaluation of the national currency, this loss in salary could, in some cases, have been as high as 60 per cent or more (Edokat 2000). The plight of university teachers in Cameroon was illustrated by a survey carried out by the National Union of Teachers of Higher Education and published in 1999 ((Edokat 2000). It was found that most of the teachers lacked minimum comfort and basic needs such as vehicles, personal houses, telephones, computers, offices, journals, and teaching materials, and were often victims of electricity and water disruptions because they could not pay their bills in time. As a result of the poor economic status of teachers, as well as the disintegration of infrastructures in the universities, there were agitations from the teachers' union for improvement in the conditions of service, and for better funding of university education. Hence, the relationship between universities and the state became increasingly tense, and academic staff were always the victims (Jumare 1997).

The situation of medical and paramedical personnel is not much different from that of university professionals. Based on anecdotal sources such as electronic and news media, it appears that, in the 1980s and 1990s, Nigeria alone lost about a quarter or more of its critical medical and allied manpower to the Western world, the Middle-East and South Africa. In most cases the immigrant countries, especially Saudi Arabia, launched recruitment missions to the countries of origin, calling on nurses, mid-wives, laboratory technologists, therapists, specialist doctors etc. working in teaching hospitals – the apex of these nation's medical establishments. Like university professional emigrants, health professionals were operating under harsh economic conditions. Wages were low, working hours were long because of the large clientele in need of care, and hospitals and clinics were in dire need of equipment and infrastructural repairs. While the situation witnessed some improvements at the dawn of the century, emigration of skilled professionals has not yet abated.

Consequences of emigration

The consequences of the emigration of African skilled persons have been examined in previous studies with respect to the impact on the individual emigrants, their origin and on the societies in which they are immigrants (Fadayomi 1996). The emphasis in this chapter is therefore on the impact of emigration on the critical skills needed for development in Africa, as well as on remittances and development, and on the development of transnational communities of emigrants in host countries.

Emigration and critical skills for Africa's development

It can not be gainsaid that one of the challenges to Africa's development in this century is the inadequate stock of high level manpower required for modernising economies, due partly to the permanent or temporary loss of critical skills. This development is considered to be serious, also because of the substantial educational investments of the various African nations in terms of scholarships, financial aid and the establishment of expensive tertiary institutions. As a result, policy makers in Africa are apt to point quickly to the net negative consequences of the emigration of skilled Africans, even while they admit some of the benefits in form of migrant remittances.

Confronted with the quest for poverty reduction and the meeting of basic needs – as set out in the eight main Millennium Development Goals (MDGs)[3] – the roles of critical African skills can not be overemphasised in respect of poverty eradication, enhancement of educational and health status of the population as well as the status of women. According to Table 3.9, the social indicators of population per physician and student/teacher ratio in most 'brain drain' African countries show relatively high ratios of inadequacy – which were considerably worse for rural communities, where the majority live – when compared to countries of immigration in the 1990s when emigration was intense.

---

3   The MDGs underscore the importance of developing a new generation of plans and programmes that focus on making economic growth more pro-poor, targeting inequality and emphasising the empowerment of women. The eight main MDGs, which were later teased out into 18 targets are: eradication of extreme poverty and hunger; achievement of universal primary education; promotion of gender equity and empowerment of women; reduction of child mortality; improvement of maternal health; combating HIV/AIDS, malaria and other diseases; and environmental sustainability.

Table 3.9: Estimates of Human Capital Indicators in major countries of brain drain and their destinations in the 1990s

Countries	Population per physician	Student/teacher ratio (secondary level)
Countries of brain drain		
Algeria	2 331	17
Ghana	22 970	19
Senegal	17 646	35
Burkina Faso	57 320	30
Mali	19 448	14
Guinea	38 961	16
Nigeria*	5 356	—
Zimbabwe*	7 181	27
Countries of destination		
Libya	957	12
Gabon	2 397	22
South Africa	1 750	33**
Saudi Arabia	656	14
United Kingdom	—	13
France	346	14
Belgium	311	—
Canada	450	14
USA	421	—

* Countries of immigration of skilled manpower from other African countries in the 1970s and early 1980s. ** Estimate was for 1984.
Sources: World Bank (1993); United Nations (1992).

These disparities in human capital formation are further worsened by emigration. Since universities are expected to be the nation's knowledge industry where technological innovations, ideas and skills are produced, the massive emigration of teachers that took place from the 1980s implies that fewer people are now able and willing to work on the development of appropriate technologies and research problems for these countries. In addition, the students who would probably have enrolled for graduate courses in the critical disciplines to promote the necessary technological capabilities have no teachers to guide their studies. Thus the much-needed intellectual capacity for the future cannot be built.

With the loss of high level medical and paramedical personnel, it has also become increasingly difficult for many teaching hospitals' departments, faculties and centres of research to run efficiently. At the same time, it has become impossible to depend on rented foreign skills because of salary differentials. Therefore most of the national and international goals of health development, such as the health-related MDGs, cannot be attained by using the available indigenous manpower. Hence, those attempting the pursuit of the international agenda on health may have to grapple with massive declines in the quality of service delivery in the short and medium term.

Emigrant remittances and socio-economic development

In spite of the afore-mentioned negative consequences of emigration, its benefits in the form of migrant remittances to their places of origin have been identified as the second largest form of capital inflow into Africa after foreign direct investments (FDIs) and are much larger than Overseas Development Assistance (ODA) (Özden & Schiff 2006). In 2001 for example, remittance to developing countries was equivalent to 42 per cent of FDIs and 260 per cent of ODA.

In terms of regional distribution, sub-Saharan Africa received 5 per cent of total global remittances, with the bulk going to Latin America and the Caribbean (Sander 2003). The region received US$ 19 billion in remittances in 2007 or 2.5 per cent of GDP. Almost three-quarters of the remittances to sub-Saharan Africa in 2007 were sent from United States and Western Europe, while the rest were sent from Gulf States, other developed countries and developing countries (Godwin Nnanna, *Business Day*, 21–23 November 2008). It is, however, conceivable that the percentage of global remittances to sub-Saharan Africa would be higher if accurate data existed as some transfers still take place via informal channels where the banking systems in countries of origin are inadequately developed. (In addition some migrants choose these informal channels because of high bank charges for money transfers.)

Remittances are expected to be additional sources of development financing in Africa by providing a lifeline, not only to communities and families to enable them to gain access to basic services such as housing, education and health, but also to national savings and investment via money and capital markets. However, the real impact of remittances on the economies of emigration countries in Africa is yet to be fully understood as, apart from their raising the level of national savings, remittances are essentially private transfers that do not directly augment the public budget. Governments also have no control over them and do not determine their destination or their use. Nor are market forces able to channel remittances to the most productive sectors or into the most innovative entrepreneurial hands to promote development (Akokpari 2006).

Another pertinent issue is that of the reliability of remittances. According to a recent view expressed on the impact of the global financial crisis on remittances (Godwin Nnanna writing in *Business Day*, 21–23 November 2008), many families in Accra and other parts of Ghana who depend on remittances from relatives in the United States and Europe for day-to-day support are being affected by the global economic meltdown which impacts negatively on their donors due to crisis-induced retrenchment and unemployment in countries of immigration. This takes a heavy toll on the daily budget of recipients via reduced levels of remittances. According to the World Bank's latest migration and development brief, published on 11 November 2008, remittance income in developing countries was expected to decline by 1 per cent from 2008–2009.

The development of transnational communities

A major fallout from emigration in general is the development of transnational migrant communities or the 'diaspora' in the countries of immigration. While the concept of 'brain drain' associates emigration with the dead end of lost human capital, there is usually no emigration without both a return flow and a substantial number of non-returning migrants who form the core transnational migrant community, often with close links to their origin through remittances and business operations. These diaspora are usually formed where relatively large numbers of a country's emigrant population take up residence in a scientifically advanced country (Patterson 2005). Diasporic communities are often supported by national governments – for example South Korea, India, China, Philippines – in their entry into information technology, in their business operations and in networking into their homelands. Ultimately their homelands became the recipients of investment – sometimes including overseas branches – from the firms in which these transnationals had, over time, achieved managerial and technical prominence (Patterson 2005). Patterson (2005) asserts that up to 30 per cent of the start-up of firms in the information technology industry in Silicon Valley, California USA was owned by Asian nationals.

Studies of migration show that migrants maintain social, political and, most importantly, economic linkages with their countries of origin even while in the process of forming transnational communities. Technological development in transportation and telecommunication has allowed migrants to maintain ties between origin and destination more strongly than ever before (Skeldon 2008). In Africa, emigrants usually move to countries of destination about which they have some information, pertaining to settlement and adjustment, employment prospects and social networks formed by chain migration involving close relatives and friends.

Chain migration is stimulated by positive conditions that pull new migrants to places where earlier migrants took up residence. Often migrants of the same ethnic group or from the same region nucleate in particular parts of receiving countries where they evolve social and economic links as well as networks to sustain their solidarity (Adepoju 1996). These African migrants have recently become more organised and often concentrate on the development of their communities of origin through their diaspora associations. These groups then refocus a substantial portion of remittances and associated investments towards community development such as the formation of community banks, support for communal projects, and so on. With the support of some African governments, diaspora associations have, in recent times, been evolving from community and ethnic groups into national organisations enthusiastic about political, social and development agendas.

Enhancing the development impact of skilled migrants from Africa

It is evident that the remittances of Africa's professional emigrants are the direct compensation for the loss, temporary or permanent, of scarce expertise needed for Africa's social and economic transformation. While the real economic value of the two sides of the emigration phenomenon remains poorly explored and has not been objectively ascertained, the countries of emigration in the continent are yearning for the development which remittances, largely in form of intra-family and personal investment transfers, are presently ill-suited for.

The perception of remittance is that it is an inflow of capital, like foreign direct investment, into the emigrant's country of origin as an additional source of investment. However, remittances may not impact on development, especially if the large part constitutes a flow in cash or kind directly to the migrant's family for consumption, or to the diaspora's communities of small rural towns and villages. The immediate effect can be to reinforce or increase inequalities between regions, or between rural and urban areas, depending on where emigrants originate.

Similarly, the discussion of skilled migration and development and the preoccupation with emigration as a source of brain drain from Africa diverts attention from the underlying developmental issues that induce emigration, such as the domestic policies towards university education and the management and retention of high level manpower in the economy. It is therefore expedient to examine how African countries can obtain maximum returns from their skilled migrants by minimising the loss of skills and managing their remittances better for development.

Many African countries have tried in the past to restrict the migration of the highly skilled in the hope of spurring development at home. Three major types of policies were adopted to influence the emigration of skilled personnel or diminish its consequences (UNCTAD 1988). In sub-Saharan Africa, regulatory or restrictive policies in the form of passport regulations and short-term exit permits were put in place – for example in Sudan in 1978–1980. Similar policies such as service bonding and national service programmes have been adopted by Ethiopia, Ghana and Nigeria since the 1970s. Another attempt was the policy of de-linking the nation's educational system from international standards in order to facilitate the absorption of professional personnel by giving employment preference to nationals with national certificates as opposed to internationally negotiable diplomas. Countries under the British colonial rule like Ghana, Nigeria and Sierra Leone created trade schools immediately after the attainment of political independence. These schools' diplomas were given more recognition than the erstwhile City and Guilds trade certificates received from United

Kingdom. A third policy was incentive-based, covering a wide range of measures to induce skilled persons to return to their countries. These are programmes aimed at providing skilled nationals abroad with information about employment opportunities at home; for example the UNDP[4] -financed Transfer of Knowledge through Expatriate Nationals provides assistance to skilled emigrants, allowing them to work in their home country for short periods of time. Another example is an International Organization for Migration (IOM) programme through which placement opportunities in the home country are identified, and then qualified people living in developed countries are approached with job offers (Pires 1992). The programme, which covered the period from 1983 to 1999, provided incentives for returnees and their dependents – such as travel expenses, installation allowances, medical and accident insurance, and so on – for an average of six months. However, by the end of the programme very few skilled migrants had been re-integrated into their countries. It did nevertheless manage to relocate about 2000 nationals to eleven participating countries over the 16 years. On the whole, neither repatriation and relocation nor previously-mentioned regulatory policies made any significant impact on reversing the brain drain (Akokpari 2006).

In sub-Sahara Africa these policies are bound to fail for as long as domestic policies of development have not addressed the underlying causes of emigration of skills, such as the availability of research facilities in higher institutions of learning, better conditions of work and pay for skilled professionals – especially in the education and health fields that are critical to human capital development. In addition, the recent democratisation of the political system in many African countries needs to be deepened in order to enhance good governance, human rights and the rule of law, which are fundamental to the effective participation of skilled Africans in the affairs of their countries without the fear of political victimisation which was rife in the last century.

Given the more recent and considerable shift in developed countries from capital goods industrialisation to the knowledge-based industries of information technology, nanotechnology and communication, labour with high levels of skilled human capital is in excess demand, thus inducing industrialised countries in the West to devise more permanent migration options for professionals from developing countries skilled in these fields. Immigration policy is thus rapidly emerging as a tool of industrial policy – as advanced industrial economies compete with each other to overcome a shortage in critical skills by attempting to attract them from the global human capital (Kapur 2001). Within this scenario, the migration of skilled African professionals has become inevitable. Therefore we need realistic policies in Africa to minimise the cost to the countries of origin of this type of migration, and to maximise its benefits by adopting an effective management mechanism to make migrant remittances more development-

---

4 United Nations Development Programme.

oriented and by using appropriate incentives to engage the diaspora in the development of Africa.

Both India and Philippines, for example, have engaged in proactive strategies to attract migrants' remittances, foster the use of formal channels, and enhance development impacts at home by granting incentives and privileges to remitters in terms of investment options, purchase of land, tax breaks, and so on (Anh 2005). In Vietnam, before 1987, recipients of migrant remittances were forced to withdraw their money in Vietnamese currency at the bank, so many preferred to receive goods and gifts that they could resell in the free market, for example medicines, clothes, cosmetics, electric and electronic devices. With the policy reforms introduced after 1987, the whole economy started to benefit. From the late 1990s until 2004, about a third of remittances were used for small-scale enterprises – as opposed to for direct consumption (Anh 2005).

In order to engage the diaspora effectively in development, African countries need to use their foreign embassies to foster good relations between host countries and the diaspora, to allow the latter to carry out their business activities in an atmosphere of peace and harmony. They should then be encouraged to develop their social capital and effectively contribute their quota to the political, social and economic development at home, for example through the establishment of institutions of information, education and communication.

The diaspora should be permanently linked to their homelands through channels that promote a knowledge of their history, through cultural events and through interaction with their people at origin, especially through electronic and news media. This effort would help in the transmission to subsequent generations of national values and aspirations, and in the promotion of nationalism. The social capital of the diaspora should be fostered by encouraging and formalising their associations, and supporting them officially and financially. As remitters, these migrants need assistance to enhance their means of livelihood – for instance by giving them access to home country resources to acquire advanced training in their countries of immigration in high value-added industries, gaining skills which can be exported home. A last point that should not be overlooked is that they often need the support of national banks for transactions and loans in their businesses at destination.

Conclusions and way forward

In recent times, countries of emigration in Africa and other developing regions have come to recognise the inevitability of the emigration of their skilled professionals to economically more advanced countries, both because of the demand for such skills, and because of the inability of African governments to regulate, restrict and sufficiently retain these skilled emigrants. Different strategies have been adopted in countries as economically and politically diverse as India, Philippines, Vietnam, China and, recently, some African countries, to attract migrants' remittances to enhance national development and to support their diaspora as viable channels for the transfer of human capital, technology and industry from developed countries (the major destination of the emigrants) to their homelands.

In order for African countries to derive maximum benefit from this strategy, there is an urgent need for a reform of the existing migration protocol into a practicable development policy that fosters formal institutions aimed at attracting migrants' remittances for national development via the money and capital markets and other investment options that are secure and attractive to the migrants. In addition, a national patronage of the diaspora through diplomatic and economic institutions needs to be put in place in their countries of abode – which is likely to enhance not only their financial capital transfer, but also their social capital, and the return of some critical skills, technology, industrial know-how and entrepreneurship.

We should also take note that, as the ongoing global crisis continues to reduce Africa's options regarding foreign investment, aid, technology and value of primary exports, a reverse in-flow of capital into African countries can be induced through sufficient socially and economically viable diaspora being attracted back to their homelands.

References

Adepoju, Aderanti. 1991. South-North Migration: The African Experience, *International Migration*, 29 (2).

Adepoju, Aderanti. 1996. The Links between Intra-continental and Inter-continental Migration in and from Africa. In *International Migration in and from Africa: Dimensions, Challenges and Prospects*. Dakar: Population, Human Resources Development in Africa (PHRDA); Stockholm: Centre for Research in International migration and Ethnic Relations (CEIFO).

Akokpari, John. 2006. Globalization, Migration and the Challenges of Development in Africa. *Perspectives on Global Development and Technology*, 5 (3).

Anh, Dang Nguyen. 2005. Enhancing the Development of Migrant Remittances and Diaspora: the Case of Vietnam, *Asia-Pacific Population Journal* 20 (3).

Danso, Kwaku. 1995. The African Brain Drain: Causes and Policy Prescriptions, *Scandinavian Journal of Development Alternatives*, 14 (1, 2).

Edokat, Tafar. 2000. *Effects of Brain Drain on Higher Education in Cameroon*. Paper presented at UNECA Regional Conference on Brain Drain and Capacity Building in Africa, Addis Ababa, 22–24 February.

Ellerman, David. 2005. Labour Migration: A Developmental Path or Low-level Trap? *Development in Practice*, 15 (5).

Fadayomi, T.O. 1994. Brain Drain from African States: Empirical Evidence and Policy Implications, *African Population Studies*, No 9, April.

Fadayomi, T.O. 1996. Brain Drain and Brain Gain in Africa: Dimensions and Consequences. In A. Adepoju & T. Hammar, *International Migration in and from Africa: Dimensions, Challenges and Prospects*. Dakar: PHRDA; Stockholm: CEIFO.

Getahun, Solomon A. 2002. Brain Drain and its Effects on Ethiopia's Institutions of Higher Learning. *African Issues*, 30 (1).

Hewitt, Cynthia Lucas. 2006. Pan-African Brain Circulation. *Perspectives on Global Development and Technology*, 5 (3).

IOM (International Organization for Migration). 2000. *World Migration Report*. Geneva: IOM.

Jumare, Ibrahim M. 1997. The Displacement of the Nigerian Academic Community, *Journal of Asian and African Studies*, XXXII (1, 2).

Kapur, Devesh. 2001. Diaspora and Technology Transfer, *Journal of Human Development*, 2 (2).

Livi-Bacci, Massimo. 1997. *South-North Migration: A comparative approach to North American and European experiences*. Paris: OECD.

Lucas, Robert E.B. 2005. *International Migration and Economic Development: Lessons from low-income countries*. Stockholm: Expert Group on Development Issues/Almqvist & Wiksell International.

Manuh, Takyiwaa, Richard Asante & Jerome Djangmah. 2002. The Brain Drain in the Higher Education Sector in Ghana, *African Issues*, XXX (1).

Oni, B. 2000. *Capacity Building Effort and Brain Drain in Nigerian Universities*. Paper presented at UNECA Regional Conference on Brain Drain and Capacity Building in Africa, Addis Ababa, 22–24 February.

Özden, Çağlarr & Maurice Schiff (eds.). 2006 *International Migration, Remittances and the Brain Drain*. New York: World Bank/Palgrave Macmillan.

Patterson, Rubin. 2005. US Diasporas and their Impacts on Homeland Technological and Socio-economic Development: How does Sub-Saharan Africa Compare? *Perspectives on Global Development and Technology*, 4: 83–123.

Pires, José. 1992. Return and Re-integration of Qualified Nationals from Developing Countries Residing Abroad: The IOM Experience, *International Migration Quarterly Review*, 30 (3, 4) 353–375.

Sako, Soumana. 2002. Brain Drain and Africa's Development: A Reflection, *African Issues*, 30 (1).

Sander C. 2003. *Migrant Remittances to Developing Countries: A Scoping Study*. Paper prepared for DFID (Department for International Development, UK). London: Bannock Consulting.

Schiff, Maurice & Çağlar Özden (eds.). 2007. *International Migration, Economic Development and Policy*. New York: World Bank/Palgrave Macmillan.

Skeldon, Ronald. 2008. International Migration as a Tool in Development Policy: A Passing Phase, *Population and Development Review*, 34 (1).

UNCTAD (United Nations Conference on Trade and Development). 1988. *Report of the 4th Meeting of Governmental Experts on Reverse Transfer of Technology*, Geneva, United Nations, 14–18 March.

UNDPI (United Nations Department of Public Information). 2003 *Africa Recovery*, 17 (2), cited in Akokpari, 2006.

UNDPI. Various years. *Africa Recovery*. Various issues, cited in Akokpari, 2006.

United Nations. 1992. *Statistical Yearbook*, 39th Edition.

United Nations. 1997. *World Population Monitoring 1997*, International Migration and Development, UN ST/ESA/SER.A/169, chapter viii.

World Bank. 1993. *Social Indicators of Development*, World Bank/Johns Hopkins University Press.

World Bank. 1995. *Rethinking Teaching Capacity in African Universities: Problems and Prospects*. Study commissioned by the Working Group on Higher Education under the Donors to African Education (DAE), No. 33, May. Washington DC: World Bank (Africa region).

CHAPTER FOUR

African Diaspora and Remittance Flows: Leveraging Poverty?

John O Oucho

Introduction

Everywhere in both the developed and developing worlds discussions on the involvement of the diaspora in homeland development dominate public discourse, even though the subject rarely features in national policies. In the true African tradition of being enthusiastic about concepts and frameworks, the African Union and its individual member states have embraced the notion that remittances from the African diaspora contribute immensely to homeland development. Without making definitive moves to develop their own datasets, the African Union and its individual member states rely exclusively on statistics from credible sources such as the World Bank and the Organisation for Economic Cooperation and Development (OECD) which have kept vital data on immigrants, their economic attributes and their links to home countries. More seems to be known about the sources than the destinations of the diaspora's involvement in homeland development and their remittances, a shortcoming which calls for wider interrogation as to whether remittances diminish or entrench poverty, or whether their impact remains an unknown quantity in the development process in Africa.

Much has changed, over the past decade or so, in the interpretation of African emigration and intra-African international migration. Although fewer Africans emigrate elsewhere than move within the continent, emigration from the continent has been the major focus in research, international discourse and policy circles, with African countries on the receiving end of concerns in the developed North which has exclusive direction of immigration policies. In the 1960s and 1970s the thesis underlining African emigration, especially of professionals and the best educated, was that it was an outrageous deprivation of human resources that were very much needed by the newly independent countries. At the same time unskilled labour migration took place but was seen as being generally more localised. (Note: this type of migration is known under a variety of names: as 'circular migration' within East Africa (Elkan 1967 in Oucho 1990: 111), as 'circulation of labour' in present-day Zambia and Zimbabwe (Mitchell 1985 in Oucho 1990: 111), or sometimes as 'circulatory migration' (Garbett 1975 in Oucho, 1990: 111).)

Since the 1980s, African international migration has been viewed as an important resource for development in African countries in terms of the resulting diaspora remittances. Yet there is no unanimity regarding the evidence and the conclusions drawn from previously-existing literature, and more work is still required on diaspora-migration-development linkages. With the emergence of Poverty Reduction Strategy Papers[1] (PRSPs) in the 1990s, and the Millennium Development Goals (MDGs) of 2000, a growing interest has focused on the linkages between diaspora (as a distinctive aspect of migration), remittances and poverty reduction in Africa. As noted in Prothero's prophetic statement (1985: 410), migration in Africa is rarely a permanent phenomenon. African international migration has become an important form of circulation, currently interpreted in terms of either circulation or transnationalism. These two terms underline the inevitability of the diaspora's involvement in African countries, and the flow of their remittances, mediated by international events and local factors.

There have been three main strands of conceptualising the international migration-development nexus (Sørensen, 2006: 89). The first strand is 'combating the root causes of migration', through reducing migration and refugee flows by generating local development, preventing and resolving conflicts, and retaining refugees in neighbouring countries or in first countries of asylum. Second is Martin and Taylor's (1996) paradoxical concept of 'migration hump', in which economic policies reduce migration in the long term, although they increase migration in the short term. Finally there is the 'transnational' approach, which views internal, regional and international migration as a basic dimension of development, underlining migration as an essential condition for socio-economic development.

These three approaches suggest that analysts of the effects of diaspora and remittances on development in general, and poverty reduction in particular, tend to address issues either within their disciplinary pursuits or based on anecdotal evidence – with either patchy empirical evidence, or even a complete lack of it. The African region convened a conference on migration, development and poverty reduction studies, as did the Asian region in March 2005 on which an informative publication has been based (IOM 2005). This work contains detailed papers on internal migration-development-poverty linkages in five countries (China, Bangladesh, India, Pakistan and Vietnam). It also presents thematic

---

1 Updated every three years, these are prepared by member countries, with input from domestic stakeholders as well as external development partners, including the World Bank and the International Monetary Fund.

issues such as migration and gender, generally about Asia and using Sri Lanka as a case study; migration, health and social protection; a case study of HIV/AIDS in south and north-east Asia; and on helping migration to improve livelihoods in China (IOM 2005). Such an approach had long since been intermittently used in Africa by students of migration working on internal migration and rural development in Nigeria (Adepoju 1976), in Malawi (Chilivumbo 1985) and in Kenya (Oucho 1996). With the donor community marginalising migration work, this research paradigm simply ground to a halt. But with the renewed interest in migration and development, it should certainly now experience a resurgence.

This chapter seeks to examine whether or not the African diaspora and their remittances do leverage development in African countries. Because of the diversity of the African region, the chapter presents selected evidence of remittance flows from both diaspora and migrant sources, and tries to examine their impact on recipient households, communities and home countries. A closer reading of the literature on African diaspora and migrant remittance flows suggests that these two types of remittances dominate journal articles from the perspective of their sources, but they say little on their impact at the receiving end. Not surprisingly, the verdict of such literature is not reliable and fails to explain the impact of the two resources in African settings.

In trying to unravel the impact of diaspora and remittances on poverty alleviation, the chapter defines and explains the diversity of the African diaspora; considers the sources, volume and value of migrant and diaspora's remittances; attempts to unpack the unknown quantum of the contribution of the diaspora to homeland development, as well as the utilisation of the remittances sent, with particular focus on poverty alleviation; and, finally, analyses whether the diaspora and their remittances leverage poverty reduction in African countries. The chapter concludes that the current fragmentary evidence on the impact of diaspora and remittances on poverty reduction in African countries precludes a conclusive verdict and that the subject requires more empirical evidence, particularly from recipient countries.

The African diaspora — conceptual issues

Definitions and characterisation of the African diaspora

Definitions and characterisation of diaspora differ — from one discipline to another and by the expectations of the diaspora on the one hand, and the identified homeland on the other. Safran (1991, cited in North-South Centre, 2006: 9) identifies four main characteristics of a diaspora: dispersal to two or more locations related to an original territory; collective mythology of homeland shared by the group and transmitted through generations to come; idealisation of return to the homeland; and ongoing relationship with the homeland. These characteristics relate to different significant diasporas that have dominated the diaspora discourse, such as the Jewish, Irish, Chinese and Indian diasporas.

The African diaspora has been defined through different epochs, underlining varying standpoints. It is not only often misunderstood, but is also too complex to interpret without exploring its nature, dimensions and changing configuration. Indeed, the notion that the African diaspora is homogeneous is both simplistic and unrealistic, given both the temporal and the spatial dimensions of African emigration to the rest of the world. To the Old World of Asia went a large slave traffic which analysts have been unable to account for successfully, and to the New World was a much larger traffic of slaves who settled Latin America and the Caribbean, currently the largest African diaspora, but with links to Africa more remote than those of the diaspora in the United States. Then a new wave of the African diaspora came with independence. As Africa looked to the developed North for educational opportunities – for its citizens to attain the high qualifications and skilled training necessary for the continent's development in the wake of colonialism, huge numbers of Africans remained overseas, forming yet another category of diaspora. Another category consists of those who relocated overseas as workers, refugees and asylum seekers, of winners of the US green card and similar opportunities. The children and grandchildren of first-generation immigrants have augmented the diaspora numbers as younger generations of Africans migrated overseas for education, work and security from repressive regimes that have left in their wake untold political and economic crises.

The African disapora is therefore a heterogeneous group of people of African descent, spanning much of Europe, Latin America and the Caribbean. There are people of African descent who constitute diasporas of particular African countries with which they identify, others of the Caribbean diaspora with no links whatsoever with the African continent, and still others who are transnational, moving easily from one country to another on account of globalisation, which has undone the effect of formerly restrictive geographical boundaries. African migrants are part of the diaspora who may be temporarily in the countries of destination; they may join the existing diaspora to stay permanently, or may be transnational whenever they engage in circular migration.

In this chapter, then, the term *diaspora* is used generically to denote people – usually of African descent – residing outside Africa, or within Africa in countries other than their own, as citizens and permanent or temporary residents, engaging in circulation as well as transnational lifestyles. Different categories of the diaspora play roles by committing their skills and knowledge to homeland development and by sending remittances which stimulate development as well as influence poverty reduction.

Remittances

Simply defined, remittances are transfers of money, goods and diverse social features, sent or brought by migrants or migrant groups back to their countries of origin or citizenship. Although the notion of remittances generally conjures up only the monetary aspect, remittances embrace both monetary and non-monetary flows, including social remittances.

The North-South Centre of the Council of Europe (2006) defines diaspora's *social remittances* as ideas, practices, mind-sets, world views, values and attitudes, norms of behaviour and social capital (knowledge, experience and expertise) that the diasporas mediate and, either consciously or unconsciously, transfer from host to home communities. African diaspora interviewed said that they obtained social remittances from different sources: through professional expertise in work places in the host countries; through values, norms and work ethics; through their socialisation and acculturation in host countries; and by constructing vast transnational networks across countries and continents, linking the process of globalisation to 'glocalisation' in their countries of origin. But as Chimhowu et al (2003, cited in Oucho 2008) caution:

> Remittances alone are unlikely to lift people out of poverty; rather it is their interplay with other economic, social and cultural factors which determine the scale and type of impact remittances can have on poverty reduction.

Although the mainstream literature is limited to north-south remittances, there are a lot of south-south remittances – since there is a substantial south-south migration, much of it intra-regional. Ratha and Shaw (2007: 6) estimate that south-south formally transmitted remittances range from 9 to 30 per cent of all forms of monetary transfers – and the figure could be higher if informal channels were taken into account. These authors also found that the total value of south-south monetary remittances was higher than that of similar north-south remittances.

Heterogeneity of the African diaspora

An important point to bear in mind is how particular groups became diasporas in their present countries of residence. Two contrasting cases – the Scottish diaspora and the Irish diaspora – are instructive for Africa (Oucho 2008: 64). On the one hand, the Scottish diaspora are not all keen on contributing to their 'home' economy, mainly because most of them are professionals who left Scotland voluntarily and do not see their country as suitable for investment, nor in any way 'needing' it. The Irish diaspora, on other hand, who were poor and unskilled, were pushed into exile by the English and took pride in their new-found ability to assist in liberating Ireland economically (*The Economist*, 20 October 2001, cited in Oucho 2008: 65). These examples are instructive to researchers and policy-makers because they are instances in which categories of emigrants have parallels with African diasporas who behave in a similar manner, and in some cases where the diasporas' desire to return or to help their homelands was rebuffed by their countries of origin or their counterparts who had stayed behind.

This chapter provides significant perspectives, reinforced by selected case studies, to provide evidence of the African diaspora's involvement in homeland development, and to explore the inflow and utilisation of remittances for poverty reduction. Generally, the African diaspora is understood in many circles to be anyone from the African continent who resides outside the continent, the duration of residence notwithstanding. Yet this notion is simplistic, and perhaps grossly myopic. Generations of the African diaspora can be thus simply identified. First, the vast majority of the African diaspora consists of descendants of the slave trade in which huge numbers of Africans were trafficked several centuries ago. They are now stable citizens of the United States, Latin America and the Caribbean, most of whom maintain only remote emotional links with Africa. Second, those from the Caribbean who subsequently migrated, mainly in the mid-twentieth century, to reside in Europe, constitute Caribbean diaspora, not African diaspora, though at times they cherish their African descent, particularly during cultural festivals. The African Union (AU) cannot and should not claim them as residents of Africa's sixth sub-region as they have had little to do with their ancestral origins. Third, within the African continent are intra-African migrants who have taken up either permanent residence or citizenship in other African countries, becoming diasporas of their respective countries of origin. Fourth, there is a relatively new category of diaspora, made up of legally and illegally immigrated workers who, because of stricter migration controls in the developed North, engage in migration circulation. Finally, Africans holding dual citizenship, although a minority, might owe their allegiance more to their second countries rather than to their countries of birth or original citizenship.

The spatial distribution of the African diaspora indicates important variations within sub-Saharan African sub-regions (Table 4.1). Migrants from Western and Eastern Africa have a similar pattern of movement towards European countries, with the foremost metropolitan powers – the UK and France – receiving most of them. Indeed, the UK stands out as the premier European country of destination. The vast majority of Central African immigrants go to France, followed by Portugal, yet another evidence of ties with former colonial powers.

The figures given in Table 4.1, from three Maghreb countries, underline the significance of northern Africa in the European migration system. From the table, it is clear that the European Mediterranean countries – France, Spain, Italy and Belgium – stand out as by far the most important immigration countries for Northern Africans, again with the metropolitan power being the largest receiver.

CHAPTER FOUR African Diaspora and Remittance Flows: Leveraging Poverty?

Table 4.1: African diaspora in the major European countries of residence by sub-Saharan African sub-region and selected Northern African countries of origin

SSA*	European country of destination (figures in thousands)						
Western	UK 210	France 163	Germany 102	Italy 80	Norway 69	Denmark 50	Sweden 20
Eastern	UK 203	France 105	Germany 35	Italy 35	Norway 29	Denmark 23	Sweden 2
Central	France 125	Portugal 36	Belgium 32	Germany 32	Spain 12	Switz. 10	Neth'lds 3
Southern	UK 100	Germany 17	Ireland 6	France 3	Neth'lds 3	Portugal 2	Switz. 1
Northern**							
Morocco (2004)	France 1113	Spain 424	Neth'lds 300	Italy 299	Belgium 293	Germany 102	UK 35
Algeria (2003)	France 1101	Spain 46	Belgium 19	Germany 18	UK 14	Italy 13	Scand. 10
Tunisia (2001-03)	France 493	Italy 101	Germany 54	Belgium 17	Neth'lds 7	Switz. 7	Other 17

Sources: *World Bank (2007), Table 4; **H de Haas (2008), Tables 2–4.

It is difficult to know the exact size of the African diaspora, though the OECD countries have data by immigrants' citizenship and/or country of birth. Estimates vary widely. For example, the American *Christian Monitor* of February 26, 2002 estimated that 15 million Nigerians (more than 1 in 10 of all Nigerians) lived outside Nigeria (Nworah 2008). With the appointment of a Special Assistant to the President on Nigerians in diaspora, and sponsoring by the Nigerians in the Diaspora Organisation (NIDO), the Federal Government of Nigeria has given impetus to Nigerians in diaspora participating more effectually in homeland development. However, the sustainability of such developments in the absence of law enforcement and policy support has been African countries' greatest failure.

Remittances – flows to Africa

Destinations, volume and value

Highlights of the destinations, volume and value of remittances to Africa, given in Table 4.2, provide informative insights, most notably for Eritrea, Cape Verde.

Table 4.2: Inflow and value of remittances to Africa by sub-region and country[2]

Sub-region and country	Remittances US$ million	% of GDP	Sub-region and country	Remittances US$ million	% of GDP
Eastern Africa	**5929**		**Western Africa**	**10 399**	
Burundi	164	22.8	Benin	263	5.5
Comoros	85	21.1	Burkina Faso	507	8.2
Eritrea	411	37.9	Cape Verde	391	34.2
Ethiopia	591	4.4	Côte d'Ivoire	282	1.6
Kenya	796	3.8	Gambia	87	17.0
Madagascar	316	5.7	Ghana	851	6.6
Malawi	102	4.6	Guinea	286	8.6
Mauritius	356	5.5	Liberia	163	25.8
Mozambique	565	7.4	Mali	739	12.5
Rwanda	149	6.0	Mauritania	103	3.9
Somalia	790	–	Niger	205	5.8
Tanzania	313	2.4	Nigeria	5397	4.7
Uganda	642	6.9	Senegal	687	7.5
Zambia	201	1.8	Sierra Leone	168	11.6
Zimbabwe	361	7.2	Togo	142	6.4
Central Africa	**2690**		**Northern Africa**	**17 614**	
Angola	969	2.2	Algeria	5399	4.7
Cameroon	267	1.5	Egypt	3637	3.4
CA Republic	73	4.9	Libya	134	0.3
Chad	137	2.1	Morocco	6116	10.7
DR Congo	636	7.4	Tunisia	769	5.1
Eq. Guinea	77	0.9			
Gabon	60	0.5			
			Southern Africa	**1979**	
			Lesotho	355	24.1
			South Africa	1489	0.6
			Swaziland	89	3.4

Source: Rural Poverty Portal http://www.ifad.org/events/remittances/maps/africa.htm, accessed 10 October 2008

---

2 Note: there are slight mismatches in the totals supplied for this table. Only countries with significant numbers have been shown.

With a huge diaspora in Europe and the rich Gulf States, Northern Africa receives a substantial amount of remittances, with Morocco always ranking among the world's top ten recipients. The *IMF Balance of Payments Statistics Yearbook 2001* ranked Egypt and Morocco fourth and eighth respectively among the top ten in 1994, Egypt alone ranked eighth in 1997 and the two countries ranked seventh and eighth respectively in 2000 (Ramamurthy 2006: 73). In Western Africa, Nigeria receives more than half the remittances of the entire block, with Ghana, Mali and Senegal, in descending order, dominating the rest of the pack. Eastern Africa is topped by Kenya, followed by Somalia (despite having no recognised government in place since 1991), Uganda and Ethiopia. Apart from Kenya, these are countries that have had political problems which left conflict in their wake, the last two attracting remittances as an important resource for national construction. The Central African countries of Angola and Democratic Republic of Congo led in remittances received. Finally, in Southern Africa, South Africa is by far the main recipient, with Lesotho second – a well-known remittance – and deferred payment – dependent economy.

Unfortunately, African countries have never had a successful means of tracking the diaspora remittances flowing to them – despite citing remittances as a current source of pride and a potential resource for investment that far exceeds the overseas development assistance (ODA) or foreign aid on which these countries have relied for more than four decades. Knowledge of the impact of migration on countries of origin is still fragmentary for three main reasons: the general paucity of good-quality data; the weak methodological foundations and poor analytical quality of much of the earlier research (Taylor 1999, cited in de Haas 2006: 567); and reliance on micro-studies (especially in Latin America and in particular Mexico) to the neglect of the major suppliers of European-bound labour migration from the South and east of the Mediterranean (Massey et al 1998, cited in de Haas 2006: 567). A recent positive development has been the emergence of several websites, among them sendmoneyhome.org, Remittance Tax Relief for International Development (Remit Aid), Africa Recruit, Livelihoods Connect, and Migrant Remittances. These organisations document remittances made to different countries of the world. Apart from these sources, which are by no means flawless, the World Bank has been a reliable source of data on remittances.

Remittances to Africa amounted to US$5.9 billion in 1990, and reached US$14 billion by 2003, though this was a mere 15 per cent of all remittance flows to the developing world. The leading African recipient countries have been Algeria, Morocco, Egypt and Nigeria. (With remittances exceeding US$1.3 million, Nigeria was by far the largest sub-Saharan African recipient, accounting for 30 to 60 per cent of the region's receipts.) The World Bank notes that remittances represented 194 per cent of the value of Eritrea's exports and 19 per cent of its GDP, and 80 per cent of Botswana's deficit (Mutume 2005), the latter – itself a major destination county – and, therefore, an important source of remittances.

Yet remittance flows are unpredictable, depending on political and economic conditions at both source and destination. Two examples illustrate these conditions: remittances to Burkina Faso have declined radically since the late 1990s following political disturbances and economic crisis in Côte d'Ivoire – the destination to which most Burkinabes had migrated and where many had settled permanently for decades; conversely, remittances to Zimbabwe have increased over recent years, albeit through unofficial sources, as Zimbabwe experienced a similar crisis (Mutume, 2005). Instability of remittance flows implies that it would be imprudent for recipient countries to put their faith in remittances as a resource for development, not least for offsetting their budgetary deficits.

The roles of the diaspora and remittances

Most governments and people in Africa have a very narrow view of the role of the diaspora. Ionescu's model says it all. She proposes a typology of diaspora: a range comprising business networks, chambers of commerce, professional networks, scientific networks, skills capacity development, community initiatives, migration and development associations, gender and development, umbrella organisations, diaspora networkings, and co-development initiatives and finances (Ionescu 2006: 27–30). According to Ionescu, therefore, any analysis of the diaspora needs to make explicit the particular type being analysed, something that this chapter makes no pretences to address.

Although previous research has shown that the roles of the diaspora and remittances are recognised at household, community and national levels, it has fallen short in distinguishing between perceived and actual impacts at the respective levels. At issue are several questions that seek answers on the best ways in which remittances can constitute a resource for development. Two pertinent questions are:
- How can governments best estimate the actual flows of both financial and social remittances?
- How can governments and international development organisations assist organised diaspora groups, such as hometown associations (HTAs) and 'home villages', to make the most effective use of collective remittances for development, without impeding local initiatives? (Sørensen 2006: 96)

These questions need to engage the attention of African governments whose growing faith in financial remittances neglects tapping the potentially significant social remittances of migrants, as well as those of HTAs. The rhetoric of African countries hardly reflects their policies towards the diaspora's financial and social remittances and the involvement of HTAs in homeland development.

Adams and Page (2003) note that remittances, as a share of a country's

GDP, have a negative and significant impact on all three standard measures of poverty – head count, poverty gap and squared poverty gap. They conclude that international migration has a strong and statistically important impact on poverty reduction in the developing world; that international remittances have a negative and statistically significant effect on all three measures of poverty; that the impact of both international migration and remittances on poverty seems to vary according to region; and that more and better data are required on poor people who send remittances through informal, unofficial channels. These research questions are still crying for answers in Africa since evidence is sporadic, and often anecdotal, constraining any meaningful generalisations.

As resources, both diaspora and remittances take the form of individuals' initiatives and pooled efforts through 'home improvement unions' and 'hometown associations' formed by migrant groups or diaspora associations in the countries of destination. Brinkerhoff notes (2006: 9) that 'diaspora organisations can act as important intermediaries between traditional development actors, and between diasporas and local communities – for example, identifying needs and priorities of local communities and communicating those to donor organisations, NGOs and diaspora members to solicit funding and expertise.'

Empirical research has provided ample evidence of unskilled migrants remitting more of their income, and more regularly, than their skilled counterparts, comparing the opportunity cost of investing in the destination countries and remitting funds back home. In this respect, unskilled, lower income migrants are better poised to combat poverty and sustain survival of households left in their countries of origin. Moreover, a burgeoning literature reports that there is a tendency for the poorer, lower-calibre migrants to embrace the extended family system – which, among other things, combats poverty – more willingly and more strongly than the higher-calibre, better resourced and more individualistic migrants, who are less inclined to send remittances back home for poverty reduction.

The finding of the Commission on Private Sector Development of the United Nations Development Programme (UNDP) notes that diasporas support entrepreneurs in their homelands with remittances, informal financing of small businesses and business advice and mentorship (Commission 2004, cited in Brinkehoff 2006: 9). This is because diasporas may be much more effective than other foreign investors, since they have a better knowledge of the local economy than investors do, and because they can combine knowledge with skills, as well as tap into networks developed abroad, to yield synergistic advantages (Brinkerhoff 2006: 9). African diasporas are best placed to understand the implications of their participation in and sending remittances for development in conflict-ridden African countries which foreign investors might be more sceptical about.

Participation of the African diaspora in homeland development can take different forms. The World Bank (2007) sees three modes of engagement with the African diaspora: permanent return to the home country; short-and long-term placements due to family, children's education, mortgages, career advancement and so on; and 'virtual return' of talents and skills. The last two seem more likely than the first as younger generations of Africans in the developed North tend to sever links with their homelands.

Previous efforts to return African brain drain in the North have had dismal outcomes. Both the 'Return of Qualified African Nationals' (RQAN), sponsored by the European Union and implemented by the IOM, and the UNDP's 'Transfer of Knowledge and Through Expatriate Nationals' (TOKTEN) programme performed below expectations. The latter was one of the programmes implemented without prior research. On evaluating RQAN, the IOM (2000) found that it lacked 'ownership' by African governments, despite these governments' appreciation and welcoming of its benefits. Nonetheless, a study of its impact in a sample of African countries (among them Ghana, Cape Verde, Uganda, Zambia and Zimbabwe) clearly suggests positive outcomes of returnees' utilisation of skills in both management and technical fields, a contribution to the financial growth of organisations through income generation and cost-saving measures, and a generally better performance by organisations (ACTS 2000). Against the lukewarm efficacy of RQAN, in 2001 the IOM initiated 'Migration for Development in Africa' (MIDA), which helps organise both placements and periodic physical and virtual migrant returns. Among its aims is the evolving of collaborative ventures with countries of destination and origin, diaspora organisations, local authorities and the private sector (IOM 2007) – but this initiative has not gone far either. These apparent failures in involving the African diaspora in homeland development imply that the diaspora have not made significant contributions to poverty reduction in African countries.

On the positive side, the World Bank (2007) expects to increase its diaspora activities through the Millennium Development Goals (MDGs), targeting poverty reduction, access to education, and health care. Yet it is only recently that the World Bank has called for commissioned surveys on migration and development in selected African countries – after failing to include sub-Saharan Africa in its recent report on international migration, economic development and policy (Özden & Schiff 2007). This is a step in the right direction, providing hope for a more focused assessment of the African diaspora's involvement in the development of their home countries. A conference at The Hague in 2006 on remittances and poverty reduction in Africa, convened by the Institute of Social Studies with the support of Oxfam-NOVIB, was a step in the right direction, and its proceedings should find a place in AU frameworks and national development programmes. In addition, organisations such as the diaspora Openhouse in Washington DC, the Development Marketplace for African diaspora in Europe, Africa Recruit, and many more national and sub-national diaspora organisations have vital agendas that should attract African diasporas to sharpen their poverty-reduction undertakings in Africa.

Potentially, these associations hold the key to poverty reduction in Africa but lack appropriate approaches to that end. Le Goff (2008) examines how remittances in 65 countries act as a stabilising force, and contribute to poverty reduction (the first of the MDGs). Drawing from other studies, she argues that: that remittances have a negative effect on the depth of poverty; that as co-insurance, they constitute an answer to the 'shocks of revenue' in migrants' countries of origin, which push people in poverty traps; that remittances promote growth more readily in countries where the financial system is less developed; that the effect of remittances on growth is greater if the political situation is bad; and that remittances can play an essential role by allowing households in developing countries to diversify their income sources. From econometric models run, the study concludes that remittances play a positive and effective role in reducing the poverty headcount and the poverty gap in migrants' countries of origin; they influence poverty reduction, especially in countries of origin with macroeconomic instability, and where households have incomes that are subject to frequent and significant fluctuations. The mixed hypotheses and empirical results of the study suggest both positive and negative impacts of remittances on poverty reduction, and require empirical research, especially in Africa, to corroborate or refute them.

Diaspora and remittances in poverty reduction in African countries

Diaspora involvement in homeland development

While the role of diaspora is easily noticeable at the macro and meso levels of society, that of remittances cuts across the whole spectrum of societal development. The influence of remittances on poverty reduction is largely indeterminate, with the literature portraying both positive and negative impacts, and in certain cases, indifferent outcomes. Part of the problem lies in the silence observed in Poverty Reduction Strategy Papers (PRSPs) on migration and its implications, such as the participation of the diaspora and the injection of remittances into homeland development. Countries where remittances have had a clear positive impact include Cape Verde, Senegal and Lesotho. Currently, virtually all large African diasporas perceive their contribution and their remittances as crucial for homeland development, even without adducing evidence as reliable as that which exists in Latin America, for instance (Neil 2003; Orozco & Fedewa 2006).

Most previous studies have found that remittances end up being consumed, rather than invested. But the distinction between consumption and investment becomes blurred when remittances cover household survival strategies, the cost of education of the next generation of household members and increased agricultural productivity. The general conclusion from previous studies of Asian migrants in the Arab world is that the diaspora use their wealth wisely, with remittances more than counterbalancing costs(Gunatilleke 1986, cited in Skeldon 2002: 78). In much of sub-Saharan Africa, where investment opportunities hardly exist, remittances no doubt lift households out of the poverty trap in which majority find themselves caught. As happens elsewhere in the developing world, remittances reduce poverty by providing families in the countries of origin with additional income, the surpluses of which end in consumption as well as investments in education and health (IOM 2006: 22).

Two important characteristics of remittances are worth underscoring: firstly they are largely unaffected by political or financial crises, tending to increase in times of hardship and, secondly, they are more equally spread among developing countries than are other financial flows (Ratha 2003, cited in IOM 2006: 23). A notable shortcoming, however, is the dearth of empirical studies providing strong evidence that contrasts remitters' with recipients' perceptions of and responses to the diaspora's contribution of remittances to homeland development.

A curious quotation from John Kenneth Galbraith (Skeldon 2002, citing Harris 2002: 119) underlines the relationship between migration and poverty:

> Migration is the oldest action against poverty. It selects those who most want help. It is good for the country to which they go; it helps to break the equilibrium of poverty in the country from which they come. What is the perversity in the human soul that causes people to resist so obvious a good?

This relationship between migration and poverty – in this chapter diaspora and their remittances on the one hand and poverty on the other – while well received in many circles, is hardly subjected to thorough analysis; hence the preponderance of anecdotal evidence. In the words of a Salvadoran sociologist, 'migration and remittances are the true economic adjustment programmes of the poor in our country' (Carlo Guillermo Ramos in Portes 2008). The expression 'our country' can be substituted with 'African countries' to underscore the dependence these countries currently have on their nationals' emigration and remittances. As Skeldon argues (2002: 80), the main challenge for policymakers is 'to facilitate the types of movement that are most likely to lead to an alleviation of poverty while protecting migrants from abuse and exploitation'.

The tendency for sub-Saharan African countries to be preoccupied with their diasporas and their remittances as resources for development might be simplistic without sound policy prescriptions. Indeed, the sudden interest of these countries in these two resources replicates reliance on foreign aid and foreign direct investment – even when the countries fail to put them to good use.

Emphasis on monetary remittances

Although this sub-section concentrates on financial remittances – that the bulk of earlier research and data do deal with – it also recognises the importance of social remittances, on which much of the literature is silent. Anthropological and migration research, as well as household surveys, underscore the importance of remittances at the micro level (household level), where they contribute to improved standards of living, better health and education, and both human and financial assets formation (Sander & Maimbo 2003: 16).

At the community level, pooled remittances by hometown associations and 'home improvement associations' are sent to sub-Saharan African countries with sizeable numbers of immigrants overseas. One example is the Kayes area in Mali which benefits from about forty immigrant associations whose pooled remittances support 146 projects with a budget of €3 million. The African Foundation for Development, quote Libercier & Schneider (1996) who estimated that over 60 per cent of the infrastructure in the Kayes villages had been sponsored by the diaspora resident in France.

Institutions working on economic development often focus on the use of remittances from a variety of perspectives. The Institute for Development Studies states that such institutions can: integrate remittances into a country's economy; employ the macroeconomic results of remittances to influence responses to productive forces (for instance in investment and trade); and ascertain the impact of remittances on national economic growth. In the policy arena, these institutions have the capacity to influence the reduction of remittance transaction costs to about 10 per cent of the current level and to help in the development of financial democracy (id21 insights 2006). It has been noted (http://www.ime.gob.mx/investgac.ones/remesa8.pdf) that remittances may reduce infant mortality by improving housing conditions and access to public services such as water; that remittances boost growth in countries with less developed financial systems because they provide an alternative way of financing investment, acting as a substitute for the domestic financial system; and that households receiving remittances tend to have better nutrition and access to health and educational services than those not receiving remittances.

Another African study (Gupta et al 2007) asserts that remittances augment recipient households' resources, smooth consumption, provide working capital and have multiplier effects through increased household spending. However, the study also cautions that the relationship between remittances and poverty is not unidirectional as poverty and the concomitant lack of economic opportunities motivate both emigration and remittance inflows. Remittances, in a variety of roles mentioned here, go a long way toward poverty reduction. Moré (2005) argues that, being gifts without a counter-flow, remittances are the best means of targeting the MDGs, in particular, poverty reduction. This implies a neglect of remittances in the MDGs. The UN Millennium project entitled 'Investing in Development: A Practical Way to Achieve the MDGs' mentions remittances in passing as a possible positive effect of migration, emphasising the need for comprehensive approaches to migration management in the context of poverty reduction. Yet migration is by no means an appropriate strategy to achieve the MDGs as its impact depends on the political, social, legal and economic environments in which the migration takes place, on available resources, as well as on the behaviour of individual migrants (IOM 2006: 20). A United Nations Economic Commission for Africa study on international migration and the achievement of MDGs notes that 'in spite of significant transfers, most African countries are still struggling with how to effectively harness the social capital by diaspora networks for...national and regional growth through migrant initiated business investments, transfer of knowledge and skills as well as the exploitation of migrant ethnic markets and enterprises' (ECA 2006: 2). It cautions, for example that 'it is pointless for an African household to receive remittances to pay for school and health care costs when there are no teachers and nurses' (ECA 2006: 13), lost by African countries as brain drain.

The place of social remittances

Much of the literature and research on remittances to Africa has dwelt on financial remittances, leaving social remittances crying out for research. And many African countries receive social remittances without recognising them as such.

Levitt (1996) identifies three types of social remittances. First, there are 'normative structures' consisting of ideas, values and beliefs, including norms for behaviour, notions about family responsibility, good governance, principles of neighbourliness and community participation, and aspirations for social mobility as well as ideas about gender, race, and class identity. The second type consists of 'systems of practice' which are actions shaped by normative structures. They include how individuals delegate household tasks, which kinds of religious rituals are engaged in; how much individuals participate in political and civic groups; organizational practices such as recruiting and socialising new group members, goal-setting and strategising, establishing leadership roles and forming interagency ties. Finally, there is 'social capital' – respect for individual migrants built up in their destination places. Social capital remittance exchanges can then occur when migrants return to live in or visit their communities of origin, or when non-migrants visit their migrant relations in the countries of destination. Social capital exchange can take place even without personal contact, through exchanges of letters, videos, cassettes, emails and telephone calls. Often, social and political leaders harness the status they acquire in the country of destination to advance their cause in their homeland.

Insights from a survey of social remittances of the African diasporas in the Netherlands and Portugal are instructive and useful for African countries (North-South Centre, 2006). In Portugal, diaspora from Cape Verde, Guinea Bissau and Senegal constitute social capital for collective action for wellbeing, using varying approaches to realise their ambitions (North-South Centre 2006: 14).

Pathways by which the African diasporas transfer social remittances vary a great deal. The North-South Centre (2006: 17-20) study found that the pathways include return, either permanently or temporarily for holidays and family visits; social affiliations when returned migrants are in contact with key political and social figures in the home countries; facilitation of transnational networks to mediate and smooth the connection of overseas and African businesses; and influencing the political climate by infusing democratic political habits, sometimes acting as pressure groups.

Unfortunately, African diasporas transmit social remittances to their home countries irregularly and unsystematically as these remittances usually do not go down well with African governments. Indeed, a number of challenges confront social remittances in African countries. The North-South Centre (2006: 23-24) found these to be: poor governance and the lack of an enabling environment in the form of personal freedom, basic civic rights, democracy and the rule of law; unwillingness of the governing elite in most countries to seek the assistance of skilled and professional diaspora for national development initiatives; and a lack of national strategies and policies that specifically target diaspora interests and encourage participation in homeland development. Even a direct policy approach such as dual citizenship – already formalised in Eritrea and Ghana, for instance – seems too tall an order for most African countries to adopt.

Migration-remittances-poverty relationship

The impact of migration and, by implication, of diaspora and remittances on poverty is complex and difficult to disentangle given the reciprocal relationship between migration and poverty. Skeldon's thesis (2002, cited in IOM 2006: 21) is that migration can both cause and be caused by poverty. And although poverty and vulnerability provide incentives to migrate, poverty can itself reduce the ability to move, due to the high transfer costs involved. Those engaged in international migration are not the poorest of the poor as migrants must of necessity have some resources to facilitate their movement (House of Commons International Development Committee, 2003, cited in IOM 2006: 21). When poorer people migrate, they are unlikely to move very far (Zolberg et al 2002, cited in IOM 2006: 21).

Interesting issues emerge from Anyanwu and Erhijakpor's (n.d.) analysis of international migration and poverty at community and household levels in Africa. The authors' findings at the community level provide some useful insights. First, remittances stimulate the formation of small-scale enterprises, thereby promoting community development. In different parts of rural Africa, recipient communities are more economically vibrant than communities that never receive returning migrants. Second, remittances ease credit constraints by providing working capital for the recipients, who consequently can engage in entrepreneurial activities. New entrepreneurial activities tend to emerge in communities receiving remittances. Finally, remittances made through migrant associations may result in the creation of new social assets and services and community physical infrastructures such as schools, health centres, roads and other community projects (Ghosh 2006; Sørensen & Pedersen 2002, both cited in Anyanwu & Erhijakpor).

On the negative side, Anyanwu and Erhijakpor (n.d.) argue that remittances tend to increase income inequality. However, at the household level, these authors found that international remittances increase family incomes, thus raising consumption and/or savings; they transfer purchasing power from relatively richer to relatively poorer family members; they reduce poverty, smooth consumption, affect labour supply, provide working capital and have multiplier effects through increased household spending; and they facilitate investment in human capital in terms of education, health and better nutrition (Lopez-Cordova 2004; Hilderbrant & McKenzie, 2005; Adams 2008, all cited in Anyanwu & Erhijakpor). These findings corroborate previous findings on the subject and require further investigation at community and household levels in different African countries.

An important point needs to be made on subtle differences between high-income and low-income emigrants. The tendency is for workers in low-income occupations to leave their families in their countries of origin and send remittances back to them, while those in higher-income occupations take their families with them to the countries of destination, and, as a result, have little obligation to remit back home. However, with increasing real estate and other opportunities in the countries of origin, large numbers of diaspora, notably the higher-status, have been sending remittances for investment purposes.

Of crucial importance are political, economic and social conditions in the countries of origin, which can either attract or repel remittances. For poverty reduction, remittances play a bigger role at the micro (household) level where consumption and survival strategies matter more than at the macro level where they are linked to national and international economic uncertainties and where the measure of poverty is markedly different.

In Africa, remittance-sending is largely optional, with a few cases where they are mandatory. For example, following the country's independence from Ethiopia in 1993, emigrant Eritreans have been sending a mandatory 2 per cent of their income as remittance to their country – this is known as 'Healing Tax' (Van Hear 2003: 2); Sudan initiated a 'Nil Value Custom Policy' on imported goods; and Egypt adopted the 'Own Exchange Import System' which permits importation only if importers can provide the necessary foreign exchange on their own, that is, outside the official foreign exchange pools (El-Sakka n.d.) Indeed, Bosnia and Eritrea provide good examples of the extent to which transnational exile communities can be mobilised to contribute to reconstruction without returning (Black et al 2000), implying that the call for return is probably overstated.

Selected African case studies

The four African case studies given here represent different types of diaspora and remittances to the countries of origin. Morocco represents the Northern African emigration to Europe and the nature and extent of Moroccan diaspora in homeland development through remittances and other means. Ghana is a classical case of successive generations of diaspora found in different parts of the world but with an exemplary commitment to Ghanaian development. Despite being a failed state, Somalia exemplifies how refugee diaspora have sustained the motherland even though it lacks an operational government. Finally, Zimbabwe represents a case where a decade-long repression and an unbearable economic crisis have forced Zimbabweans out of the country to live elsewhere in southern Africa and Europe, from where their remittances have sustained relatives and friends left behind. Only selected studies are cited and the highlights of some case studies provided to give readers a lead to what they could study in greater depth.

Morocco

In the view of de Haas (2005), recent research on Moroccan migration and development has painted an optimistic picture after the pessimistic studies of the 1970s (which saw migration as the cause of underdevelopment). His study of international migrant households in the Todgha valley oasis in Morocco suggests a strong and significant association between migration and household income, with the main dividing line noticeable between households with access to international remittances and those without it (de Haas, 2006: 569). But the tendency for Morocco to exclude emigrants from the civil service for their lifetime, curtailing deployment of their knowledge and skills upon return, minimises their potential to return and invest (de Haas 2005: 1273). This phenomenon exists in many more African countries, even where emigration is depicted as brain gain and migrants as potential investors in homeland development.

In countering the 'migration pessimists', the 'new economics of labour migration' (NELM) school examines both positive and negative effects of migration from the developing world by placing the behaviour of individual migrants within the wider societal context and considering the household, rather than the individual, as the most appropriate decision-making unit (Taylor 1999, cited in de Haas 2006: 566). The study found a strong and significant association between migration participation and household income. Distinct differences were observed: between households with and households without access to international remittances (as already mentioned); between non-migrant and internal migrant households, and between current indirect and returned international households (571). The study concludes with a cautionary remark: while migration may contribute positively to social and economic development at the origins of migration, the impact is 'potential' rather than predetermined because, among other things, migration impacts are highly context-sensitive (579).

Ghana

As the first sub-Saharan African mainland state to become independent (in 1957), Ghana was conceived by the founders of the nation to become a model independent African state. Unfortunately, from 1966 to the 1990s, successive military overthrows of government forced Ghanaians to flee the country and to make their homes virtually everywhere in the world (Van Hear 2003). Added to this was continued economic decay from the 1970s through the 1990s. By the mid-1990s it seemed that, despite Ghana's economic recovery, emigration streams were growing, particularly because of the basic migration patterns and contacts that had been established over the previous decades (Peil 1995: 358). Once emigration begins and contacts flourish, it becomes difficult to stem the tide – in fact it is likely to increase. (Literature on the Ghanaian diaspora and remittances is too copious to cite comprehensively in this chapter.)

Research on Ghanaian migrants has revealed diverse perspectives. Among them are the impact of elite return migrants to the country and to its neighbour, Côte d'Ivoire (Asiedu 2003; Ammassari 2004); the economic impact of the Netherlands-based Ghanaian diaspora on Ghana's rural development (Kabki et al 2004), and the impact of Ghanaian remittances on the country's poverty and inequality (Adams et al 2008).

From the data analysed and the evidence provided, the last-mentioned study concludes that the size of poverty reduction depends on the type of remittances being received; that, generally, international remittances have a greater impact on reducing poverty than those from internal migrants; and that both internal and international remittances have a negative impact on inequality as measured by the Gini coefficient[3] (Adams et al 2008: 23). This conclusion refutes previous findings that tend to emphasise the positive impacts of remittances in and to the country. In Ghana, Schoorl et al (2000, cited in Sander & Maimbo 2003: 17) found, in 1999–2000, that 70 per cent of remittances were used for recurrent expenditure (school fees, health care and so on) and less than 30 per cent were invested in assets (land, cattle and construction). In Mali, Martin et al (2002, cited in Sander & Maimbo 2003: 17) noted that 80 to 90 per cent of remittances in the mid-1990s went to general household consumption.

The importance attached to remittances is shown by the systematic data collection on remittances by the Bank of Ghana, one of the few national banks in Africa to do this (Higazi 2005: 4). Remittances increased from US$6 million in 1996 to US$44 million in 2002 (5). While some studies report that Netherlands-based Ghanaians' send a substantial proportion of remittances by informal means (Mazzacato et al 2004, cited in Higazi 2005), including the hand-carrying of cash (Africa Recruit 2003; Blackwell & Seddon 2004, both cited in Higazi 2005), or through informal channels such as Ghanaian-owned shops or small businesses in their countries of residence (Higazi 2005). Others refute this, citing formal means such as through banks or by money transfer – through organisations such as Western Union and MoneyGram – as the most common ways of transmitting remittances (Anarfi et al 2003, cited in Higazi 2005). A survey of Ghanaians who had returned to their country between August 2000 and January 2001 reports the bulk of remittances as going for family or household economic strategy (Tiemoko 2003, cited in Hizagi 2005), which must include poverty reduction.

The Ghanaian diaspora belongs to two types of diaspora associations: Ghanaian (particularly Pentecostal) churches and ethnic associations (Akyeampong 200:208, cited in Higazi 2005). The latter often send back to Ghana either money or commodities such as clothes and schoolbooks, and in the poor region of Brong Ahafo they have supported district assemblies (Akologo 2004, cited in Higazi 2005).

Finally, a recent study by Adams et al (2008), which explores the impact of remittances on poverty and inequality in Ghana, captures both internal and international dimensions of migration, using the 2005/06 Ghana Living Standards Survey (GLSS 5). It focuses on transfers received in money, food and non-food goods, from both internal and international sources. By applying

---

3 A measure of statistical dispersion, commonly used as a measure of inequality of income distribution (or of wealth distribution).

a series of econometric models, the study found that households receiving internal remittances (that is from within Ghana) have the lowest mean per capita expenditure and the highest observed poverty, on average, of all the household groups; that households receiving international remittances (from sources outside Ghana) have the highest mean per capita expenditure and the lowest observed poverty, on average, of all the household groups; that international remittances have a greater impact than internal ones on poverty reduction; and that both internal and international remittances have a negative impact on income inequality, as measured by the Gini coefficient. The study concludes that poverty reduction depends on the type of remittances being received, which leads us to caution that it is important for researchers to ascertain the kind of poverty being addressed.

Somalia and Somaliland

Somalis are among those refugees who live in virtually all world regions with diaspora remaining in strong contact with not only Somalis back home but also others in diaspora. In the 1990, Somalis were recorded in more than 60 countries (Van Hear 2003: 1). This diaspora has attracted considerable research on the migration-development nexus in Somalia (Gundel 2003), on migrant transfers as a development tool in Somaliland (Hansen 2004) as well as in Somalia (Lindley 2006), and the importance of overseas connections in the livelihoods of Somali refugees in Kenya (Horst 2002).

Somalis have gone through cycles of warfare with their neighbours and among themselves along clan lines, invalidating any notion that they are a homogeneous group. The Somali diaspora is a consequence of traditional mobile livelihood patterns, colonialism, labour migration, and the humanitarian disasters of the late 1980s, through the early 1990s, and continuing to the present day. Averse to a life in exiled silence, the Somali have maintained strong contact with home, reinforced by new technology (IRIN 2000, cited in Sørensen 2006: 94). Two significant diaspora groups sustain development activities in Somaliland and Somalia: firstly the Somaliland Forum, which through internet-based discussions became an association for the development of the homeland's human resources; and secondly Somali peace and equality activists – women (daughters, nieces and sisters) who, through sending remittances, support large numbers of families in Somalia/Somaliland (Sørensen, 2006: 94). These are the significant sustenance mechanisms in Somalia, which ceased to be a viable state in 1991, and in Somaliland, which exists despite being slighted by the rest of the world.

Remittances to Somalia can be explained in two main phases. The first crop of emigrants to the Gulf states in the 1970s sent remittances through the *franco-valuta* system, in which foreign exchange was transferred to traders who would import commodities for Somali markets and then give the cash to the migrants' families. This system was banned in 1982 as undermining the Somali regime's patron-client mechanisms (Marchal 1996: 5, cited in Gundel 2003: 246). More recently, remittances have been sent through private companies known as *xawilaad* (Horst 2002). The Somali word *xawil*, derived from Arabic, means 'transfer', usually of money or responsibilities. Thus *xawilaad* is an informal system of value transfer that operates in almost every part of the world (Horst et al 2002, cited in Horst 2002). This system is operated by Somalis, both for sending remittances and for business transactions which rely on electronic technology, to facilitate business as well as deepen Somali transnational relations (Horst 2002).

Primarily, the Somali remittances act as an invaluable cushion for the social safety net, for example refugees in camps in Dadaab in Kenya receive child-to-parent remittances from Europe, Australia, Canada and the United States. In these camps, the Somali diaspora on the one hand remains a force assisting in the peace process as well as in rebuilding their homeland, and on the other it is a destabilising force continuing to finance warring parties in the homeland (Horst 2002). Remittances have changed the socio-economic environment both positively and negatively. The latter include the expenses incurred by the senders in tracing recipients; the insecurity of the intended recipients as *shifta* (shady characters or notorious criminals) hover around, terrorising them; and the creation of a dependency syndrome. Nonetheless, *xawilaad* maintains survival and improves private accumulation among Somalis whose situation would have been worse without it.

Amounts of Somali remittances range from US$140 million per annum in one study to US$800 million in another, though, as Horst (2002) cautions, what matters is not so much the amount remitted but the effects of the remittances on the lives of the recipients.

In Somaliland, the returned diaspora have been engaged in opening small-scale businesses (restaurants, beauty salons, transport companies, supermarkets and kiosks) through the savings they made abroad, and they also invest in land and housing (Sørensen 2006: 91). In two separate studies Hansen (2004) and King (2003) consider diaspora transfers an important tool in Somaliland's development. While one-third of monthly remittances received in Hargeisa goes to investment in the construction industry and other businesses, two-thirds supports the livelihood of about a quarter of households (King 2003: 27).

One of the most positive developments has been the spontaneous and self-organised return of Somalilanders in recent years. By 2002, several research and higher education institutions were headed and staffed by returnees and, with funds raised in the diaspora, a large number of returnees had founded primary or secondary schools, and were teaching in them. It is believed, however, that some Somalilanders may become 'revolving returnees' who, after a presumed 'permanent' return, still go back to Europe or North America, for a variety of reasons: inability to renew their contracts within the 'development industry'; having failed in their business efforts; or inability to convince their families in the wider diaspora overseas to join them (Hansen 2004; Ambroso 2002, cited in Sørenson 2006: 93).

The commitment of Somali and Somaliland diasporas to their homeland provides a lesson for the rest of Africa. Among other things, it shows evidence of a hyper-nationalism that can emerge after a prolonged conflict, which provides both challenges and opportunities for the diasporas to remain mindful of their nations and relatives as well as their friends back home.

Zimbabwe

After attaining independence in 1980, Zimbabwe grew into an economic powerhouse, before plunging into political and economic chaos over the last decade, forcing Zimbabweans of all walks of life to flee to all parts of the world. A survey carried out in Zimbabwe in 2001 found, though, that Zimbabweans were generally not well-travelled and that those who had travelled had mostly gone to other southern African countries (Tevera & Crush, 2003: 28–29). But that was the lull before the storm. When the economic crunch began, Zimbabweans move to countries further afield, very much as Ghanaians had done earlier.

It is important to note that, unlike Somalis/Somalilanders and Ghanaians, Zimbabweans emigrated largely because of an economic crisis of unprecedented proportions. The Association of Zimbabweans Based Abroad has become a galvanising force for Zimbabweans of all walks of wife, united in reaction to the terrible events back home. Today, Zimbabweans remaining in the country would not be able to survive without the diaspora remittances, monetary and non-monetary. It is relatively easy for the Zimbabwean diaspora to remit extremely small amounts of money for pitiable exchange rates, with an inflation rate at home of a level never before recorded in any country's history. Not surprisingly, 28 per cent of Zimbabweans make remittances to support family and friends, with the bulk of these being made through family or friends going back to the country. From the UK and South Africa, most Zimbabweans send non-monetary gifts, with food items dominating those sent, or taken home, from South Africa (IOM 2006: 178, 182). In Zimbabwe, mere survival counts more than all other needs, hence the importance of food items in remittance inflows to the country.

With respect to contact and socialisation in their destination countries, Zimbabweans in the UK and South Africa participate mostly in informal social activities, with just less than half taking part in activities with Zimbabwe-based people or organisations. Zimbabweans in diaspora in different countries also hold internet discussion groups, engage in political activities, send monetary as well non-monetary remittances to each other, and engage in business associations (IOM 2006: 185–186). Bloch's (2005) survey of Zimbabweans in the UK and South Africa underlines the=importance of diaspora in Zimbabwe's survival. Thus Zimbabweans have increasingly=become ambivalent about where they belong, or have consciously elected to become transnational.

Two other studies highlight the significance of remittances to households in Zimbabwe. Bracking and Sachikonye (2006) provide a detailed picture regarding remittances, poverty reduction and the informalisation of household wellbeing in Zimbabwe. The distribution of remitters suggests that about 25 per cent of them were based in the UK and about 23 per cent in South Africa, the UK hosting about 31 per cent of Zimbabweans, compared to 34 per cent in southern Africa (South Africa, Botswana and Namibia), though it is likely that the southern African – and particularly South African – figures have risen considerably since this study was done. Interestingly, children-to-parents remittances dominate, followed by inter-sibling remittances (Bracking & Sachikonye 2006: 21), evidence of the younger generations having emigrated as their older relatives remain at home, in an ever-deteriorating economy. The authors' categorisation of remittances – into productive, consumptionist, speculative, survivalist/exit, exit and performative/culture – is perhaps the most exhaustive and realistic treatment of remittances to a country where households are sustained only by remittances.

Return of the diaspora: myth or reality?
Return migration of their skilled and professional nationals in the diaspora is one option on which African countries pin their hopes, and one tried by the UNDP and the IOM without much success. However, in this age of IT technology, the notion of virtual return is, in many instances, becoming more popular than that of physical return. Indeed, as Skeldon remarks (2005, cited in Oucho, 2008: 62), for return to be desirable, there has to be something positive for skilled migrants to return to. Building on the work of Bovernkerk, King defines return migration as 'a process whereby people return to their country or place of origin after a significant period in another country or region' (Bovernkerk 1974 and King 2000: 80, both cited in IOM 2001: 18). Cerase (1974, cited in IOM 2001: 22) took the debate a step further by identifying four types of return. Firstly the *return of failure* by migrants who failed to overcome the 'traumatic shock' in the new

abode, or were unable to adjust to the new environment; second the *return of conservatism*, made by migrants who migrated to pursue the specific objective of saving a significant portion of their income to realise their plans back home (and do not aim at changing the social context they left before migrating); third is the *return of motivation* by migrants who stay in the host society long enough to start referring to its value system and, when they do eventually return home, are prepared to make use of the skills they acquired there; and lastly the *return of retirement* by migrants who have terminated their working lives and go back home to retire. This characterisation of return possibilities is unclear, it seems, to African governments, not least with respect to the households and communities that could benefit from diaspora support, including remittances.

Consideration of several return schemes point to why they have failed in Africa (Oucho 2008). First, the conditions that sparked the emigration of professionals and highly-trained Africans have deteriorated rather than improved in their countries of origin. Returning doctors and nurses find run-down health programmes with obsolete or irreparable equipment; teachers return to schools with poor learning environments or grossly lacking in basic facilities; university lectures are confronted with intolerably large classes, lack of equipment and poor research facilities, including lack of research funds; and returning migrants with capital and entrepreneurial skills cannot afford to invest in a risky economic environment ravaged by crime, corruption and bad governance. Second, the public service (represented by national governments) is supposed to benefit from return migrants, but its representatives merely sign agreements with the IOM or other parties, and hardly adhere to the provisions of these agreements. Finally, those returning often have a most shocking homecoming where relatives merely await gifts from them and do not wish to collaborate with them in whatever initiatives they propose (Oucho 2008: 225). More reasons could be given were it not for lack of space.

Ethiopia is one country whose diaspora has been in favour of return, especially virtual return. But it is doubtful whether even Ethiopians who appreciate the need for virtual return would do so to a country with strict controls on the use of the internet and mobile phones. Another problem for virtual returnees is that even countries with better IT facilities rarely maintain them well enough for sustained usage. There have been physical returns by Nigerians and Ghanaians in diaspora but how sustainable these will be is open to question. On returning, the diaspora would probably not work easily with their professional or business colleagues who had not emigrated. Indeed there have been stories of lost trust between such parties, with attempts made by those who stayed behind to complicate the re-entry of their diaspora colleagues.

Conclusion and the way forward

Previous research on the African diaspora and remittance flows to Africa has generated inconclusive findings. It has concentrated on the sources of these two resources and neglected studying their effects at the destinations where they are expected to make a difference. Future research will have to address this shortcoming, emulating the research undertaken by the Southern African Migration Project on migration, remittances and development in that sub-region (Pendleton et al 2006).

For African countries to harness diasporas and remittances in their development process, they need to formulate policies in which they involve the diaspora, improve the investment environment, and be constantly responsive to changes that positively affect the utilisation of the two resources. Policy frameworks and programmes focusing on the diaspora and remittances could benefit from those already elaborated in Latin America where the two resources have made significant contributions.

African countries should incorporate the contribution of their diaspora and remittances in national development planning and programmes. This could be done through sustained engagement with the diaspora in multiple facets of development.

It should be remembered that there still exists little clarity in the analysis of the impacts on each other of migration and poverty – Waddington and Sabates-Wheeler (2003) remind us that poverty may induce people to migrate to improve their livelihoods and that migrants may in turn become further impoverished and more vulnerable. More importantly, future research must encompass a study of the effects of social remittances to African countries – a subject which the research community, policy makers and national planners have so far sadly neglected.

This chapter ends with a note on a theme which the author has propagated over the last two decades: that Africa needs a series of 'African migration surveys' in the mould of the Demographic and Health Surveys which have been running since the 1980s. If the African Union is serious about implementing its migration and development frameworks and the Economic Commission for Africa is willing to serve its member states better regarding migration and development interrelations, they should prevail on national statistics offices across the continent to launch well-resourced migration data surveys.

Finally, both internal and international migration and their inherent consequences should be factored into PRSPs and the MDGs as well as the numerous national-specific terminal year 'visions', thereby making them an integral part of mitigating and eventually eradicating poverty from the African scene. NEPAD is now as good as dead but its conceptualisation for the utilisation of African resources – including the return of the diaspora – offers much promise for the future.

References

ACTS (African Centre for Technology Studies). 2000. Return and Reintegration of African Nationals Programme (RQAN III), Phase 3 Report. Nairobi: ACTS.

Adams, R.H. & J. Page. 2003. *The Impact of Migration and Remittances on Poverty*, Poverty Reduction Group, World Bank. Paper prepared for DFID/World Bank Conference on Migrant Remittances, London, 9–10 October.

Adams, R.H., A. Cuecuecha & J. Page. 2008. Remittances, Consumption and Investment in Ghana. In *World Bank Policy Research Working Paper* 4515. Washington DC: World Bank.

Adepoju, A. 1976. *Rural Migration and Development in Nigeria*. Ile Ife: University of Ife, Department of Demography and Social Statistics.

Ammassari, S. 2004. From nation-building to entrepreneurship: the impact of elite return migrants in Côte d'Ivoire and Ghana, *Population, Space and Place*, special issue on Transnational Migration, Return and Development in West Africa, 10 (2) 133–154.

Anyanwu, J.C. & A.O. Erhijakpor. Do International Remittances Affect Poverty in Africa? http://www.afdb.org/pls/portal/url/ITEM/581F2A4BB74515DE040C00AOC3D77BF.

Asiedu, A.B. 2003. *Some Benefits of Migrants Return Visits to Ghana*. Paper presented to the International Workshop on Migration and Poverty in West Africa, Sussex Centre for Migration Research, University of Sussex, 13–14 March.

Black, R., K. Koser & N. Al-Ali. 2000. The Mobilisation and Participation of Transnational Exile Communities in Post-Conflict Reconstruction: A Comparison of Bosnia and Eritrea, Trans national Communities Programme. http:www.transcomm.ox.ac.uk/wwwroot/black.htm (accessed 14 June 2009).

Bloch, Alice. 2005. *The Development Potential of Zimbabweans in the Diaspora: A Survey of Zimbabweans Living in the UK and South Africa*. Migration Research Series no. 17. Geneva: International Organization for Migration.

Bracking, S. & L. Sachikonye. 2006. *Remittances, Poverty Reduction and the Informalisation of Household Wellbeing in Zimbabwe*, GPRG-WPS-045. Global Poverty Research Group.

Brinkerhoff, Jennifer M. 2006. Diasporas, Skills Transfer, and Remittances: Evolving Perceptions and Potential. In C.G. & J.M Brinkerhoff (eds.) *Converting Migration Drains into Gains: Harnessing the Resources of Overseas Professionals*. Asian Development Bank.

Chilivumbo, A. 1985. *Migration and Uneven Development in Malawi*. Latham, MD: University Press of America.

De Haas, H. 2005. International migration, remittances and development: myths and facts, *Third World Quarterly* 26 (8) 1269–1284.

De Haas, H. 2006. Migration, remittances and regional development in Southern Morocco, *Geoforum* 37: 565–580.

De Haas, H. 2008. North African Migration Systems: Evolution, Transformations and Development Linkages. In S. Castles & R.D. Wise (eds.) *Migration and Development: Perspectives from the South*. Geneva: International Organization for Migration.

ECA (Economic Commission for Africa). 2006. *International Migration and the Achievement of the MDGs in Africa*. Paper for the International Symposium on International Migration and Development, Population Division, Department of Economic and Social Affairs, United Nations Secretariat, Turin, Italy, 28–30 June.

El-Sakka, M.I.T. n.d. Migration remittances: Policy Options for Host and Countries of Origin. Final report of research project CC023, Kuwait University, College of Administrative Sciences, Department of Economics.

Gundel, J. 2003. The Migration-Development Nexus: Somalia case study. In N. van Hear & N.N. Sørensen (eds.) *The Migration-Development Nexus*. Geneva: IOM.

Gupta, S., C. Pattillo & S. Wagh. 2007. Making remittances work for Africa, *Finance and Development*, 44 (2).

Hansen, P. 2004. *Migrant Transfers as a Development Tool: The Case of Somaliland*, Working Paper no. 2004/15. Copenhagen: Danish Institute for International Studies.

Higazi, A. 2005. *Ghana Country Study*. Part of the report on Informal Remittance Systems in Africa, Caribbean and the Pacific (ACP) countries. Oxford: ESRC Centre on Migration, Policy and Society (COMPAS), University of Oxford.

Horst, Cindy. 2002. *Xawilaad: The Importance of Overseas Connections in the Livelihoods of Somali Refugees in the Dadaab Refugee Camps of Kenya*, WPTC-02-14. Amsterdam Research Institute for Global Issues and Development Studies, University of Amsterdam.

ID21 insights 60. 2006. *Sending money home: can remittances reduce poverty?* IDS, University of Sussex. http:www.id21.org/insights/insights60/index.html (accessed 9 June 2009).

IOM (International Organization for Migration). 2000. Evaluation of Phase III of the Programme for the Return of Qualified African Nationals. Geneva: IOM, Office of Programme Evaluation.

IOM. 2001. *Harnessing the Potential of Migration and Return to Promote Development*, Migration Research Series No.5. Geneva: IOM.

IOM. 2005. *Migration, Development and Poverty Reduction in Asia*. Geneva: IOM.

IOM. 2006. *Migration for Development: Within and Beyond Frontiers*. Geneva: IOM.

IOM. 2007. *Evaluation of the Migration for Development in Africa (MIDA) Initiative as an Illustration of IOM's Approach to Making Migration work for Development*. Geneva: IOM, Office of the Inspector General.

Ionescu, Dina. 2006. *Engaging Diasporas as Development Partners for Home and Destination Countries: Challenges for Policymakers*, Migration Research Series No. 26. Geneva: International Organization for Migration.

Kabki, M., V. Mazzucato & E. Appiah 2004. *Wo benane a eye bebre*: the economic impact of remittances of the Netherlands-based Ghanaian migrants on rural Ashanti, *Population*,

Space and Place, Special Issue on Transnational Migration, Return and Development in West Africa, 10 (2): 85–97.

King, A., with A.M. Mohamed & S.I. Addou. 2003. Report for FEWS-net, *Hargeisa Urban Household Economy Assessment.* FEWS-Net (USAID Famine Early Warning System Network).

Le Goff, M. 2008. *How remittances contribute to poverty reduction: a stabilising effect.* Université Montesquieu-Bordeaux IV, 13 October. http://ged.u-bordeaux4.fr/LeGoff_Transferts_migrants.pdf (accessed 14 June 2009).

Levitt, Peggy. 1996. *Social Remittances – culture as a development tool.* Wellesley MA: Wellesley College. http://idbdocs.iadb.org/wesdocs/getdocument-asapx?docnum=561717 (accessed on 22 October 2008).

Libercier, Marie-Hélène & Hartmut Schneider. 1996. *Migrants: Partners in Development Co-operation,* Paris: OECD.

Lindley, A. 2006. *Migrant Remittances in the Context of Crisis in Somali Society: A Case Study of Hargeisa,* Background Paper, Humanitarian Policy Group. London: Overseas Development Institute.

Martin, P. & J.E. Taylor. 1996. The Anatomy of a Migration Hump. In J.E. Taylor (ed.) *Development Strategy, Employment and Migration: Insights from Models.* Paris: OECD Development Centre.

Moré, I. 2005. *Remittances Reduce Poverty in sub-Saharan Africa.* Demography & Population – ARI no. 136/2005 (translated from Spanish). Madrid: Real Instituto Elcano. http://www.realinstitutoelcano.org/analisis/854/More854vale.pdf

Mutume, G. 2005. Workers' remittances: a boon to development, *Africa Renewal,* 19 (3) 1–9.

Neil, K. 2003. *Using Remittances and Circular Migration to Drive Development,* Migration Information Source. Washington DC: Migration Policy Institute.

North-South Centre of the Council of Europe. 2006. *Social Remittances of the African Diasporas in Europe: Case Studies – Netherlands and Portugal.* Strasbourg: Council of Europe.

Nworah, U. 2008. Study on Nigerian Diaspora, *Global Politician,* 2 December.

Orozco, M. & R. Fedewa. 2006. *Leveraging Efforts on Remittances and Financial Intermediation,* Working Paper 24. Washington DC: Inter-American Development Bank, Integration and Regional Programs Department.

Oucho, J.O. 1990. *Migrant Linkages in Africa: Retrospect and Prospect,* Commissioned paper for UAPS Conference on the Role of Migration in African Development: Issues and Policies for the '90s, 19–24 February. Dakar: Union for African Population Studies.

Oucho, J.O. 1996. *Urban Migrants and Rural Development in Kenya.* Nairobi: Nairobi University Press.

Oucho, J.O. 2008. African Brain Drain and Gain, Diaspora and Remittances: More Rhetoric than Action. In A. Adepoju, T. Naerssen & A. Zoomers (eds.) *International Migration and National Development in sub-Saharan Africa.* Leiden, Netherlands: Brill.

Özden, C. & M. Schiff. 2007. *International Migration, Economic Development & Development Policy*. London: World Bank and Palgrave Macmillan.

Peil, Margaret. 1995. Ghanaians Abroad, *African Affairs* 94: 345–367.

Pendleton, W., J. Crush, E. Campbell, T. Green, H. Simelane, D. Tevera & F. de Vletter. 2006. *Migration, Remittances and Development in Southern Africa*. Migration Policy Series No. 44. Cape Town: IDASA; Montreal: Queen's University.

Prothero, R.M. 1985. The context of circulation in West Africa. In M. Chapman & R.M. Prothero (eds.) *Circulation in Third World Countries*. London: Routledge & Kegan Paul.

Portes, A. 2008. Migration and Development: A Conceptual Review of the Evidence. In S. Castles & R.D. Wise (eds.) *Migration and Development: Perspectives from the South*. Geneva: International Organization for Migration.

Ramamurthy, B. 2006. Remittances and Labour Source Countries. In K. Tamas & J. Palme (eds.) *Globalizing Migration Regimes*. Aldeshot, UK: Ashgate.

Ratha, D. & W. Shaw. 2007. *South-South Migration and Remittances*, Migration Information Source. Washington DC: Migration Policy Institute.

Sander, C. & S.M. Maimbo. 2003. *Migrant Labor Remittances in Africa: Reducing Obstacles to Developmental Contributions*, Africa Region Working Papers Series No. 64. Washington DC: World Bank.

Skeldon, R. 2002. Migration and poverty, *Asia-Pacific Population Journal* 17 (4) 67–82.

Sørensen, Ninna N. 2006. Migration, Development and Conflict. In K. Tamas & J. Palme (eds.) *Globalizing Migration Regimes: New Challenges in Transnational Cooperation*. Aldershot, UK: Ashgate.

Tevera, D.S. & J. Crush. 2003. *The New Brain Drain from Zimbabwe*, Migration Policy Series No. 29. Cape Town: IDASA; Ontario: Queen's University: Southern African Migration Project.

Van Hear, N. 2003. *Refugee Diasporas, Remittances, Development and Conflict*, Migration Information Source. Washington DC: Migration Policy Institute.

Waddington, H. & R. Sabates-Wheeler. 2003. *How Does Poverty Affect Migration Choice? A Review of Literature*. Working Paper T3, Institute of Development Studies, Development Research Centre on Migration, Globalisation & Poverty, University of Sussex.

World Bank. 2007. Concept Note: *Mobilizing the African Diaspora for Development*. Washington DC: Capacity Development Management Action Plan Unit (AFTCD), Operational Quality and Knowledge Services Department, September 7.

CHAPTER FIVE

Irregular Migration within and to the Republic of South Africa and from the African Continent to the European Union: Tapping Latent Energy of the Youth

Eugene K Campbell

Introduction

Largely due to the globalisation process, international migration has increased remarkably since 1989. The International Organization for Migration (IOM) estimates that there were 191 million people living outside their home countries in 2005. This represents an increase of 80 per cent over what it had been five years earlier. The total number of irregular migrants globally is estimated at between 30 and 40 million, representing about 15 to 20 per cent of all migrants (IOM 2007). Meanwhile, the International Labour Organization (ILO) estimates that in 1991 there were 2.6 million irregular migrants in Western Europe alone. By 1998 this figure had increased to 3 million (Romero-Ortuno 2004). Due to scarce empirical research on irregular migrants, very limited data exists on volumes of irregular migration or on the characteristics, activities and aspirations of migrants in Africa. Some work has been done in the European Union (EU) and South Africa, but the elusive nature of these migrants renders the results unreliable.

International migrant movements and residence in non-origin countries without possession of valid travel and/or residence documents have been referred to by various epithets, including 'illegal', 'irregular', 'undocumented' and 'clandestine'. But several scholars have now eschewed the use of 'illegal' because of its derogatory implications. In the end, the question is whether irregular migration is a problem; and overwhelmingly the answer is 'yes'. Few scholars have actually examined all aspects of the problem, thereby giving the impression that the fault is mostly with irregular migrants themselves.

Realising that there is a problem and that it affects government's internal security strategies as much as it affects the public, what are governments actually doing about it? They apprehend migrants, construct border fences (some electrified, as in South Africa) and inflate the budgets of border patrol and internal security units. This approach mainly achieves unnecessary expenditure of tax-payers' money, including that spent on deportations. It does not address the critical problems associated with irregular migration (such as unemployment, xenophobia, bad governance and crime). It certainly did not help the Zimbabweans who escaped the terrible assault by Robert Mugabe's henchmen to become victims of the fatal xenophobic onslaught from South Africans in May/June 2008.

A very good approach to examining the positive side of irregular migration was provided by De Genova (2002). He called attention to the role of migration legislation in criminalising a part of labour migration that had previously been accepted as normal. This has unfortunately introduced an epistemological dimension to the way that migrants are treated by governments and by the public. It is effectively responsible for the public perception that the presence of African (and indeed dark-skinned) migrants in a society is synonymous with unemployment, crime and prostitution. However, this paper does not explore the sympathetic approach to irregular migration in detail, but instead describes the practice in Africa within historical and contemporary situations.

The concept 'irregular' is used here as a convenient alternative to 'illegal'. 'Illegal' implies unlawful to the extent that such migrations may be interpreted as constituting a criminal offence (Campbell 2007). It is being increasingly realised, however, that irregular migrants are forced by failed political economies to eke out a living in some other country with a much better political economy. Though 'irregular' also implies derogation and may not quite satisfy those who prefer 'undocumented', it seems to reflect the behaviour better than 'undocumented', because there is indeed some documentation of such movement, notwithstanding its poor reliability. The term 'migrant' is used throughout this chapter in reference to both immigrants and emigrants. Irregular migration is defined here as the movement of labour between countries without valid travel permit, or remaining in a country beyond the expiration of a visitor or residence visa. It also includes refugees who remain in a country after their application for asylum status has been rejected. It is also acknowledged that refugees may become illegal migrants when they leave a refugee camp (Zlotnik 2003).

This paper examines the patterns, causes and consequences of irregular migration to and within South Africa, and similarly from the Maghreb to the EU. It includes a short section on policy strategies that have been implemented, as well as strategies that should be considered, especially by African governments, to minimise the cost to governments and migrants of irregular migration. Whereas conventional labour migration is about skills transfer, irregular migration involves people, mostly men, with low or no skills. They are usually hardest hit by unemployment and low wages, both of which make it very difficult to obtain entry visa into countries where preference is for skilled labour. Although human trafficking falls within the broad spectrum of irregular migration, it will not be addressed in detail here because its complexity requires that it be dealt with in much more detail than is possible in this chapter.

The greatest obstacle to producing scholarly articles on irregular migration is poor access to data. Research in this area is hampered by the elusiveness of the target population. Their lack of formalised residence status generally compels them to stay away from people. When interviewed, the reliability of their responses is questionable because extreme trust in the interviewer is needed for them to respond truthfully. But the factor that probably did the most damage to studies in this area was the tendency of donors, from the 1970s to the 1990s, to focus research grants in areas of reproductive health – almost to the exclusion of migration studies. Reference to this by De Genova (2002: 421) was strongly echoed by Black (2003), whose passionate appeal for research into irregular migration and refugees should be often repeated by migration scholars in these days of increased displacement of people.

History of irregular migration in Africa

The history of irregular migration extends over several generations prior to the twentieth century. Irregularity of migration exists because of the existence of territorial borders within which national governments implement policies related to social, economic and political activities. One of the mechanisms that ensures human development in each spatial territory is the enactment of laws which aim to ensure the regulation of human movement into and out of a country. Territorial security is therefore nominally ensured by requiring all migrants to be in possession of valid travel documents when they enter or leave a country. These documents are essentially passport and visa, in the absence of which temporary travel permits may be used. Migration therefore becomes irregular when a non-citizen violates the requirement for entering a country or staying in it. Thus irregular migration is not only about crossing international borders without valid documents, it includes migrants who entered a country normally ('legally') but stayed beyond the maximum period granted, without obtaining permission from the government to do so. Because of the involuntary nature of refugee movements, refugees, who are often granted only limited terms of residence, in this way easily join the ranks of irregular migrants (Black 2003).

The origin of irregular migration may be found in the Chinese Exclusion Act which was passed in the USA in 1882, which effectively banned the immigration of Chinese people (Lui 2007). Prior to this act the term 'irregular migration' did not exist. When migration began in the Maghreb, it had nothing to do with Africans moving to Europe. The Maghreb became involved because of its convenience as a transit point when Jews were assisted in migrating irregularly from Europe to the Mandate of Palestine between 1939 and 1945, following the British restriction of Jews wishing to enter Palestine (Palestine Facts 2009.) Migration to South Africa began in the early nineteenth century, but it is unlikely to have attracted much irregular immigration because the mechanisms for such activity hardly existed at that time.

The advent of irregular migration in South Africa may be traced to the apartheid laws which restricted the residence of non-white people. Through bilateral agreements with several southern African countries, the South African government recruited foreign labour through the Employment Bureau of Africa (TEBA) to work in its mines. This was necessitated by labour scarcity in South Africa and poor employment opportunities in pre-independence southern African countries. Encouraged by tribal chiefs, thousands of foreign nationals migrated to work in South African mines, farms and the domestic sector within the cities. Men went mostly to work in the mines and farms while the domestic sector was dominated by women (Taylor 1986; Crush 1999; Crush et al 2005). In 1920, there were 99 950 contract workers from Botswana[1], Lesotho, Malawi, Mozambique, Swaziland, Zambia and Zimbabwe in South African mines, and by 1921 the number of foreign-born Africans in South Africa had increased to 279 819 (see Tables 5.1 and 5.2).

As early as the 1920s South Africa was already attracting irregular migration of men and women. Women were much more disadvantaged than men in getting work. Since there were few jobs apart from domestic work and street hawking, some were forced to resort to more demeaning activities such as prostitution. 'The journey south for "illegal" migrants was for many years a fairly hazardous undertaking. Migrants had to pay for their own transport or travel on foot, often stopping to work en route to their final destination' (Crush 2000: 17). This is not unlike current movement from Zimbabwe, except that South Africa had no erected border post then. Hence the 'legal' issue at that time referred to whether or not an immigrant had valid documents to be in the country.

The number of foreign mine workers and foreign-born Africans in South Africa peaked in 1970, after a slight decline in recruitment in the 1960s. This may be partly explained by negative post-independence attitudes towards apartheid South Africa in several southern African countries. Zambia, Tanzania and Malawi took a dim view of labour migration to South Africa, with Zambia and Tanzania withdrawing their mine workers shortly after independence, while Malawi did so in 1972 (Crush et al 2005). The policies which restricted migration to South African mines triggered irregular migration to South Africa in pursuit of employment and higher living standards in South Africa's multi-sectoral economy. Initially, employment of irregular migrants was concentrated in the commercial farm sector, mostly on farms close to the borders of Zimbabwe and Mozambique (Crush 1999). But political changes in the 1990s probably

---

1 For convenience these and similar countries are referred to here by their current names.

enhanced opportunities for irregular employment in urban centres such as Johannesburg and Durban, and it was the social and environmental effects of this change that drew the most attention to the increasing inflow of irregular migrants to the country. As the new economics of labour migration (NELM) theory states, a person who has migrated once finds it easier to make subsequent migrations, because the risks are not as restrictive as was the case the first time (Taylor 1999).

In West Africa, the situation was more or less similar to that in southern Africa except that the main employment attractions were agriculture and commerce. Prior to the political demarcation of Africa in 1885, migration in West Africa went on without the limiting effects of borders. The Zarma people who came to Northern Ghana from Niger as warriors were able to proceed further into the country to be assimilated as settlers in southern Ghana (see Painter 1988). Likewise the Lebanese who entered West Africa in the early twentieth century perceived the region as favourable to settling and engaging in commerce. Many other Africans also moved between West African countries, settled and engaged in trade, fishing, and so on in the destination countries. Nigerians, Ghanaians and Liberians migrated to Sierra Leone, Sierra Leonean Creoles easily found new homes in Nigeria and Ghana, while francophone nationals and Nigerians migrated to Ghana to work in the farms and to trade (Peil 1971). Indeed, this was the case up to the end of colonial period, after which political independence was accompanied by several legislative restrictions on entry into countries such as Sierra Leone, Nigeria, Gabon and Botswana (Adepoju 1984). Currently it appears that these restrictions are not necessarily recognised where people of the same ethnic group straddle a border between two countries. It is common practice for this group of people to use man-made gaps in border fences to cross over to a neighbouring country to visit, etc. At the official border between Sierra Leone and Liberia, for instance, people in this category who own farms nearby in the next country are usually the first to be permitted to cross over when the border gates are open; and they do so without the usual travel documents. However, though the entry of migrants into these countries and the activities they took part in seemed legal initially, hundreds of thousands of these migrants subsequently found themselves living and working in the host country irregularly, or being treated as though that was the case. In the process, several Lebanese relocated from Guinea and Côte d'Ivoire to Sierra Leone and Ghana. Ghanaian fishermen were summarily expelled from Sierra Leone in the 1960s when their occupational activities were deemed to have negative effects on the environment. Adepoju (1984, 1995a) listed a number of cases where irregular immigrants were expelled from West and other African countries during the mid-1960s. In another place he wrote:

> Côte d'Ivoire expelled about 16 000 Beninoise, Senegal expelled Ghanaians from its borders; 800 Nigerians were expelled from Cameroon, Sierra Leone and Guinea, while the Côte d'Ivoire expelled Ghanaian fishermen. In 1964

the Zaire government expelled Rwandese refugees after they participated in the Mulelist uprisings in the country. In 1978, Burundi expelled 40 000–50 000 Zaireans, mostly Bembe refugees, from the 1964 Mulelist rebellion, and jobless migrant workers. In apparent retaliation Zaire quickly evicted Burundian Hutu refugees from the farms on which the UNHCR had earlier settled them in 1974 on the grounds that these were needed for the returnees. In 1971, Zambia expelled all aliens – about 150 000 nationals of Zimbabwe, Botswana, Zaire, Tanzania and Somalia – without valid work permits...50 000 Asians [were expelled] from Uganda in 1972. (Adepoju 1995a: 167)

But the most dramatic of these events occurred in 1969 when over one million irregular immigrants were expelled from Ghana, many of whom had been in the country for several generations and did not consider their residence status irregular. The Ghanaian case demonstrates how political and economic developments and legislation relegated seemingly regular residents to the status of irregular migrants. The government of President Busia inherited a failed economy with high unemployment and inflation rates. With immigrants seeming to be the more resourceful, they became the target of a vicious campaign to intensify the localisation process. Seen as perpetrators of the economic woes of Ghana, a burst of nationalism triggered the passing of the Aliens Compliance Order in 1969. This order required all immigrants without valid residence status to obtain it within two weeks or leave the country (an action that is strikingly similar to the treatment of Jews in Germany in the 1930s and Indians who were pushed out of Uganda in the 1970s). The total number of 'migrants' deported from Ghana is uncertain; but it is estimated, officially and otherwise, to be between 213 750 and 1.5 million (Adomako-Sarfoh 1974; Adepoju 1995a, 1995b; Makinwa-Adebusoye 1995; Akyeampong 2006). Significantly 66 per cent of the Lebanese whose commercial and industrial enterprises had contributed much to Ghana's economy felt obliged to leave the country and moved to Côte d'Ivoire and other nearby countries (Akyeampong 2006).

The large number of people expelled from Ghana and other African countries reveals the uncertainty of the regular status of migrants in Africa. It also says much about the porous nature of African borders before and immediately after independence. Furthermore, it exposes the deceit that goes on in various African societies regarding treatment of regular and irregular migrants in their territories. The economic events that led to the Aliens Compliance Order were actually not the making of the 'irregular' migration. A major determinant of the unemployment and inflation was the dramatic fall in world cocoa prices, excessive expenditure on ill-conceived social and infrastructural development, and rampant corruption. By 1963 the budget deficit of Ghana was £50 million sterling (Hansen 1968; Price 1984). But as Hansen notes, this was not the first time that cocoa, the primary agricultural product of Ghana, had declined in value. Due to viral infection, cocoa production fell during the late 1940s, leading to a fall in national income. Imported goods were in short supply while wage increases and increased prices of other products fuelled inflation.

Subsequent to the exodus of irregular migrants from Ghana, various steps were taken to assist the localisation process and improve the living conditions of nationals. The Ghanaian Business Promotion Act No. 334 was passed in 1970 in an attempt to ensure this. As a result, for instance, non-nationals were barred from owning business enterprises which accrued returns of £200 000 sterling or more (Ahooja-Patel 1974). But the economy did not revive. As Adomako-Sarfoh (1974) laments, there is a strong possibility that the government did not consider the effects of the Aliens Compliance Order on an economy that that had grown for over half a century largely from the efforts of non-nationals. By 1975 the Ghanaian economy had collapsed and it took the determined efforts of a young military officer, Jerry Rawlings who assumed executive leadership through a military coup d'état in 1979, to get it back on track twenty years later.

The Nigerian case is included in this section because of a chain of events that led to the expulsion of irregular immigrants in Nigeria. A similar concern about irregular migrants during the early 1980s led to a parliamentary Act which resulted in the expulsion of over two million migrants (mostly Ghanaians) from Nigeria, in 1983 and in 1985 (Adepoju 1995b; Makinwa-Adebusoye 1995). Nigeria's oil revenue and its implications for urban job creation diverted valuable skills from agriculture to the rapidly-modernising urban sector. While uncontrolled rural-urban migration put increasing pressure on the job market, agricultural production fell. As Joseph (1978: 231) reported, cocoa output fell 'from 350 000 tonnes in 1970 to 196 000 in 1975–6…The country which was once the world's largest producer of palm oil and groundnuts now [imported] these commodities to satisfy its domestic needs.' The importation of food and inflation increased during this period, and by 1982 the politicians seemed to have no alternative but to hunt down illegal immigrants for mass deportation. It should be noted that about 77 per cent of all West Africans who were migrants in Nigeria at that time (including the highly-skilled) were irregular migrants (Makinwa-Adebusoye 1995). However, the decision to expel irregular migrants did not have the same public support it had had in Ghana fourteen years earlier. Many nationals protected irregular migrants, leaving far fewer deportees than had been initially anticipated.

The Nigerian government was much more considerate to irregular migrants than the Ghanaians had been, extending the two weeks notice by four weeks (Adepoju 1984). Still, the expulsion was deplored by international organisations. Among the 1½ million deportees, the greatest number was Ghanaian (700 000). Nigeriens comprised 180 000 of the deportees, while 120 000 were Cameroonians, 150 000 Chadians, 5000 Togolese and 5000 Beninoise. Considering the Ghanaians who left in the second round of expulsions in 1985, the total was much higher, at between 900 000 and 1.2 million (Akyeampong 2006). Contrary to the generally expected profile of irregular migrants, those in Nigeria were a mix of unskilled and skilled. They included university professors, teachers, lawyers, accountants and medical professionals. In 1983, these categories of migrants were allowed more time to regularise their stay in Nigeria, and most of them were not expelled.

Why irregular migration?

Generally, economic factors, porous borders and corruption are among the motivators of migration that lead to the irregular residence of migrants in host countries. Another factor was that in countries such as Sierra Leone, Liberia and Zimbabwe, where political economies declined significantly, the application time for passports and visas, and their financial cost, tended to rise considerably, putting these items out of reach of most people, especially women. But this would not have been the reason for most irregular migration before 1970, because restrictions on immigration at that time were minor, and the conditions that produced brain drain in Africa had not reached the economically debilitating proportions they attained in the 1970s and 1980s. Much of the irregularity in migration occurred through financial and employment problems, and other negative circumstances that changed migrants' residence status from regular to irregular.

The position that many migrant families in Ghana found themselves in 1969 may have been due to negligence on the part of immigration officers. The affected individuals may have wrongly concluded that, since they had stayed in the country for a long time and had benefited from opportunities normally reserved for citizens, it made no difference whether they possessed a valid residence permit or not. As events in practically every African country where migrants were expelled shows, this opinion is convenient for all until the national economy weakens to the extent that citizens begin to express concern about employment, inflation and rights. Migrants, especially irregular migrants, then become the objects of exclusion by government officials in the hope that this would keep the 'natives' quiet.

In the case of the Lebanese, the majority had entered Africa legally. According to Akyeampong (2006) the first of them landed in Senegal accidentally, while on their way to the USA. But the favourable African climate and opportunities for lucrative business encouraged increasing numbers after the beginning of World War I. As a people in diaspora their intention was to stay in Africa permanently (as was the case with Lebanese living elsewhere). Indeed, very few applied for Lebanese citizenship when offered the opportunity to do so (Akyeampong 2006). But while most took citizenship of the African country they were in, others stayed without such commitment. These were subsequently trapped by the Aliens Compliance Order in Ghana in 1969 and deported as illegal immigrants.

Irregular migration in the past has contributed much to development in host countries. It provided guaranteed profits for South African mining companies and farmers because the migrants provided cheap labour. In West Africa it helped to develop the economies of several countries (Ghana, Sierra Leone, Liberia, Senegal, etc.). It also boosted the fishing industry in Sierra Leone and Liberia. In Nigeria it helped to develop skills through education and sustain life through the health sector. It contributed to the country's financial growth and developed the transport, infrastructure and manufacturing industries. It also assisted families in home countries through remittances.

Irregular migration in southern Africa and to South Africa

Contemporary issues on irregular migration in southern Africa involve migration both to and within South Africa as well as African migration to Europe. Though the South African government became more open to the rest of Africa in the late 1980s it was in the early 1990s that South Africa's attraction to Africans really blossomed. This is partly because several countries that had not permitted their citizens to visit or work in South Africa rescinded this policy when apartheid was formally ended in 1994. Moreover, the attraction to Zimbabwe – where almost a quarter of a million African migrants were employed in 1961 – and to Zambia had dwindled remarkably as their economies declined (Crush et al 2005).

The surge of migration interest in South Africa was partly because the lifting of apartheid occurred at a time of serious economic and political turmoil in most other parts of sub-Saharan Africa. The economies of Sierra Leone, Nigeria, DRC, Tanzania, Zambia and Uganda had crashed. Ghana was just emerging from a similar fate which began in the mid-1970s, and Liberia, Ethiopia, Sudan and Somalia were engulfed in bloody civil wars (Lewis 1996; Abraham 2001; Smith 1997; Crowder 1987; Collier 2002). The brain drain that accompanied these unstable political economies had resulted in most professionals of these countries living and working in Europe, the USA and Canada. Thousands of students who went to study in western countries did not return after graduating. In addition, a substantial proportion of skilled and semi-skilled Africans left to work in other African countries, especially South Africa, Botswana and Namibia. Many did so irregularly or entered South Africa with valid documents but stayed on after their residence or visitor permit expired. Most irregular migrants in these countries are employed in commercial agriculture, construction, the restaurant, hotel and domestic sectors, as well as in informal trade (Waller 2006; Crush 1999).

It would be futile to attempt to determine the number of irregular migrants in South Africa because of the diversity of the existing estimates. According to Waller (2006), the Human Sciences Research Council estimate of 2.5 to 4 million came under harsh criticism for being inflated, and was subsequently withdrawn. A political statement in 1998 by Chief Mangosuthu Buthelezi who was then Minister of Home Affairs increased the range to 5 million – all of these being figures which Crush (1999) found contentious. The widely acknowledged paucity of irregular migration data reflects inadequacy in the amount and the depth of research that has been done on migration. As Black (2003) states, there is an urgent need to focus research on migration issues in order to obtain the basic information required to develop policies on irregular migration.

Because of the legal and social implications of staying in a country without valid documents, most irregular migrants maintain a perpetual state of 'invisibility' and are therefore not easy to identify or interview. It would take determined effort by donor agencies to mobilise qualitative data of this population. What presently gives some idea of the trend of irregular migration are figures of deportations. Table 5.3 reveals a substantial increase in the total number of deportees from South Africa between 1994 and 1999, with figures of 90 692 and 183 861 respectively, indicating an average annual growth rate of 15.2 per cent over that period. The marked increase in deportations may have been an effect of the government's restriction of movement into the country. According to Crush and Williams (1999), legal immigration of mine workers to South Africa fell at a time when irregular migration seemed to be on the rise – quite probably because of the expense of legal immigration. Still, the increase in deportations may reflect an intensified search for irregular migrants rather than an increase in irregular immigration. The appropriateness of an intensified search is questionable, considering that between 1995 and 1997 the government offered three amnesties to migrants who wished to normalise their status and obtain permanent residence in South Africa. The amnesties probably explain the fall in deportations in 2000 and a slower annual growth rate of deportations (3.5%) between 2000 and 2004.

It is clear from Table 5.3 that, until the recent crisis in Zimbabwe, Mozambicans formed the bulk of all irregular migrants in South Africa. Their dominance reflects a long period of movement into South Africa as hundreds of thousands fled the civil conflict of the 1980s and early 1990s to seek refuge. Others entered to escape hunger due to the drought in Mozambique. It was an easy transformation of these groups from 'refugees' to irregular migrants, as they desperately sought employment in the urban centres, thereby abandoning the refugee shelters prepared for them in the rural north-east (Brunk 1996).

Though Zimbabweans formed the second largest group of irregular migrants in South Africa, between 1994 and 1999 their numbers grew annually at a much faster rate (27.0%) than the Mozambicans'. From 2000 to 2004 irregular migration from Zimbabwe grew annually by 12 per cent (8.5 percentage points more than the corresponding growth rate of Mozambicans). This implies that the economic and political situations in Zimbabwe have had a greater effect on the living conditions of its nationals than did the political and climate conditions in Mozambique. The additional constraints to leaving Zimbabwe through regular channels may have fuelled the rapid increase of irregular migration to South Africa. In order to restrict Zimbabwean movement to the UK, the British government raised its visa fee for Zimbabweans quite substantially – one of the strategies for restricting migrant entry is periodic increment of visa fees.

From a survey of brain drain in Zimbabwe, Tevera (2005) observed that applications for British visas remained very high, even after the fees were increased by 65 per cent in May 2003 and by a further 21.3 per cent in October of that year. The introduction of special US visas for Zimbabweans did prompt a reduction in emigration of the unskilled to the USA. Meanwhile the response to stricter immigration control by the South African government was mixed. In 2000 South Africa introduced a new Immigration Act which required Zimbabweans entering its territory to have valid passport, passport photograph and visa. Even though the measures were tightened further in August 2003 with the introduction of additional requirements such as a bank statement, letter of invitation and repatriation guarantee fee, Zimbabweans continued to apply for visas in greater numbers. Meanwhile, border jumpers increased in number, while others gave false information in order to meet the requirements for entering South Africa. Almost three-quarters of Zimbabwean students who took part in the 2003 survey had given a great deal of consideration to leaving Zimbabwe, and 80 per cent of them intended to be away for at least two years. In addition, 33 per cent said that they wanted to take up 'permanent residence' status wherever it was that they moved to, while 31 per cent preferred to become citizens of their destination country (Tevera 2005).

Botswana - a transit country

Among the indicators of irregular routes to South Africa is the nationality of applicants for amnesty. This is not to suggest that every applicant was an irregular migrant. But in the USA in 1988, amnesty provided irregular migrants an opportunity to validate their stay in the country. Of all the applications submitted for the 1996 South African amnesty, 146 675 were Mozambique nationals, 25 405 were from Zimbabwe, 15 647 Lesotho, 7744 Malawi, 2898 Swaziland, 1626 Botswana, 1042 Zambia, 207 Tanzania, 145 Angola, 122 Mauritius and 91 Namibia (Crush 1999). There must have been several land routes taken by these border jumpers to get to South Africa. What is certain is that the routes originated or went through these nine countries.

Botswana is one of the transit countries used by migrants to reach countries such South Africa, Zambia, Tanzania and Zimbabwe. It has historically been a transit station for refugees and travellers who moved northward from South Africa to escape violent conflict in their own country. This is how several waves of refugees from South Africa came to settle in Botswana in the nineteenth century. Between 1976 and 1978 about 10 000 refugees who escaped the apartheid regime of South Africa to seek asylum in Zambia and Tanzania went through Botswana, whose government was exceptionally sympathetic to refugees. Among those who decided to stay in Botswana, thousands were granted Botswana citizenship (Campbell 2003).

Botswana was a popular destination of Zimbabwean refugees in the 1970s, and remains so to irregular migrants from that country. The deportation figures in Table 5.4 indicate a very high increase in Zimbabweans entering or staying in Botswana irregularly from 2000 to 2007. From official reports it appears that 95 percent of all deportees from Botswana are Zimbabweans (Botswana Ministry of Immigration and Citizenship 2008). The average annual growth rate of irregular migrants in Botswana between 2000 and 2007 was 28.1 per cent. This rapid increase in the volume of irregular Zimbabwean migrants in Botswana is partly due to geographical proximity, and also to a cultural relationship between the two countries. The north-eastern part of Botswana is dominated by the Bakalanga whose ancestry may be traced through Zimbabwe. The Bakalanga initially came to Botswana from South Africa in the nineteenth century and settled in the north. When a civil conflict forced them to flee, a great number of them were given refuge in Zimbabwe in 1947. They finally returned to Botswana in 1958 (Dube 2002).

Zimbabweans enjoy several social and health privileges in Botswana that migrants of other nationalities may not have access to. But employment opportunities in Botswana are very limited and it is illegal to employ irregular migrants in the country. It is quite likely that many irregular migrants use Botswana as a transit post, within a stepwise migration to South Africa, which has a much bigger employment market. The most common employers of irregular migrants in Botswana are in the domestic and construction sectors. As is the case in every country, women also earn income from prostitution.

Factors influencing irregular migration in South Africa

Since 1990 Zimbabwe's economy has experienced considerable strain. But the most harm to its economy was triggered by the ZANU PF party's decision in 2000 to redistribute highly productive white-owned farms to black nationals (Bracking 2005; Moyo & Yeros 2005). Poverty among Zimbabweans has increased dramatically since the 2002 elections due to international backlash in response to the re-election of Robert Mugabe, the inability of blacks to maintain the commercial value of the land and Mugabe's political excesses. This has forced scores of thousands of young Zimbabwean men and women to leave the country and take refuge in South Africa. Many of them enter South Africa without valid travel and/or residence documents.

History also plays an important role in encouraging irregular migration in South Africa. The country has been a major and continuous importer of labour from neighbouring countries since the nineteenth century. A multiplier effect of this is the development of the idea that full employment exists in the country, notwithstanding the glaring evidence of high unemployment among the unskilled (van Heerden et al 2006; Kingdon & Knight 2003; Mundi Index 2007). This optimistic perception of employment and income opportunities is a well-known phenomenon, which usually occurs where there is significantly large economic gap between two neighbouring nations.

Table 5.5 reveals the persistence of such a gap between South Africa and the neighbouring countries, including Mozambique and Zimbabwe, from which most of her irregular migrants originate. The table also shows that the economic gap between South Africa and Mozambique was the highest in southern Africa from 1992 to 1999. An effect of geographical proximity is that Mozambique's contribution to irregular migrants in South Africa remains dominant even though the Zambia–South Africa economic gap has been the highest gap since 2004. The difference between South Africa and Zimbabwe's economies has consistently been lower than that between South Africa and Zambia, but Zambia does not feature highly in irregular migration to South Africa because of the greater geographical distance between the two countries, relatively good governance and the history of Zambian government restrictions on labour migration to South Africa. Likewise, though Malawi's economy is very far from that of South Africa, there are relatively few Malawians in South Africa without valid documents, partly due to the geographical distance between the two countries. To reach South Africa, irregular migrants from Malawi and Zambia would have to travel through multiple international borders without valid travel documents, which would increase the risk of being apprehended.

It may appear that most irregular migrants in South Africa and Botswana are cross-border migrants. However, notwithstanding the porous nature of the border, it is very unlikely that most irregular migrants enter South Africa without valid documents. As Crush (1999) observed, the majority would be likely to enter legally and stay on irregularly when their tourist permits expire and there is no valid way of extending it. Indeed the number of non-citizens who overstayed in South Africa between 1990 and 1996 increased annually by 53 per cent – from 18 399 in 1990 to 233 472 in 1996 (computed from Table 10 in Crush 1999). Another contributor to the high rate of irregular migration in South Africa is culture. The emergence of a powerful Zulu kingdom under Shaka, and the resulting wave of wars in South Africa, led to the forced movement of the Tswana, Basotho, Ndebele, and others to neighbouring territories, where they have lived in diaspora ever since (Solomon 1996). Where one group of people share ethnic identity with another group in a different country, it may be tempting to believe that people can move as freely in the foreign country as their ancestral 'cousins' do.

From the foregoing it is evident that, as Massey (1990) observed, theory-based perception among scholars that international migration is solely influenced by differential and poor development at the source is inaccurate. Family and organisation decisions also influence irregular movements within southern Africa. The frequency and magnitude of personal remittances made by migrants is usually associated with altruism which develops from migrants' awareness of the additional financial and material needs within their origin households that they are expected to contribute towards. The basics of these expectations are discussed within the family before the migrant leaves home. Organisational influence on irregular migration appears in the form of the returns expected from migration to South Africa. Among the conditions agreed between the governments of South Africa and countries from which mine workers were recruited has been the official transfer of deferred payments (60% of migrants' earnings) to the home country.

A further contribution to rapid increase of irregular migration to South Africa is the change of attitude of governments towards the use of the electrified fence in the northern part of the country. This fence was constructed in the mid-1980s to discourage irregular border-crossing, particularly from Mozambique, and it was designed so that it could be switched between 'lethal' and 'alarm' modes. Initially, the government maintained it at lethal mode with fatal consequences to over 100 individuals who attempted to jump the border. Since 1990 the fence has been kept on alarm mode only (Campbell 2007). Though the fence has been reinforced since 1990, its length has made it difficult to police, thereby providing irregular border jumpers a convenient path into South Africa.

Public attitudes towards irregular migrants

In 1997 the Southern African Migration Project (SAMP) conducted a random sample survey to obtain South Africans' opinions about irregular migration in their country. The data showed that public attitudes towards irregular migration were generally unfavourable. About a third of black, coloured and Asian South Africans supported the deportation of irregular migrants, while for whites the figure was a little lower (29%). Whites seemed to be most concerned about the national economy and supported the deportation of migrants who did not contribute to South Africa's economy (Mattes et al 1999). Only 4 per cent of respondents opposed the deporting of irregular migrants, and almost 60 per cent opposed granting amnesty to irregular migrants. Whites seemed considerably more threatened by the continued legal presence of irregular migrants than others, with 76 per cent of them opposing amnesty. This fear may be partly attributed to the association of irregular immigrants with a rise in crime in South Africa when the SAMP study was done.

Negative opinion of irregular migration is not confined to South Africans. The 2001 SAMP study of nationals' attitudes toward immigrants in southern Africa revealed a high public intolerance of irregular migrants (SAMP 2001). The recent waves of violent physical attacks on migrants by citizens in South Africa may have created the impression that South Africans are the most intolerant of irregular migrants in southern Africa. This perception already existed when two Mozambicans were fatally attacked in a moving train by South Africans in 2000.

However, Table 5.6 indicates that Namibians and Batswana are even less tolerant of irregular migrants than South Africans are. Paradoxically, even nationals such as Mozambicans and Zambians, who have themselves been victimised by xenophobic reactions to their presence in major destinations like South Africa and Botswana (Crush 2000; Nyamnjoh 2002; Campbell 2003; Campbell & Oucho 2003; Crush & Pendleton 2004) are apparently also intolerant of irregular migrants. Over half of Mozambicans and Zimbabweans would support a policy by their government that denied legal protection to irregular migrants. The only subjects on which they gave fairly low support (see Table 5.6) were tax increases for reinforced border control and turning on the electric fence (switching the South African fence from alarm to lethal mode). This may largely be explained by high poverty levels and by the fact that Mozambicans in particular have suffered quite seriously from the fatal effect of this fence when it was in lethal mode in the 1980s. According to the table, the most tolerant of irregular migrants are the Swazis (citizens of Swaziland).

The general intolerance of irregular migrants in southern Africa is not unique to the region. It reflects the perception of people who respect the belief that irregular migration contravenes laws that dictate the process of international migration. Campbell (2003) noted that Botswana citizens, for instance, adhere very highly to the law. Hence, while irregular migration benefits employers, it exposes the general population to the risk of their peaceful existence being violated by people from this group of migrants. In effect, the general perception is that, the moment individuals begin to live in a country without the 'legal' right to do so, they constitute a security risk and should therefore forfeit the right to benefit from the social and economic opportunities established within the laws of the country. However, most irregular movements are fuelled by a poverty that could have serious, or even fatal, effects on the individual, and others who depend on them, if there were no possible way for them to migrate.

The Maghreb as transit and origin of irregular migrants

Migration from the Maghreb to Europe is not new. Its history goes back to the early nineteenth century. However, it has attracted increasing attention since 1990, not just because of the remarkable rise in the volume of irregular migration through that region, but because of the extreme risk that young men and women take in order to seek better living conditions in Europe.

The major destinations of irregular migrants coming from or through the Maghreb are France, Spain, Netherlands, Italy, Belgium and Germany, and the major sources are Morocco, Tunisia and Algeria in the Maghreb, and Senegal, Nigeria and Ghana in West Africa. Most of these migrants are aided across to convenient destinations in Spain and Italy by networks of people-smugglers. The historically most popular transit routes in the Maghreb are from Morocco and Tunisia to Europe, with the corresponding routes in the EU being from Spain and Italy to the Americas. Algeria and Libya are also important transit centres, especially for West Africans, who are increasingly using the Maghreb routes. These routes are currently popular because the strategic alliances between Morocco, Tunisia and Spain have made irregular movements through the first two countries increasingly difficult.

While Western Europe was a major emigration area after World War II, its rapid economic development helped to stabilise its population by the mid-1960s, and by 1980 it had become a net importer of migrants. In the 1980s increased restrictions on visa requirements in northern Europe (which used to be the final destination of migrants from the Maghreb), together with rising economic development in Spain and Italy, transformed these countries from transit to destination for migrants from the Maghreb (Apap 1997). From an economic perspective, income differential does play an important role in motivating irregular migration from the Maghreb to the EU. For instance the average income in Spain, where about 400 000 Moroccans live, is about thirteen times greater than that of Morocco (Briscoe 2004; Sadiqi 2007b). The income gap between Spain and West Africa is much wider.

There were an estimated 400 000 irregular migrants in Italy in 1998, about 200 000 in Spain (in the 1990s), 500 000 in France, and 370 000 in Greece (Icduygu & Unalan 2001). It is quite difficult to attempt the journey by land and sea on one's own, even though a few actually do so. A large proportion of migrants are assisted by networks of people-smugglers who have made trafficking into a lucrative business. Out of 566 Sierra Leone asylum seekers who arrived in the Netherlands in 2000, 97 per cent had been assisted by smugglers (van Moppes 2006). The corresponding figures for those from Somalia and Sudan are 681 (98%) and 433 (99%) respectively. But the proportions obtained from a survey in West and North Africa and Europe are much lower (60 to 70%) (Icduygu & Unalan 2001). Not all attempts to enter Spain succeed; many irregular migrants are apprehended at the border and turned away. With increasing border controls on the traditional routes, irregular migrants and traffickers are seeking out new routes where border controls are relatively weak. Turkey is one of the alternate transit routes used, so much so that between 1994 and 2004 almost 9400 irregular migrants were arrested by the Turkish authorities (Baldwin-Edwards 2005). As was observed in the figures of irregular movement to South Africa, there are conflicting statistics on similar migrations from North Africa to the EU. What is certain is that the total number would be in the hundreds of thousands.

Out of 144 090 Moroccans expelled from Spain in 1996, 97 per cent were turned back at the border (Carella & Pace 2001), a figure which demonstrates the effectiveness of border controls in the EU. This statistic also shows that in a year there are indeed hundreds of thousands of attempts made by Africans to enter the EU. Chiuri et al (2002) reported that 54 428 irregular migrants were apprehended in the EU in just the third quarter of 1999, while Italy expelled 130 791 in 2000. Spain and Italy have the highest number of migrants in Europe and irregular migrants form a substantial part of the total immigrants. In the 1990s the usual irregular migrants were joined by groups of youth fleeing the hazards of failed political economies in West Africa. In 1990, 127 600 Africans, most of them Moroccans and Tunisians, had their status in Italy regularised (Carella & Pace 2001). Six years after the Italian regularisation of migrants, Spain regularised the stay of 108 321 of those who had lived there irregularly. Most of these were African migrants from the Maghreb and the rest of Africa.

Migration risk

The passage to the European Union is much more complex and financially costly than migration in southern Africa. For the smugglers of irregular migrants, the process is a business and it is quite lucrative. The estimated cost of smuggling an individual to Spain or Italy by air has been put as high as close to US$15 000 (van Moppes 2006). This however seems to be on the high side, even where the fee includes handling, board, lodging and other expenses such as a residency fee. Still, the high cost of air travel makes most individuals prefer to travel the more risky way – by land and sea. A reasonable estimate of the cost of the boat trip from Senegal to the Spanish coast is about US$1311, while the total expense on a journey from West Africa to the Canary Islands is over US$4626 (van Moppes 2006). It costs less to cross by canoe (the most perilous mode) than by a relatively comfortable boat. Still, concessions may be made by special arrangement between the migrant and smuggler, which would require an initial payment. This is more likely to be done where the migrant is a woman and subsequent payments would usually be made through prostitution (van Moppes 2006).

The most significant factor in the preference of West Africans for the Maghreb route is its geographic proximity to Spain and Italy, via the Straits of Gibraltar or Sicily. The three most popular entry points to Spain from Morocco are Barbate, Algeciras and Gibraltar – only 25, 27 and 32 nautical miles (46, 50 and 60 kilometres) separate them (respectively) from Tangier in Morocco. Though the exit and entry points are close to each other, travelling by small boats across the strait is perilous because of the turbulent waters around the Spanish coast. The misfortunes of many youths who have perished while attempting to cross the Mediterranean from North Africa has attracted the attention of NGOs. The most extreme example of the dangers that crossing the Atlantic Ocean and the Mediterranean Sea offers is the journey from Senegal to Spain. Senegal is a major transit centre for irregular migrations from West African countries. The journey begins with land, sea or air travel from places such as Sierra Leone, Mali, Niger, Ghana, Nigeria and Gambia to Senegal and is generally organised by traffickers who demand payment of between US$500 and US$1000 from each person. The illegal migrants are usually men between the ages of 15 and 40 years. But women are increasingly participating in desperate efforts to escape poverty in a region where unemployment is over 60 per cent. One such trip from

Senegal to the Canary Islands of Spain, in December 2006, took twelve days to execute. With very little food and water in a boat that had drifted off course, less than half of the 105 men who started the journey survived, and all needed medical attention ('Group from Senegal risks all to reach Europe', *International Herald Tribune*,http://www.iht.com/articles/2006/12/20/news/senegal.phd. In October 2003, thirty-seven Moroccan men died when their boat sank as they were about to reach the Spanish coast at Andalusia (Briscoe 2004). Hundreds of Africans have perished in the Mediterranean as they tried to reach Spain, while others have lost their lives from bullet wounds at borders and from dehydration exhaustion as they tried to cross the desert. IRIN (2008) reported a shooting incident that occurred during border-jumping in which twelve Malians lost their lives. Murder and injury by armed robbers are also among the risks these migrants are exposed to, especially those who take the Sahara Desert route to the North African coast.

Migration from (or through) the Maghreb may take weeks or even months and years, depending on the route and place of departure, and the obstacles on the way. Mostly it is achieved in step-wise movements (Icduygu & Unalan 2001). A likely bad experience in irregular migration is loss of money paid to people-smugglers. Some smugglers do not accompany their clients to the final destination because of the step-wise movement of most irregular migrations in the Maghreb. A subsequent caretaker may not be as trustworthy as the previous one, and temporary housing conditions may not provide the security needed to avoid loosing cash to thieves. Another problem is the health status of migrants, which may deteriorate due to the shameful conditions of housing and transport in the quest to reach Spain or Italy. Due to their skin colour and language, West Africans usually avoid the Moroccan cities, preferring to take refuge in remote parts of the country. Missnana Forest, north of Tangier, for example, was a known area of refuge to many North and West Africans awaiting assistance to travel to Spain. About 3000 West Africans, mostly Nigerians, were once housed there in very poor housing and under hostile weather conditions. According to Briscoe (2004: 2) 'food is occasional, pregnant women dehydrate, fevers propagate, and the little money going round is hoarded for that final voyage across the Strait'. By 2005 the place had become deserted because the migrants fled from the dangerous conditions in the camp to seek refuge elsewhere.

Due to the increasing volume of irregular migrants, the frequency of deaths, and the association with drug trafficking, the governments of Spain and Italy have intensified measures to discourage these movements. The Berlusconi regime vowed to imprison irregular migrants to reduce crime in Italy. But it backed down from this position two months later because of international criticism ('Berlusconi backtracks on illegal immigration', *Irish Times*, 4 June 2008). Still, it is likely that the Italian government's position on immigration could become more restrictive in future, making it even more difficult for irregular migrants to enter and stay in that country.

Factors influencing movement in the Maghreb

Political crises

The 1990s was a period of political crises in West Africa. The unrest followed years of devastated economies which were the outcome of rampant corruption and political dictatorships. But there was also a long-standing issue involved. In Liberia and Sierra Leone historical but silent ethnic conflicts between the settler descendants of freed slaves and the indigenous people finally erupted in violent and bloody ethnic wars (Abraham 2001; Jones 2004; Husband 1998). The settlement of groups of ex-slaves from the USA and the West Indies in Liberia from 1822 had introduced an elitist minority population, Americo-Liberians, as rulers of the country (Akpan 1973). The xenophobic attitude of the settlers towards the indigènes fuelled tensions between the two, culminating in bloody coup d'état in April 1980. The subsequent excesses of Samuel Doe, the coup leader and national President, led to one of Africa's bloodiest civil wars and destroyed the economy, key social structures and the infrastructure of Liberia. Though democracy was recently restored in the country the socioeconomic situation is still poor. Forty-five per cent of the youth are illiterate, 68 per cent of those between fifteen and twenty years of age do not know what a classroom looks like, 88 per cent of the youth are unemployed and 75 per cent of the total population lives on less than one dollar a day (WCRWC 2007).

The situation is similar in Sierra Leone where freed slaves from Britain, the Caribbean and slave ships were settled from 1792. Considering themselves 'black Englishmen' (Dixon-Fyle & Cole 2006), and being more educated and dominant in administration, politics and the economies, they maintained an air of superiority and disdain towards the indigènes. Although the social and economic dominance of the Creoles, as the settlers are called, hardly existed after independence in 1961, this position has never been forgotten by the indigènes. Hence, though the civil war in Sierra Leone was born out of decades of rampant corruption by the All People's Congress Party, the storming of Freetown by the rebels in 1997 and 1999 was designed to punish Creoles for having implemented xenophobic attitudes on indigènes in the past. The civil war worsened the already poor economic, social and infrastructural state into which Sierra Leone had deteriorated after becoming bankrupt in 1980 (Smith 1997; Cline-Cole 2003; Keen 2003). The youth suffered the most, being kidnapped and used as child soldiers or sex slaves and starved of education. Eighty-two per cent of Sierra Leonean youth are unemployed and national poverty rate is 70 per cent (Okojie 2003; IMF 2005). Youth living in such depressing conditions would be more easily influenced to seek employment in countries with better economic and social status.

In Tunisia, 1984 was heralded by a bloody revolt which subsequently spread to Morocco. These disturbances were signs of serious economic problems in the Maghreb (Seddon 1984; Contreras 2007). Mass demonstrations were not new in this region; but the motivating factor in the 1984 violence was the injection into government politics of an IMF Structural Adjustment Programme similar to those in West and East Africa.

Socioeconomic factors

Post-independence economic troubles in several West African states have influenced the on-going high levels of social degeneration in the region, which has had the effect of fuelling south-north migration of unskilled youth. Indeed, the Moroccan students in a survey of emigration intentions were right when they identified social, economic and historical factors as the primary motivators of migration to the Maghreb (Sadiqi 2007a). The military coups d'état which accompanied political and economic crises in Ghana, Nigeria, Sierra Leone, Congo, Uganda, Ethiopia, Mali, Burkina Faso, Chad, Central African Republic, and some other places, from the 1960s to the 1980s highlighted the importance of national security, a sector that received little recognition from the public and international media. Having assumed political and economic power, the new military elites did much to demonstrate their role in the political economy by engaging in excessive expenditure on arms, ostensibly to improve the image of the military. Notwithstanding the notion that increased defence spending boosts economic growth (Antonakis 1977; Biswas & Ram 1986; Kusi 1994), the indications are that this had a negative impact on national economic growth in West Africa (Kusi 1994; Heo 1998).

Educational investment also contributed to economic problems in anglophone West Africa. Logistic difficulties such as an inadequate supply of teachers, and the huge financial cost of implementing education policies in Sierra Leone and Nigeria strained the economy and compromised educational standards (Csapo 1983; Banya 1993). Corruption, expenditure on non-necessities such as the conference of the Organisation of African Unity in 1980 worsened the economic problem in Sierra Leone. Meanwhile Nigeria's economic problems were compounded by a bloated employment rate, poor population census data, government's erroneous anticipation of continuous inflow of huge wealth from oil, poor implementation of the Udoji Commission's recommended public service salary increases, corruption, and reckless government overspending (Joseph 1978; Csapo 1983). High fertility and population growth also impacted on the fragile economies of West Africa. However, this seemed to have been a blessing to West Africans whose labour was required in the low skills sectors in Europe, partly as a result of decades of implementing effective family planning in western countries.

Consequences of irregular migration

Economic

Data inadequacy makes it difficult to quantify accurately the economic returns of irregular migration of Africans to the EU. What is definite is that the agricultural sector in Spain and Italy needs labour from Africa, because of a shortage of such labour in Europe. The fall in fruit prices in the early 1990s coincided with an increase in farm production costs and made it necessary for European farmers to seek cheaper labour. Decades of implementing fertility regulation and social development has left the EU with increasingly high labour costs. Political and economic crises have remarkably reduced payment for labour in the Maghreb and West Africa, and this region has thus increasingly become a source of cheap labour to European farmers in areas where the demand for unskilled labour could not be met locally. Access to irregular migrants helps countries like Spain compete more favourably with agricultural products from the Maghreb region (Fuentes 2000). It may be argued that, just as the private sector in the USA saves billions of dollars annually from utilising irregular migrants (Huddle 1995), so does the EU private sector accrue huge profits from using cheap – and often irregular – African labour.

Meanwhile rural areas in the Maghreb and West African countries have lost tens of thousands of young men whose productive capacity at home could, under favourable economic conditions, have helped reduce income risk. Senegal's fishing industry loses many young men each year as they risk their lives across savage waters attempting to reach the Spanish coast. But though several efforts have been made – for instance through education – to stem the exit of irregular migrants, these have apparently not been effective (IRIN 2006). However, the migrants arguably compensate by remitting money and goods home. Thus Moroccans, Tunisians, Algerians, Senegalese, Malians and others invest in their country by migration to the EU. While short term remittances may be low and occasional, regularisation of stay in Europe would improve the situation (Carella & Pace 2001; Briscoe 2004; IRIN 2008).

Similarly irregular migrants contribute substantially to the economies of South Africa and Botswana. The utility of these migrants to South Africa is not easily quantifiable because of poor statistics on irregular migrants. However speculations may be made from the number of African workers whose residency has been regularised. Out of 13 297 irregular migrants apprehended in 1982 in South Africa, 4639 received exemption certificates to work in the country. Similar exemption was granted to 4793 irregular migrants the following year (de Vletter 1985). The granting of these exemptions should, however, be put in the context of the economic environment at the time. The global economic recession in the first half of the 1980s affected South Africa as much as it did Mozambique, Zimbabwe, Botswana, Swaziland and Lesotho the neighbouring states from which irregular migrants mostly came (Lodge et al 1992). Meanwhile southern Africa was experiencing the disturbing effects of drought and food insecurity. There was, in addition, a decline in foreign labour recruitment due to decisions in Zambia, Tanzania and Malawi to terminate labour supply while efforts by South African white workers unions to protect their jobs from blacks seemed to be making progress (Burawoy 1976). These factors may have placed much pressure on employers to seek the desired cheap labour through clandestine means. The risk of this behaviour pattern leaking to national employment authorities should be lower with migrants (especially irregular migrants) than with locals. No legitimate business organisation would admit to having irregular migrants in their employ. It may be conjectured therefore that the granting of exemption certificates was effectively recognition of the significant contributions irregular migrants had made to private sector production and savings. In considering Burawoy's (1976) discussion on the issue of employers' savings and on the concept 'cheap', some caution should be exercised regarding this cheapness of irregular labour and its effect on the savings of employers. However, it is logical to conclude that the 'cheapness' was deemed significant by employers; otherwise there would not have been a sustained demand for this type of labour.

Sending remittances home is also important for migrants in Africa because many seek work in South Africa, Botswana and Europe primarily to assist their home households. According to Sadiqi (2007a), over 1.2 million people in Morocco have managed to stay above the poverty line only because their migrant relatives remit money from developed countries. A SAMP study has revealed that a large number of households in Botswana, Lesotho, Swaziland, Mozambique and Zimbabwe likewise receive considerable remittances (Pendleton et al 2006).

The most preferred method of transmitting remittance is to bring it home personally and in southern Africa this is often done around major public holidays – or at the migrant's own convenience. The other likely channel of transfer used by irregular migrants is a trusted person, including a bus driver. Though the SAMP studies indicate that remittances make an important contribution to households, there are questions about the significance of the contribution. As Burawoy (1976) observed, and SAMP studies also revealed, remittance is not a unidirectional occurrence. It flows between the home household and the migrant as well as in the more usually spoken-of opposite direction. The extent of migrants' altruism, households' capacity to assist migrants, anticipated expenditure of income from work and remittances, demographic changes, and income changes within the household all influence the level of satisfaction that recipients at home derive from the net flow of remittances. Though Lucas's (1982) study did not reveal significant effects of remittances in Botswana, the SAMP studies indicate that recipients of remittances from migrants are usually satisfied with the contribution they make to meeting household needs. Otherwise, the wives and parents of the youth who make the south-north movement to Europe would surely do more to discourage them. Irregular migrants who succeed in living permanently at their destination contribute towards the formation and development of present-day diasporas in South Africa and the EU. Notwithstanding the tentative nature of the definition of the modern diaspora, van Dijk (1997) identified a community of 15 000 Ghanaians living as a diaspora in the Netherlands, including both legal and irregular migrants.

Xenophobia

There are several negative factors associated with irregular migration and many of them are attitudinal. Hostility stems from a morbid suspicion of the intentions of migrants who do not have permission from the host government to be in the country. Its roots are found in the basic mistrust that human beings hold towards those who seem different. Between races this attitude is frequently described as racism, while within the same racial group, it is referred to as xenophobia. In May 2008 South African citizens viciously attacked 'foreigners' in several cities, and by mid-June at least sixty people had been killed ('More than 2200 Zimbabweans await repatriation from South Africa', *ChinaView*, 17 June 2008). The official version is that the intended targets were irregular migrants, but the assault also affected African migrants with legal residence status. The South African incident sent an alarm wave throughout the world because it happened in the only African country with an anti-xenophobia plan of action. This syndrome is seen as a deep-seated feeling which usually lies dormant until it is triggered by economic and political events (Campbell 2003).

As demonstrated earlier, South Africans, and most southern Africans, have little tolerance for irregular migrants. But there are also indications that the level of intolerance in the region is part of the inherent xenophobia that pervades much of the region. While feelings of resentment towards other people are essentially bad, they are not always without reason. Data from the NIPS study by SAMP reveal that 40 per cent of southern Africans have heard of a citizen who was denied a job because it went to a migrant (SAMP 2001). In addition, 28 per cent knew someone who had been affected the same way, while about 11 per cent had personally been denied jobs which went to migrants. However, the data do not include information about the differential in skills and qualifications of the affected citizens and migrants. What is clear is that Zimbabwean irregular migrants are often preferred in the construction industry because they produce better quality goods and charge substantially less than nationals with similar skills. A good number of Zimbabweans are better educated than the work they do may imply. As with many migrants internationally, they are frequently forced by circumstances to accept jobs that need skills different from what they can offer, or are below – or way below – their skills level.

Some of the attitudes of locals towards migrants are simply bizarre. Ten per cent of southern Africans want their governments to prohibit entry of migrants, and 38 per cent are opposed to the granting of permanent residence to foreigners.

Generally, Namibians, Batswana and Mozambicans were more strongly in favour of restrictive policies than South Africans were. But South Africans seemed more prone to violence than the rest. The highest proportion (39%) of respondents who said they would take part in actions to stop migrants from moving into their neighbourhood was South African (SAMP, 2001). They were also the most likely to take part in actions that would stop migrant entrepreneurship in their community, stop migrant offspring from sitting in the same classroom as their own children, and stop migrants becoming their co-workers (42%, 43% and 37%, respectively). It is within this context that the attacks on foreigners in South Africa should be viewed. In addition to all this is the global fear that irregular migrants are highly likely to commit crime.

The news media are among the worst culprits in propagating misconceptions about the 'clandestine' intentions of irregular migrants. An example of their alarmist approach is this quotation from the South African *Financial Mail*: 'The high rate of crime and violence – mainly gun-running, drug trafficking and armed robbery – is directly related to the rising number of "illegal" migrants in South Africa' (Danso & McDonald, 2001). Politicians also foster public resentment toward irregular migrants. A widely cited remark by a South African politician is that they aggravate 'the crime situation and [rob] South Africans of jobs' (Campbell 2007). This is at best a half truth because it is unlikely that migrants would operate at these levels without assistance from nationals who know the territory well. Social networks that assist irregular migrants operate as much as possible within limits of the law. Where legal lapses occur it would be difficult to exclude the effects of national collaborators. Where there is the illusion that jobs are being 'stolen' by irregular migrants, this may be partly because migrants are willing to work for less pay than nationals would accept. But while doing so they forgo the opportunities available to regular migrants to improve their skills – a process which contributes positively to brain circulation. Owing to the duration and nature of jobs that irregular migrants take on, it is unlikely that they would make significant progress on the occupational scale. Hence their contribution to economic development when they return home may not be comparable to that of skilled legal migrants.

Health impacts

The health aspect of irregular migration is most frequently associated with women and prostitution. Poverty is a major factor influencing prostitution, and, as the bulk of irregular migrants are within critical stages of poverty, many women migrants are forced by circumstances to eke out a living by trading their body for money. But gone are the days when individuals took voluntary decisions to work as prostitutes. In South Africa the sex trade is now dominated by prostitutes who have virtually no control over their own lives. They are brought into the country as sex slaves, though most of them hardly realise initially that is to be their fate.

The main African sources of South African sex slaves are Lesotho, Mozambique and Malawi (Woolman & Bishop 2006), but many others are recruited outside Africa, mostly in Thailand. Because these women have been tricked by human traffickers into working in an illegal commercial sector in South Africa, their de facto status in the country is also irregular. As do people in many countries throughout the world, South Africans perceive prostitutes (both voluntary and coerced) as among the main distributors of HIV/AIDS. The prevalence of HIV in South Africa was 29 per cent in 2006 – up by four percentage points from the 2001 figure (AVERT 2007).

A similar situation exists in Europe where migrants from sub-Saharan Africa contribute about 19 per cent to the heterosexual transmission of HIV. A study of prostitutes in Spain revealed that women from sub-Saharan Africa had the highest incidence of HIV, hepatitis B, bacterial vaginosis and acute sexually-transmitted infections in the country (Del Amo et al 2004; Del Amo et al 2005). Domestic work and street hawking within sub-Saharan Africa are dominated by women, and a considerable number of them are irregular migrants. In an effort to maximise income, several of these women occasionally participate in non-institutionalised prostitution which exposes them to HIV infection.

Migrants also bring non-sexual diseases to their destinations, and irregular migrants in particular are frequently exposed to the physical effects of anxiety, excessive smoking and poor diet. Due to fear of apprehension and expulsion, many of them do not seek medical assistance from clinics or hospitals. Non-communicable health problems such as infertility have social and biological effects which need medical attention. Cultural myths and taboos are also barriers to migrants' access to appropriate solution to their problems. Migrants generally have greater health problems than citizens of destination countries, with variations existing among different migrant groups of different social and economic backgrounds and migrant status. Irregular migrants are the most affected by communicable and congenital diseases, especially because the health policies of destination countries seldom favour their needs. According to Yebei (2000) irregular migrants in the Netherlands are not entitled to social services from the state nor are their expenses on health care reimbursed by the state. Yet for several reasons, including poor nutrition, many irregular migrants in the Netherlands who suffer from infertility could not get adequate medical attention.

The epidemiology of destination areas is adversely affected by the migration of Africans. Patient screening in the EU has revealed an abundance of tuberculosis (TB) among African migrants, thereby suggesting that Africans fleeing TB-endemic areas of political and economic turmoil contribute towards increasing TB prevalence in the EU – where the disease had been almost eradicated earlier in the twentieth century (Rieder et al 1994; Gushulak & MacPherson 2006). The increasing volume of migrants, tourists and business travellers from Africa to Europe has also increased the chances that a continent that was malaria-free for several decades has become exposed to the disease. Cuadros et al (2002) described a case of malaria in a Spanish woman who had no history of proximity to the disease. She probably contracted malaria because her house in Spain was near a stream where it was suspected that mosquitoes could have been breeding. Though preventative measures such as regular fumigation are taken by airlines to avoid intercontinental transfer of diseases, the vectors can be lodged in baggage and could cross that way. Similarly, irregular migrants may inadvertently carry such vectors to Europe in their clothes and baggage. The overall effect is that practically all major destinations of irregular migrants are increasingly at risk of epidemics of diseases that had been locally eradicated earlier in the twentieth century.

Africans have lower life expectancy (53 years) in general than Europeans. In addition to this are trauma and other physical factors associated with irregular migration. Hence, mortality is higher among African migrants in the EU than among native-born Europeans. As an example: a study in Belgium revealed that native-born Belgians have higher life expectancy than migrants from Morocco. The lowest life expectancy found was among migrants from sub-Saharan Africa (Deboosere & Gadeyne 2005).

Policy implications

Among the difficulties involved in scientific analyses of irregular migration are the differing positions taken by governments and non-governmental organisations (NGOs). Traditionally, governments are not in favour of this practice while NGOs tend to be somewhat sympathetic. Though details are undocumented, it appears that irregular migrants have contributed to social welfare and pension schemes in Europe and South Africa, even when they hardly benefit from them. For a while in the 1990s the German pension scheme was sustained by migrant workers (Baldwin-Edwards 1997). Irregular migrants in the EU benefit from education grants but do not necessarily have access to healthcare from the state. Because of the language and social capital problems which migrants experience in destination countries, many do not actually get to enjoy these benefits before they are deported or their status is regularised. Poor treatment from government and employment officials has made some European NGOs concerned that not enough is being done to protect these migrants, especially the women. Spanish NGOs have been encouraged by increasingly positive media response to the problem to adopt positive attitudes to the consequences of migration and to be more proactive in migration policy-making (NGO 2005).

In an effort to eradicate irregular migration in their countries, several governments have implemented 'integration' policies. In this regard, millions of migrants throughout the world have had their status regularised. Most notable among these is the granting of amnesty in the United Stated to 3.2 million irregular migrants in 1986. Migrant regularisation began in Europe in the 1970s with 12 000 in Belgium in 1974 and 15 000 in the Netherlands in 1975 (De Genova

2002). Since then, hundreds of thousands of migrants in Europe have been regularised. South Africa also offered amnesty to irregular migrants several times in the 1980s and 1990s. Governments' rationale for these amnesties is based on the conviction that it would 'integrate' the 'alien' population within a superbly civilised social order. This interpretation of 'integration' implies that granting regularisation and amnesty to migrants is the passport with which they would access social, political and economic opportunities just like any other person in the country.

However, as Danso and McDonald (2001) observed, many irregular migrants in South Africa did not think the stated benefits of the amnesties outweighed the net social cost and decided not to apply for them. The concept 'integrate' in this sense is patronising. Moreover, integration does not provide a watertight solution to the negative consequences of irregular migration or migration in general. It is clear that among South Africans there is a fine line between regular and irregular migrants. Migrants are perceived to be mostly irregular, and as exploiting the country of its limited economic resources (Dodson 2001; Campbell 2007). In the wake of the South African xenophobic attacks on migrants in May and June 2008, and the threat this posed to tourist confidence in the country and its hosting the FIFA (football) World Cup in 2010, the government proposed integrating irregular migrants into local society. But this incident was a symptom of wider socioeconomic problems in the country, especially a very high unemployment level among the unskilled. Migrant integration could aggravate this problem if it were not accompanied by very good employment-creation strategies. The 'pro-elitist' employment strategy of Thabo Mbeki had not changed when he resigned the presidency, and it is widely anticipated that the new president, Jacob Zuma, will institute a strategy aimed at minimising unemployment of the unskilled.

International cooperation is crucial to the successful management of irregular migration (Campbell 2007). At the instigation of EU countries, North Africa seems to be faring well in the area of 'external dimension'. This is because EU countries have moved from a traditionally conservative approach to a more or less democratic one. One of the alternatives that may be adopted within the 'external dimension' framework is for the EU to dialogue with sending and transit countries about stemming irregular migration. A second approach is to influence migrants' choice of destinations, including addressing causes of migration and improving migrant access to social welfare services (Boswell 2003). Within this framework, Spain has offered lucrative employment opportunities to Africans who might otherwise have been forced to take risky marine routes to Europe. Meanwhile, Britain, Senegal and Morocco now cooperate with Spain to combat irregular migration more effectively (Davis 2006; E Nash & C Soares, *Independent*, 26 June 2007[2]).

---

2 http://www.independent.co.uk/news/world/europe/spain-offers-jobs-and-visas-to-fight-illegal-migration-454645.html

Several scholars and politicians perceive the free movement of people between countries as the key to curbing irregular migration. However, this idea was vehemently opposed by Botswana and South Africa when the Protocol on the Facilitation of Movement of Persons was drafted by the Southern African Development Community (SADC) (Campbell 2007). These countries are economically the most prosperous in the region and their prolonged resistance to the Protocol may have been influenced by experiences in West Africa after a similar protocol was passed. In 1980, five years after the Economic Community of West African States (ECOWAS) was established, the Protocol on Free Movement of Persons and Rights of Residence and Establishment was signed by member states. It provided for non-visa entry of citizens of ECOWAS states into any ECOWAS country, and a stay of up to 90 days. As Adepoju (2002) observed, this was undoubtedly a significant achievement for the region. However its introduction occurred during a period of economic prosperity in Nigeria but recession in most West African states. The resultant rush of labour to Nigeria, and the failure of migrants/tourists to regularise their stay, created a pool of over one million irregular migrants in the country and triggered the mass deportations of 1983 and 1985. In 1993 another violation of the Protocol occurred when the government of Côte d'Ivoire stripped Alassane Ouattara of his right of inclusive citizenship because one of his parents was born in Burkina Faso. This came just a year after the revised protocol was signed. It is therefore not surprising that several states in sub-Saharan Africa would hesitate to adopt a protocol that allowed free movement of persons into their territories.

Research

No region in the world has developed migration strategies which guarantee sustained peace and the minimisation of irregular migration. As mentioned earlier, one of the reasons for this is the complex nature of the migration process. This has discouraged demographers and other social scientists from seriously and continuously researching current and emerging migration issues. At the African Parliamentary Conference on Migration in Rabat in May 2008, parliamentarians acknowledged the urgent need for comprehensive and sustained migration research. Migration is really no more complex than fertility and mortality, and the wealth of theories of migration is testimony to this. What apparently distinguished the other subject areas from migration was the serious health risks associated with reproduction and child care, while the risks associated with migration were considered insignificant. Before 1980, migration was not widely perceived be a serious health issue; the economic and social models focused on economic and social risks. But global experiences indicate that international migration involves serious health risks, and may indeed have fatal consequences.

With an increasing number of young professional and semi-skilled men and women engaging in international migration, there is growing risk to the health and life expectancy of the youth. It is now essential to find solutions to the negative aspects of international migration (both regular and irregular). There are numerous indicators of the determinants, patterns and consequences of regular and irregular migration. But the available data is unreliable, inconsistent and haphazard. What is urgently required is the strengthening of a reliable data bank, and a common communication channel that would inform scholars and policy-makers about the directions that problem-solving efforts are taking. In this regard, this paper calls for developed and developing states to undertake longitudinal World Migration Surveys, as was done through the World Fertility Surveys and Demographic Health Surveys. These surveys would serve to inform migration policies as well as monitor progress and identify problems during their implementation. If, as Widgren and Martin (2002) predict, migration will increase for the next 21 years, now is the time to obtain reliable data that would ensure its eventual decline – as well as the maximisation of returns from migration, and the minimisation of its costs.

Summary and conclusion

Irregular migration to South Africa has been in practice since the colonial era; but it became an issue of concern to African governments during the post-independence era. Since the 1960s irregular migrants have been expelled from several African countries. The most dramatic of these events have occurred in Ghana, Nigeria and South Africa, where the total number of deportees exceed one million. From the mid-1980s, irregular migration flows to the EU have occurred increasingly from the Maghreb and West Africa. Although statistics exist about irregular migration in Africa, they are unreliable estimates. Very limited empirical research has been done in this area, which makes it extremely difficult to determine the demographic, economic and social characteristics of the migrants.

Public opinion on migration tends to be unfavourable, but it does not have to remain so. The migrants are labour migrants who were forced by economic and social limitations to move by irregular means and routes. They deserve to be treated with civility and not hostility. But for the public to be objective on this issue there needs to be a wealth of data to inform that level of rationalisation. Until then irregular migrants will continue to be perceived as criminals, job thieves and distributors of sexually transmitted infections.

Table 5.1: Numbers of contract labour migrants to South African mines, 1920 – 1990

Year	Country of origin									Total
	Angola	Botswana	Lesotho	Malawi	Mozambique	Swaziland	Tanzania	Zambia	Zimbabwe	Other	
1920	0	2 112	10 439	354	77 921	3 449	0	12	179	5 484	99 950
1925	0	2 547	14 256	136	73 210	3 999	0	4	68	14	94 234
1930	0	3 151	22 306	0	77 828	4 345	183	0	44	5	99 355
1935	0	7 505	34 788	49	62 576	6 865	109	570	27	9	112 498
1940	698	14 427	52 044	8 037	74 693	7 152	0	2 725	8 112	70	168 058
1945	8 711	10 102	36 414	4 973	78 588	5 688	1 461	27	8 301	4 732	158 967
1950	9 767	12 390	34 467	7 831	86 246	6 619	5 495	3 102	2 073	4 826	172 816
1955	8 801	14 195	36 332	12 407	99 449	6 682	8 758	3 849	162	2 299	192 934
1960	12 364	21 404	48 842	21 934	101 733	6 623	14 025	5 292	747	844	233 808
1965	11 169	23 630	54 819	38 580	89 191	5 580	404	5 898	653	2 686	232 610
1970	4 125	20 461	63 988	78 492	93 203	6 269	0	0	3	972	265 143
1975	3 431	20 291	78 114	27 904	97 216	8 391	0	0	2 485	12	220 293
1980	5	17 763	96 309	13 569	39 539	8 090	0	0	5 770	1 404	182 449
1985	0	18 079	97 639	16 849	50 126	12 365	0	0	0	4	196 068
1990	0	15 720	108 780	72	50 104	17 816	0	0	2	0	192 044

Source: Crush, 2000:15.

CHAPTER FIVE   Irregular Migration: Tapping Latent Energy of the Youth

Table 5.2: Foreign-born Africans in South Africa, 1911–1985

Country of birth	1911	1921	1936	1946	1951	1960*	1970	1980	1985
Angola	0	0	28	6 716	6 322	68	3 859	589	392
Botswana	5 020	11 959	4 048	38 559	51 017	21 658	49 469	33 366	26 015
Lesotho	75 132	111 733	163 838	199 327	219 065	73 639	157 499	172 879	135 563
Malawi	4 573	2 2122	17 657	61 005	63 655	23 608	110 777	36 087	28 712
Mozambique	114 976	110 245	98 031	141 417	161 240	35 857	142 512	64 813	63 561
Namibia	2 230	2 926	1 879	4 990	4 129	1 073	2 518	10 342	9 210
Swaziland	21 662	29 177	31 092	33 738	42 914	17 836	29 167	31 981	30 722
Tanzania	0	0	118	2 937	7 127	225	288	145	887
Zambia	2 158	0	12 189	13 515	13 544	2 996	2 194	1 495	926
Zimbabwe	2 526	0	2 167	32 034	32 697	11 805	13 392	20 552	7 019
Other	930	5 146	2 730	22 569	4 282	857	4 369	4 234	14 003
Total	229 207	279 819	333 777	556 807	605 992	189 622	516 044	376 483	317 010

* Note: Figures include mine workers except in 1960.

Source: Crush, 2000: 15.

Table 5.3: Number of deportations from South Africa per year; to three countries of origin

Country	1994	1995	1996	1997	1998	1999	2000	2001	2002	2003	2004
Mozambique	71 279	131 689	157 425	146 285	141 506	123 961	84 738	94 404	83 695	82 067	81 619
Zimbabwe	12 931	17 549	14 651	21 673	28 548	42 769	45 922	47 697	38 118	55 753	72 112
Lesotho	4 073	4 087	3 344	4 077	4 900	6 003	5 871	5 977	5 278	7 447	7 468
Other	2 409	3 759	5 293	4 316	6 332	11 128	9 044	8 045	8 779	9 541	5 938
Total	90 692	157 084	180 713	176 351	181 286	183 861	145 575	156 123	135 870	154 808	167 137

Source: Waller, 2006.

Table 5.4: Numbers of irregular migrants deported from Botswana

Year	Number deported
2000	13 191
2001	22 511
2002	35 889
2003	36 724
2004	57 808
2005	46 580
2006	58 464
2007	74 570

Source: Botswana Ministry of Immigration & Citizenship, 2008.

Table 5.5: Number of times by which the GDP per capita of South Africa exceeds those of other countries in southern Africa

Country/region	Year			
	1992	1999	2004	2007
Botswana	1.235	0.970	1. 267	0.957
Malawi	12. 600	15. 286	17. 211	12.198
Mozambique	31. 500	22. 929	9. 909	9.598
Zambia	6. 000	8. 676	12. 263	11.710
Zimbabwe	3 .938	4. 458	4. 500	6.036
Lesotho	5. 362	4. 721	3. 303	2.698
Swaziland	3. 072	2. 112	2. 074	2.265
Namibia	n/a	1. 521	2. 010	1.444
Sub-saharan*	6. 866	6. 172	5. 874	5.855
West Africa	6 .146	9. 441	9. 168	8.805
East Africa	10. 957	12. 346	10 .548	9.924
Central Africa	5. 478	10. 700	8 .681	8.547

* Other than the countries above.

Source: Population Reference Bureau, World Population Data Sheet: 1992/1999/2004/2007.

CHAPTER FIVE   Irregular Migration: Tapping Latent Energy of the Youth

Table 5.6: Nationals' support of government policies to minimise irregular migration, by country of enumeration (%)

Support policy	South Africa	Namibia	Botswana	Zimbabwe	Mozambique	Swaziland
Police right to detain suspected irregular migrants	82.4	95.1	87.6	77.5	88.3	56.9
Foreigners to carry identification always	74.9	89.6	82.0	65.7	92.3	47.7
Increase tax to assist border patrol	20.6	49.9	37.7	14.6	35.7	11.4
Use army to patrol border	82.6	94.6	94.9	62.0	71.7	73.3
Allocate more money to border protection	61.1	80.7	68.5	39.8	61.0	51.4
Punish employers of irregular migrants	81.1	94.8	95.4	57.7	86.6	66.0
Turn on electric fence (to lethal mode)	60.4	79.8	62.7	47.5	22.9	33.7
No freedom of speech for irregular migrants	85.5	90.9	94.8	82.9	84.5	87.3
No voting right for irregular migrants	88.7	98.8	98.4	90.4	96.1	95.8
No legal protection of irregular migrants	62.1	64.7	59.9	50.4	57.3	46.2
No social service to irregular migrants	65.4	49.9	77.3	46.5	33.9	40.7

Source: SAMP, 2001; raw data from 2001 NIPS survey.

References

Abraham, A. 2001. Dancing with the Chameleon: Sierra Leone and the Elusive Quest for Peace, *Journal of Comparative African Studies*, 19 (2) 205–228.

Adepoju, A. 1984. Illegals and Expulsion in Africa: Nigerian experience, *International Migration Review*, 18 (8) 426–436.

Adepoju, A. 1995a. The Politics of International Migration in Post-Colonial Africa. In *The Cambridge Survey of World Migration*. Cambridge: Cambridge University Press.

Adepoju, A. 1995b. Emigration dynamics in sub-Saharan Africa, *International Migration*, 33 (3, 4) 315–390.

Adepoju, A. 2002. Fostering Free Movement of Persons in West Africa: Achievements, constraints and prospects for intraregional migration, *International Migration*, 40 (2) 3–28.

Adomako-Sarfoh, J. 1974. The Effects of the Expulsion of Migrant Workers on Ghana's Economy, with particular reference to the Cocoa Industry. In S. Amin (ed.) *Modern Migrations in West Africa*, 138–155. Oxford: Oxford University Press.

Ahooja-Patel K. 1974. Regulations Governing the Employment of Non-Nationals in West Africa. In S. Amin (ed.) *Modern Migrations in Western Africa*, 170–187. Oxford: Oxford University Press.

Akpan, M.B. 1973. Black Imperialism: Americo-Liberian rule over the African peoples of Liberia, 1841–1964, *Canadian Journal of African Studies*, 7 (2) 217–236.

Akyeampong E.K. 2006. Race, Identity and Citizenship in Black Africa: The case of the Lebanese in Ghana, *Africa* 76 (3) 297–323.

Antonakis, N. 1997. Military Expenditure and Economic Growth in Greece, 1960–90, *Journal of Peace Research*, 34 (1) 89–100.

Apap, J. 1997. Citizenship Rights and Migration Policies: The case of Maghreb migrants in Italy and Spain. In R. King & R. Black (eds.) *Southern Europe and the New Immigrations*, 138–157. Eastbourne: Sussex Academic Press.

AVERT. 2007. *South Africa: HIV and AIDS Statistics*. Horsham, West Sussex: AVERT (AVERTing HIV and AIDS). http://www.avert.org/safricastats.htm.

Baldwin-Edwards, M. 1997. *Third Country Nationals and Welfare Systems in the European Union*. Jean Monnet Working Paper in Comparative and International Politics. Catania, Italy: University of Catania, Department of Political Studies.

Baldwin-Edwards, M. 2005. *Migration in the Middle East and Mediterranean*, Region Study prepared for Global Commission on International Migration.

Banya, K. 1993. Illiteracy, Colonial Legacy and Education: the case of modern Sierra Leone, *Comparative Education*, 29 (2) 159–170.

Biswas, B. & R. Ram. 1986. Military Expenditures and Economic Growth in Less Developed Countries: an augmented model and further evidence, *Economic Development and Cultural Change*, 34 (2) 361–372.

Black, R. 2003. Breaking the Convention: Researching the "Illegal" Migration of Refugees to Europe, *Antipode* 35: 34–54.
Boswell, C. 2003. The 'External Dimension' of EU Immigration and Asylum Policy, *International Affairs*, 79 (3) 619–638.
Botswana Ministry of Immigration and Citizenship. 2008. *Requesting Data on Illegal Migrants (a letter)*. Gaborone: Ministry of Immigration and Citizenship.
Bracking, S. 2005. Development denied: Autocratic Militarism in Post-Election Zimbabwe, *Review of African Political Economy*, 32 (104; 105) 341–357.
Briscoe, I. 2004. Dreaming of Spain: Migration and Morocco, *Open Democracy*, May 1–5.
Brunk, M. 1996. *Undocumented Migration to South Africa: More Questions than Answers Institute for Democracy in South Africa*. Cape Town: Idasa.
Burawoy, M. 1976. The Functions and Reproduction of Migrant Labour: Comparative material from Southern Africa and the United States, *The American Journal of Sociology*, 81 (5) 1050–1087.
Campbell, E.K. 2003. Attitudes of Botswana Citizens Towards Immigrants: Signs of xenophobia? *International Migration*, 41 (4) 71–111.
Campbell, E.K. 2007. Reflections on Illegal Migrations, Botswana and South Africa, *African Population Studies*, 21 (2) 23–44.
Campbell, E.K. & J. Oucho. 2003. Changing Attitudes to Immigration and Refugee Policy in Botswana. SAMP Migration Policy Series 28. Cape Town: Southern African Migration Project.
Carella, M. & R. Pace. 2001. Some Migration Dynamics Specific to Southern Europe: South-North and East-West axis, *International Migration*, 39 (4) 63–99.
Chiuri, M.C., G. De Arcangelis & G. Ferri. 2002. Crises in the Countries of Origin and Illegal Migration into Italy. European Commission.
Cline-Cole, R. 2003. Perspectives from Yet Other Places, Spaces and Voices: A commentary on Michael Watts' 'Development and Governmentality', *Singapore Journal of Tropical Geography*, 24 (1) 38–48.
Collier, P. 2002. On the Incidence of Civil War in Africa, *Journal of Conflict Resolution*, 46 (1) 13–28.
Contreras, A.I.P. 2007. Recent History of the Maghreb: A Sociological Approach, *Language and Intercultural Communication*, 7 (2) 109–121.
Crowder, M. 1987. Whose Dream Was It Anyway? Twenty-Five Years of African Independence, *African Affairs*, 86 (342) 7–24.
Crush, J. 1999. The Discourse and Dimensions of Irregularity in Post-Apartheid South Africa, *International Migration*, 37 (1) 125–151.
Crush J. 2000. Migration Past: An Historical Overview of Cross-Border Movement in Southern Africa. In D.A. McDonald (ed.) *On Borders*, New York: St. Martin's Press.
Crush, J. & W. Pendleton. 2004. *Regionalizing Xenophobia? Citizen Attitudes to Immigration and Refugee Policy in Southern Africa*, SAMP Migration Policy Series 30. Cape Town: Idasa.
Crush, J. & V. Williams. 1999. *The New South Africans?: The Immigration Amnesties and their Aftermath*. Cape Town: Idasa.

Crush, J., V. Williams & S. Peberdy. 2005. International Migration and the Southern African Region, Background paper for the Global Commission for International Migration.

Csapo, M. 1983. Universal Primary Education in Nigeria: its Problems and Implications, *African Studies Review*, 26 (1) 91–106.

Cuadros, J., M.J. Calvente, A. Benito, J. Averalo, M.A. Calero, J. Segura et al. 2002. Plasmodium Ovale Malaria Acquired in Central Spain, *Emerging Infectious Diseases*, 8 (12) 1506–1508.

Danso, R. & D.A. McDonald. 2001. Writing Xenophobia: Immigration and the Press in Post-Apartheid South Africa, *Africa Today*, 48 (3) 115–137.

Davis, J. 2006. Spain, Senegal Agree to Continue Cooperation on Illegal Migration Issue, *Voice of America*, 6 December.http://www.voanews.com/english/archive/2006-12/

De Genova, N.P. 2002. Migrant "Illegality" and Deportability in Everyday Life, *Annual Review of Anthropology*, 31: 419–447.

De Vletter, F. 1985. Recent Trends and Prospects of Black Migration to South Africa, *The Journal of Modern African Studies*, 23 (4) 667–702.

Deboosere, P. & S. Gadeyne. 2005. Adult migrant Mortality Advantage in Belgium: Evidence using census and registration data, *Population*, 60 (5; 6) 655–698.

Del Amo, J., G. Broring, F.F. Hamers, A. Infuso & K. Fenton. 2004. Monitoring HIV/AIDS in Europe's Migrant Communities and Ethnic Minorities, *AIDS*, 18 (14) 1867–1873.

Del Amo J., C. Gonzalez, J. Losana, P. Clavo, L. Munoz et al. 2005. Influence of Age and Geographical Origin in the Prevalence of High Risk Human Papillomavirus in Migrant Female Sex Workers in Spain, *Sexually transmitted Infections*, 81: 79–84.

Dixon-Fyle, M. & G. Cole (eds.). 2006. *New Perspectives on the Sierra Leone Krio*. New York: Peter Lang Publishing Inc.

Dodson, B. 2001. Shades of Xenophobia: In-migrants and Immigrants in Mizamoyethu, Cape Town, *Canadian Journal of African Studies*, 34 (1) 124–148.

Dube, M. 2002. Botswana: The Hidden Shame of Tribalism, *Africanews*, 76. www.peacelink.it/afrinews/76issue/p4.html. Fuentes, F.J.M. 2000. Immigration Policies in Spain: Between External Constraints and Domestic Demand for Unskilled Labour, Paper presented at the ECPR Joint Sessions of Workshops, Copenhagen.

Gushlak, B.D. & D.W. MacPherson. 2006. The basic principles of migration health: Population mobility and gaps in disease prevalence, *Emerging Themes in Epidemiology*, 3 (3).

Hansen, E. 1968. Ghana: Background to Revolution, *Transition* 35: 24–28.

Heo, U. 1998. Modeling the Defense-Growth Relationship around the Globe, *Journal of Conflict Resolution*, 42 (5) 637–657.

Huddle, D.L. 1995. The net national cost of illegal immigration into the United States, *Current World Leaders*, 38 (2) 11–34.

Husband, M. 1998. *The Liberian Civil War*. London: Routledge.

Icduygu, A. & T. Unalan. 2001. *Tides Between Mediterranean Shores: Undocumented Migration in the south of Europe*, Conference Paper, 10SSP General Population conference XXIV, Brazil: Session S26.

IMF (International Monetary Fund). 2005. *Sierra Leone: Poverty Reduction Strategy*, IMF Country Report, No.05/191.

IOM (International Organization for Migration). 2007. *Global Estimates and Trends*. http://www.iom.int/jahia/jahia/pid/254.

IRIN (Integrated Regional Information Networks). 2006. *Senegal: Migration – a mother's load*. http://www.irinnews.org/report.aspx?reportid=61484.

IRIN 2008. *MALI: Culture of migration faces new realities*. Humanitarian News and Analysis, United Nations. http://www.irinnews.org/Report.aspx?ReportId=61471 (accessed 16 June 2009).

Jones, E.S. 2004. Recalling the senseless rice riots of 1979, *The Perspective*. 27 July.

Joseph, R.A. 1978. Affluence and underdevelopment: the Nigerian experience, *The Journal of Modern African Studies*, 16 (2) 221–239.

Keen D. 2003. Greedy elites, dwindling resources, alienated youths: The anatomy of protracted violence in Sierra Leone, *International Politics and Society*, 2.

Kingdon, G.G. & J. Knight. 2003. *Unemployment in South Africa: the Nature of the Beast*. Oxford: Centre for the Study of African Economies, Oxford University.

Kusi, N.K. 1994. Economic growth and defense spending in developing countries: a causal analysis, *The Journal of Conflict Resolution*, 38 (1) 152–159.

Lewis, P. 1996. From prebendalism to predation: The political economy of decline in Nigeria, *The Journal of Modern African Studies*, 34 (1) 79–103.

Lodge, T., B. Nasson, S. Mufson, K. Shubane & N. Sithole. 1992. *All, Here and Now: Black Politics in South Africa in the 1980s*. London: C Hurst & Co.

Lucas, R.E. 1982. Outmigration, remittances and investment in rural areas. In *Migration in Botswana: Patterns, Causes and Consequences*, National Migration Study Vol. 3; Gaborone: Government Printers. 627–653.

Lui, C. 2007. How illegal immigration was born, *American Heritage*. http://www.americanheritage.com/articles/web/20070507.

Makinwa-Adebusoye, P.K. 1995. Emigration dynamics in West Africa, *International Migration*, 33 (3, 4) 435–467.

Massey, D.S. 1990. The social and economic origins of immigration. *Annals of the American Academy of Political and Social Science*, 510: 60–72.

Mattes, R., D.M. Taylor, D.A. McDonald, A. Poore & W. Richmond. 1999. *Still Waiting for the Barbarians: SA Attitudes to Immigrants and Immigration*, Migration Policy Series No.14. Cape Town: Southern African Migration Project.

Moyo, S. & P. Yeros. 2005. Land occupations and reforms in Zimbabwe: Toward the national democratic revolution. In S. Moyo & P. Yeros (eds.) *Resurgence of Rural Movements in Africa, Asia and Latin America*. London: Zed Books.

Mundi Index. 2007. *South Africa Unemployment Rate*. www.indexmundi.com/south-africa/unemployment-rate.html.

NGO (Non-Governmental Organizations, Council of Europe). 2005. *General Report: INGO Forum on Integration of Migrants in Europe: What Role for NGO?* Council of Europe.

Nyamnjoh, F.B. 2002. Local attitudes towards citizenship and foreigners in Botswana: An appraisal of recent press stories, *Journal of Southern African Studies*, 28 (4) 755–775.

Okojie, C.E.E. 2003. *Employment Creation for Youth in Africa: The Gender Dimension*. Paper presented at Expert Group Meeting on Jobs for Youth: National Strategies for Employment Promotion, 15–16 January. Geneva.

Painter, T.M. 1988. From warriors to migrants: Critical perspectives on early migrations among the Zarma of Niger, *Africa*, 58 (1) 87–100.

Palestine Facts. 2009. *Why did the British oppose Jewish immigration to Palestine?*, British Mandate, Palestine Facts website: http://www.palestinefacts.org/pf_mandate_oppose_immigration.php.

Peil, M. 1971. The expulsion of West Africa aliens, *Journal of Modern African Studies*, 9 (2) 205–229.

Pendleton, W., J. Crush, E. Campbell, T. Green, H. Simelane, D. Tevera & F. de Vletter. 2006. *Migration, Remittances and Development in Southern Africa*, Migration Policy Series No. 44. Cape Town: Southern African Migration Project.

Price, R.M. 1984. Neo-colonialism and Ghana's economic decline: A critical assessment, *Canadian Journal of African Studies*, 18 (1) 163–193.

Rieder, H.L., J.P. Zellweger, M.C. Raviglione, S.T. Keizer & G.B. Migliori. 1994. Tuberculosis control in Europe and international migration, *European Respiratory Journal*, 7: 1545–1553.

Romero-Ortuno, R. 2004. Access to health care for illegal immigrants in the EU: Should we be concerned? *European Journal of Health Law*, 11: 245–272.

SAMP (Southern African Migration Project). 2001. *National Attitudes to Immigration and Refugee Policies (NIPS) Tables*. Johannesburg: SAMP.

Sadiqi, F. 2007a. *Intentions, Causes and Consequences of Moroccan Migration*. Florence, Italy: Euro-Mediterranean Consortium for Applied Research on International Migration.

Sadiqi, F. 2007b. *The General Profile of the Migrant in Morocco*. Florence, Italy: Euro-Mediterranean Consortium for Applied Research on International Migration.

Seddon, D. 1984. *Winter of discontent: Economic crisis in Tunisia and Morocco*. Merip Reports, 127: 7–16. Washington DC: Middle East Research and Information Project

Smith, G.H. 1997. The dichotomy of politics and corruption in a neopatrimonial state: Evidence from Sierra Leone, 1968–1993, *Issue: A Journal of Opinion*, 25 (1) 58–62.

Solomon, H. 1996. Strategic perspectives on illegal immigration into South Africa, *African Security Review*, 5 (4) 10–14.

Taylor, J. 1986. Some consequences of recent reductions in mine labour recruitment in Botswana, *Geography*, 71: 34–45.

Taylor J.E. 1999. The new economics of labour migration and the role of remittances in the migration process, *International Migration*, 37: 63–86.

Tevera, D.S. 2005. *Early Departures: The Emigration Potential of Zimbabwean Students*, Migration Policy Series No.39. Cape Town: Southern African Migration Project.

Van Heerden, J., R. Gerlagh, J. Blignant, M. Horridge, S. Hess, R. Mabugu & M. Mabugu. 2006. Searching for triple dividends in South Africa: Fighting CO_2 pollution and poverty while promoting growth, *Energy Journal*, 27: 113–141.

Van Moppes, D. 2006. *The African Migration Movement: Routes to Europe*, Working Paper, Migration and Development Series, Radboud University, Nijmegen, Netherlands.

WCRWC. 2007. *Build the Peace: Creating Economic Opportunities in Post-Conflict Liberia.* New York: Women's Commission for Refugee Women and Children.

Waller, L. 2006. *Irregular Migration to South Africa During the First Ten Years of Democracy*, Migration Policy Series No.19. Cape Town: Southern African Migration Project.

Widgren, J. & P. Martin. 2002. Managing migration: The role of economic instruments, *International Migration*, 40 (5) 213–229.

Woolman, S. & M. Bishop. 2006. State as pimp: Sexual slavery in South Africa, *Development South Africa*, 23 (3) 385–400.

Yebei, V.N. 2000. Unmet needs, beliefs and treatment-seeking for infertility among migrant Ghanaian women in the Netherlands, *Reproductive Health Matters*, 8 (16) 134–141.

Zlotnik, H. 2003. Migrants' rights, forced migration and migration policy in Africa, presented at the Conference in African Migration in Comparative Perspectives, June 4–7. Johannesburg.

CHAPTER SIX

Institutional Framework for the Management of Migrants, Data and Information in Africa

Adejumoke Alice Afolayan

Introduction

The rationale for an institutional framework for the management of migrants, data and information globally, and in particular in Africa, is the formulation and implementation of an effective migration policy. This demands a well-designed institutional framework to coordinate the diverse linkages between migration and development. These linkages manifest as both external and internal factors that determine the causes, courses and consequences of migration. The internal factors relate to migrants as individual persons; they are the personal characteristics of migrants and potential migrants that make them behave or act in the way they do when they respond to the environment around them, and which impact on their persons, as well as on the source and destination regions. On the other hand, the external factors are happenings both in the individual African countries from which migrants moved out, and also in regional economic bodies within Africa and in destination countries outside the continent. The diverse external factors include social, economic and political factors that are of concern to African governments in their management of migrants, data and information.

The economic factors are captured by data – for example the labour force market, the growth of different sectors of the economy, employment and remittances – which are considered in relation to their direct and indirect connections with migration. Demographic changes (fertility and mortality), health, education, social networks and other indicators of social capital are the core data for the social factors. Data on political factors cover the form of governance and security, among others. In essence, not only are these data numerous, diverse and complex, they are collected, collated and published by various different ministries, agencies and non-governmental organisations (NGOs), often with purposes in mind other than migration.

Coupled with these factors is the challenge of inadequate data and information on migrants and migrations in Africa. Consequently, the linkages between migration and development that are made are often only inferred, and vaguely understood. There is therefore a need for an institutional framework that would collect, collate and coordinate relevant data and information on migrants, within and outside Africa, effectively and on a sustainable basis so that the managing bodies – the various governments – would have viable migration policies.

The management of migrants, data and information, briefly defined, consists of planning, organising, directing and assessing any available data that could be used to examine the causes, courses and consequences of migration. Information on managing the courses and consequences of migration covers the categories and numbers of migrants to plan for, and the type of care or control that the different categories of migrants would require. Management would also entail reviewing and/or assessing the performance of activities carried out in implementing the migration policy. There are also other aspects of development, which governments or their designated agencies or commission would have to monitor. All these added together make the management of migrants, data and information a multifarious exercise, involving diverse governmental administrative units, as well as other international agencies, non-governmental bodies, and others.

The development plans and activities of many African governments have, however, not reflected sufficient consideration of migration factors, nor of a management system that would keep track of the dynamics of migration. This situation not only weakens management, but also downplays the importance of migration in the overall planning of individual countries, and of the bigger regional body and the entire continent of Africa. The need is therefore pressing, as the awareness of the positive aspects of migration becomes more accurately gauged and better harnessed.

Up to the recent past, migration issues have been handled as an adjunct issue in many African states, regional bodies and in the entire continent. Migration issues have, in many instances, featured merely as sub-sections of economic or population policies. In some other cases they have been a part of the mandates of government organisations, international agencies and non-governmental organisations, which have their focus on issues other than the migration issue. Many of the plans and activities of African governments' policies have touched on improvement in the living standards of their people, their quality of life, the promotion of health and welfare, human rights, reduction of the population growth rate, and rural-urban differences –among others. The policies fail to set out clearly how these aspects of plans and activities impact on migration, and vice versa. They also do not focus on how to harness the positive side of migration, while reducing or regulating its negatives. Moreover, in many African governments' ministries, international agencies and non-governmental organisations have worked as separate units, with very few of them sharing data, information and practices on migration issues. The situation can, therefore, be summed up by saying that a laissez-faire attitude to migration issues and an ad hoc manner of handling them has contributed to the underachievement of the development goals by many African states. More recently the challenge posed by inadequate data and information in the formulation of a migration policy is being addressed by many African governments. The efforts made so far are, however, mostly speculative.

This chapter is, therefore, based on the above-outlined background, and considers the topic of an institutional framework for the management of migrants in three sections. The first section is an examination of the model for comprehensive migration management proposed by the International Organization for Migration, (IOM). It is presented as the norm for analysing any institutional framework that could be adopted for managing migrants, data and information. The second section deals with the institutional framework adopted in three cases: in a selected African country (Nigeria), in some regional bodies, and by the African Union. This section ends with a description of some institutional frameworks offered by other international agencies on the management of migration in Africa. The third section presents a summary and suggestions for a way forward in order to achieve the set objective of formulating and implementing a viable migration policy.

Review of the IOM Conceptual Model for Migration Management

The IOM 'Conceptual Model' for comprehensive migration management (IOM 2004a) reviewed here as the norm or yardstick from which we can deduce what form, or forms, an institutional framework for the management of migrants, data and information should take. However, since the model does not indicate details of the institutional framework, this review goes beyond merely presenting the model and highlights the institutions necessary for the implementation of its rationale and its goals. The rationale for the model is presented first, after which the model itself is discussed.

Rationale for the IOM Model

The various stages of the migration process involve different elements of management. These stages are linked, and involve different actors or partners, and different policies on economics, trade, labour, social issues, cultural issues, health issues, the rights of migrants, and the obligations of states at national, regional and international levels. The management of the various stages also happens at different levels. Some of these cover conditions on travel and entry, return, integration or reintegration, and acquisition of a nationality. Others concern border management, admission, refusal or removal of migrants, as well as consequences of migration, such as diasporas, the protection of migrants, and health issues.

These complex sets of relationships bring to the fore the need for a global understanding of migration management, and a concerted approach to it. The IOM migration management model is presented as 'an organisational tool that can help governments and civil society focus on the complexities of the growing migration portfolio'.[1] Also, the model serves as a 'framework for public discussion and offers principles for managing migration in an orderly way and for controlling irregular migration'. It is, further, a pointer that effective management of migration 'can only begin to be achieved if there is a clear understanding of the trends and flows in migration movement, based on the collection, sharing and analysis of migration data between states'. International cooperation can, therefore, be forged, rather than unilateral approaches being adopted in managing labour migration. The model explains here that latter would lead only to ad hoc movements of labour, with an oversupply of labour in some countries and a 'drain' or undersupply in others.

In addition, the IOM model captures the need for regulating migration. For example, the model notes that 'in order to address trafficking in persons, States need to share law enforcement information to understand and follow patterns and to break up organised crime networks. Unilateral efforts would yield minimal results, if any, in this area'. Besides, it continues, 'effective migration management requires cooperation and dialogue, not only among states, but also among all interested stakeholders, including international organizations, non-governmental organizations, and the private sector'.

The IOM model

Figure 6.1 depicts the IOM model diagrammatically. The first box shows the institution for managing the four main areas of migration management. It has three subsections. The first is policy. This indicates the major institution or the coordinator as being the government or state. Since the onus for formulating diverse policies, including migration policy, is on the state, it has to synchronise and coordinate migration policy within its overall activities for the good of the nation and societies within it. The premise for this is that 'migration policy is based on national objectives and usually derives from, and relates to, other elements of public policy, for example, labour market policy, foreign policy and demographic policy' (IOM 2004a).

---

1 Quotations in this sub-section are from IOM 2004a – the IOM 'Conceptual Model for Comprehensive Migration Management'.

The second subsection of the first box refers to legislation. This 'gives concrete expression to migration policy and provides the authority for the measures required to manage migration'. Again, legislation indicates a subset of the institution that the government employs or makes use of to guide and control migration matters. This includes 'recruitment and selection, authorizing entry, granting of residency, border inspection, response to illegal entry and stay, and removal of persons from the territory of the State'.

The third subsection is the resulting administrative organisation. This 'assigns and coordinates the various functions involved in managing migration within a coherent framework of operational responsibility and accountability'. In essence, the state is the helm institution for the management of migration – including related data, and information.

In addition, it is the state that sets the goals of the IOM model, which is the promotion rather than the restricting of migration. Ideally, it perceives migration as a net positive force or process. As a result, the state will facilitate migration in areas in which it is seen as a positive force; regulate it when it is inimical; and, for the special group, the forced migrants, its goal is to assist or care for them.

The next level, represented in the diagram as a row of four boxes, depicts the four main areas of migration management that the state should coordinate. These are migration and development, facilitating migration, regulating migration and seeing to a special type of migration, forced migration. These four areas are later described as migration management 'goals'. The state, as the highest level of governance, is the only institutional body that can harness adequately the ramified nature of these four areas of managing migration.

The cross-cutting management and activities, which the four areas of migration management entail, are depicted by the last level (lowest box) of the diagram. Again, the box shows that the management of migration, data and information cannot but involve a myriad of institutions, agencies and non-governmental organisations, whose overall activities and performances have to be coordinated and synchronised by the state for an effective migration policy.

Since policy formulation is dependent on available data and information, examples of the numerous migration-related policy issues and concerns (or the relevant data and information required) are given. In addition, the premises or concerns are well-brought out in the enunciated goals, as the quotations in the next sections of this chapter will indicate.

Figure 6.1 IOM model for comprehensive migration management

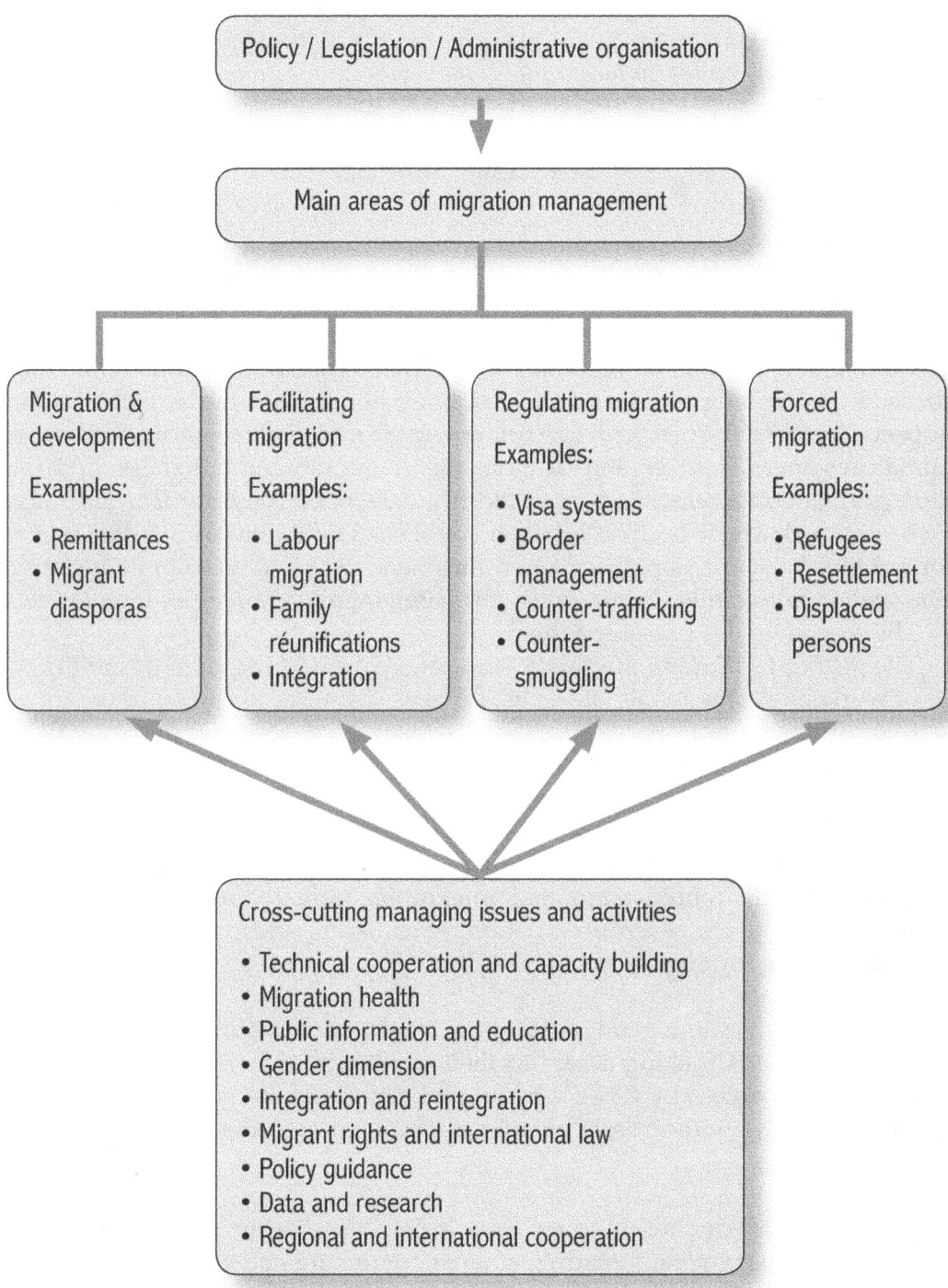

Source: IOM 2004a.

The four IOM goals (see below) make plain the data and information necessary for their achievement, and indirectly indicate which authorities and institutions need to collect, collate and furnish data, and the information needed for managing migrants, data and information.

The first goal, managing migration and development (see the first of the boxes in Figure 6.1) is described as follows:

> The goal of managing migration and development is to help harness the development potential of migration for individual migrants and societies.

The activities involved in achieving this goal cut across many aspects of livelihood of the citizens and migrants resident within a nation, and of opportunities and challenges in other parts of the world. They include data on factors and consequences of migration, such as economic imbalances, trade, globalisation impacts, conflicts, the nature of governance, environmental factors and disasters, human resources, sources and destinations of migrants, remittances, and the demographic characteristics of migrants in the diasporas. These are data generated by, or assumed to have been collected and published by, different arms of the state, for drawing up various policies, often for policies other than migration policy. The need for a collating institution for the latter, therefore, becomes imperative.

The second goal is presented thus:

> The goal of facilitating migration is to safeguard and improve the ability of workers, professionals, students, trainees, families, tourists and others in order for them to move safely and efficiently between countries with minimal delay and with proper authorization.

Again, the data and information required for achieving the set goal are many, and cut across diverse spheres of government operation. They include labour migration, family reunification and integration. Equally many and diverse would have to be the institutions collecting, collating and publishing the data and information for migration policy.

The third goal:

> The goal of regulating migration is to help governments and societies to know who is seeking access to their territories and to take measures that prevent access by those who are not authorized to enter. Replacing irregular flows with orderly, regular migration serves the interests of all governments.

The data and information required to achieve this goal include visa systems, and border management, including counter-trafficking and counter-smuggling measures. The institutions involved in this would also need to be many, with a unified institution to tailor the data and information towards the formulation and implementation of migration policies; or, when necessary, reviews of policy.

The fourth and last goal:
The goal of managing forced migration is to help people move out of danger during emergencies and to return afterwards. Refugees and displaced persons are a distinct category of "people on the move" deserving special attention. Managing forced migration involves finding solutions for Internally Displaced Persons (IDPs), refugees, former fighters, victims of ethnic engineering and populations in transition and recovery environments.

In general, the state needs to oversee the diverse, cross-cutting activities associated with these four main areas of management of migration. These are given by the IOM in terms of coordinating activities in the following: technical cooperation and capacity-building, migrants' rights, promoting international laws, migrants' health, public information and education, the gender dimension of migration, integration and reintegration, policy debate and guidance, data and research, and regional and international cooperation on issues pertaining to migrants.

The links between the four main areas of migration management clearly bring out the necessity for an institutional framework that would coordinate the different activities, even though this is not explicitly stated in the IOM model. Such an institutional framework would consist of levels of management under a unified body that would coordinate all the other levels.

The management of migrants would entail collecting, collating and organising data and information in an accessible and usable manner for creating meaningful and effective migration policy – among other policies of the State – by sub-institutions directed, monitored and coordinated by the unified, central institution. It would also require knowledge of the numbers and categories of migrants. This would be with the view of assessing migrant needs, the provisions that need to be put in place, and the mechanisms that would have to be adopted in resolving the problems and challenges that confront the nation, and, in particular, the migrants under consideration.

The next sections consider the current situation in a selected African country, and in two regional bodies, examining the activities of the IOM in a specific part of the continent, and in the continent as a whole, with regard to migration policies. The cases considered are Nigeria, the Economic Community of West African states (ECOWAS) – with special reference to Nigeria, and the Southern African Development Community (SADC), through the 'Migration Dialogue for Southern Africa' (MIDSA). The activities of the IOM are considered in the form of projects on migration for development in Africa. Some details of the International Dialogue on Migration (2001) and the joint Africa-EU projects are also presented, as pertinent to the discussion.

Nigeria

Draft institutional framework for implementing national policy on migration

A realisation of the marginal, laissez-faire attitude of the Nigerian government on migration matters, as depicted in the 1988 and 2004 Nigerian 'National Policy on Population' has led to the recent draft of a National Policy on Migration. For example, the only reference made to an institutional framework for managing migration in the 2004 Population Policy for Nigeria gives the Ministry of Internal Affairs as its main involved institution. This ministry is to 'regulate the outflow, inflow and stay of immigrants in the country. It is also to collect data on international migration and transmit same to National Population Commission for analysis and dissemination' (Federal Republic of Nigeria 1989).

Even though the National Policy on Migration in Nigeria is still in its draft form, it offers us a working template to examine. A review of parts of the draft follows, examining the institutions that would be handling the different activities for the implementation of the policy.

The draft proposes the establishment of an 'Agency/Commission' to coordinate all stakeholders in the field of migration. This implies that the thinking of the government is towards having a centralised body, called an Agency/Commission, to coordinate all such activities. In all its twenty-one objectives, this Commission is to serve as a guide for all government and non-governmental organisations, agencies and nations on migration activities. Also, it is to coordinate the activities of nationals' resident abroad, aiming for a harmonious end to any problem.

The draft aims of the Commission include helping stem the migration of Nigerian professionals – a matter that had previously been addressed in a haphazard manner – reducing the impact of 'brain drain' through the development of organised labour migration; and seeing to the signing of bilateral labour migration agreements. This is to be executed by institutions that are well-informed on data and information pertaining to the source country, Nigeria, and to destination countries.

Furthermore, the Commission is to facilitate the negotiated and voluntary repatriation of Nigerian irregular migrants. Other bodies that would be involved in the management of migrants include diaspora groups, professional and student bodies in both Nigeria and destination countries, and the Nigerian National Volunteers Service.

In essence, the goal of the proposed Commission is the coordination of the varied institutions for a successful, viable migration policy in Nigeria.

ECOWAS

Challenges of management of migration

The ECOWAS Common Position on Migration (ECOWAS 2007b) highlighted the need for an institutional framework for managing migration in the region. A premise for this document was that there is an increasing awareness of the cross-cutting nature of migration in regional integration and development. This awareness has been enhanced by the regional body's Protocol on Free Movement of Persons, Rights of Residence and Establishments in Member States since 1978. In addition, the dynamics of globalisation are felt all over the world, including in the ECOWAS region. ECOWAS is, therefore, prioritising the effective management of migration as an international phenomenon.

The major migration management pillar of the ECOWAS document – that of facilitating migration among its member states – has, however, long been hampered by a lack of adequate data and information. Most often, estimates of numbers of diverse types of migrations taking place in the region come from incomplete statistics=with respect to the forcefully displaced – that is expelled irregular ECOWAS aliens (Afolayan 1988) and returned trafficked children and women (NAPTIP 2003), among others. ECOWAS is yet to establish an institution geared mainly to data collection, analysis and dissemination – to monitor factors influencing the volume, direction and consequences of migration within and outside the regional body. Consequently, ECOWAS has not been able to manage effectively the diverse types of migrants, data and information in the region.

As an example: estimates indicate that there are differences in the demographic characteristics of ECOWAS and those of the main destination for its emigrants, Europe. In 2005, young people aged less than 20, and less than 25, formed 56 and 65 per cent respectively of the ECOWAS population, as against 23 and 30 per cent respectively for Europe – less than half as many. The higher percentages of dependent population in the former region, apart from serving as an explanatory factor for migration, are a piece of knowledge that could be utilised either for facilitating the beneficiary aspects of migration or for regulating its negatives. But without adequate, on-going and up-to-date data and information, any policy adopted would be defective. Consequently there is a need for an institution to collect relevant data and information for effective migration policy.

Facilitating migration in ECOWAS within an institutional framework

Activities aimed at facilitating migration among ECOWAS member states include the issuance of ECOWAS travel documents, the organisation of training for migration personnel, the ratification of the UN Convention on Protection of Migrant Workers' Rights, the handling of under- or un-employment in West Africa, and the harmonisation of labour laws on professionals. Others are the removal of forms of harassments along roads connecting member states, the setting up of joint border posts, markets, health centres, shared schools and the support of border development. The development of good-neighbourly relations is also to be promoted.

The institutions that would see to the implementation of these objectives are yet to be specified. Such institutions are likely to include security outfits, ministries of foreign affairs, justice and health, and education on issues of labour and productivity and security.

Regulating migration in ECOWAS within an institutional framework

In the fight against traffickers, ECOWAS aims to take issue with all bodies promoting the recruitment, transportation and exploitation of irregular migrants, in particular women and children. Member states are to cooperate with host countries on measures aimed at the return of irregular migrants. They are also to implement measures regarding the reinsertion of returnees, as well as the broadening of current capacities for combating irregular migration by sea to include irregular fishing in West African territorial water bodies (ECOWAS 2008).

Many institutions would be involved in implementing these varied activities, which a central unit should coordinate. The location of the central institution, its mandates and working principles are points that must be considered before effective management can be achieved.

Other aspects of migration management in the ECOWAS region touch on ensuring media coverage of ECOWAS initiatives; strengthening assistance for dismantling criminal organisations; rehabilitating victims of trafficking; harmonising national legislation against human trafficking, and promoting a 'solidarity for victims' fund, among others.

In the wider policy frame, these aspects come under the activities of different government ministries, NGOs, international agencies and faith-based programmes. The need for a coordinating institution, though paramount, is yet to be made explicit.

ECOWAS Initial Plan of Action against Trafficking in Persons

At the end of 2001, ECOWAS set up an Initial Plan of Action against Trafficking in Persons for 2002–2003, and later another for 2008–2011. These plans outline the actions deemed most urgent in the struggle against trafficking in persons to be taken by member states within these time periods. They are both much more explicit about a regional institutional framework than those on national migration plans (ECOWAS 2007b) and on the facilitation of migration in the region (ECOWAS 2001). This is understandable since many African states have yet to formulate and implement any national policy on migration. Moreover, the region's Protocol on Free Mobility of Persons, Goods and Services is yet to be fully implemented by all member states.

Briefly discussed, as part of its legal framework and policy development against trafficking in persons in the region, the activities to be carried out by each member state are mainly through four bodies: the national government, its administrative structures, a National Task Force on Trafficking in Persons and the ECOWAS Trafficking in Persons Unit.

If it has not yet done so, each state is to ratify and fully implement certain conventions, charters and laws pertaining to migration issues. This would involve, for example, supporting the provisions of the UN Convention Against Transnational Organized Crime, and the Protocol to Prevent, Suppress, and Punish Trafficking in Persons, especially Women and Children. The administrative structures, including the legislative and immigration offices, are expected to implement the amended immigration and emigration regulations of the state and the newly-established system of repatriation. Member states were, for example, called upon to:

> Consider adopting legislative or other appropriate measures that permit victims of trafficking in persons to remain in their territory, temporarily or permanently, in appropriate cases; and…give appropriate consideration to humanitarian and compassionate factors in the consideration of permitting victims of trafficking to remain in their territory. (ECOWAS 2001: 3)
>
> …take responsibility for victims of trafficking in persons, who are their nationals, or persons with the right of permanent residence in their territory at the time of entry into the territory of the receiving State by facilitating and accepting, with due regard for the safety of such persons, the return of such persons without undue or unreasonable delay. (ECOWAS 2001: 4)
>
> …take measures that permit the denial of entry into the country and/or the revocation of visas of persons wanted for the commission of crimes related to the trafficking in persons. (ECOWAS 2001: 4)

According to the two ECOWAS Initiative Action Plans, 2002–2003 and 2008–2011, the National Task Force that was to be established was to:

> …bring together relevant Ministries and Agencies in developing policy and taking action against trafficking in persons, and calling on Inter-Governmental Organizations, Non-Governmental Organizations, and other representatives of civil society, as necessary. (ECOWAS 2001: 4)

Also, the National Task Force shall:

> …develop recommendations for a national plan of action against trafficking in persons. The National Task Force should also monitor and report through their government to the ECOWAS Secretariat on the progress of the implementation of this Initial Plan of Action. (ECOWAS 2001: 4)

An ECOWAS Trafficking in Persons Unit is to be established within the ECOWAS Secretariat. Its task would be to coordinate efforts to combat trafficking in persons. Pending its establishment, the Legal Department of ECOWAS Executive Secretariat would carry out the function (ECOWAS 2001: 5).

About the same can be said of the institutions for the protection and support of victims of trafficking in persons. These include the Ministries of Justice and Social Affairs of the national government, local NGOs, and inter-governmental organisations (IGOs) – the latter two bodies to assist with material support and expertise, as required (ECOWAS 2001: 5).

For 'Prevention [of trafficking] and Awareness Raising', the two Initial Plans of Action (2002–2003 and 2008–2011) specified the following as recommended agents: government social service agencies, government media and public education agencies, media outlets, local NGOs, and international NGOs and IGOs, particularly the IOM, ILO and UNICEF (ECOWAS 2007a). Two sets of activities, one of collection, exchange and analysis of information, and the other specialisation and training, are to be carried out by the ministries and agencies of each national government. These include passport offices and immigration agencies, law enforcement agencies, border control agencies, social service agencies, national statistical offices and government personnel and training agencies. Others are international bodies, such as the crime-prevention agency ODCCP/CICP, Interpol, and other relevant IGOs. Travel and identity documents are to be handled by national government passport offices and immigration agencies, while the last-listed activity, the monitoring and evaluation of the Initial Plan of Action at national level, is for government agencies. These units are to report to a government task force (ECOWAS 2002: 9–11).

In general, the activities on regulating trafficking in ECOWAS are to be staffed by relevant national institutions – which do not need to be the same in each member state. The coordinating unit at national level is the individual member state's National Task Force, whose activities are again to be coordinated by the ECOWAS Trafficking in Persons Unit.

One clear-cut achievement of the different plans has been the establishment of a National Task Force against Trafficking in Persons in Ghana and Nigeria, while efforts are being made by some other ECOWAS states on other strategies and activities.

The next sub-sections deal in more detail with trafficking of persons in Nigeria.

Institutional framework and resources used against trafficking of children and women in Nigeria

The institutional framework against the trafficking of children and women in Nigeria is seen as a means of regulating migration, according to the IOM model considered earlier on. This form of migration needs to be discouraged in every way possible, so the institutions involved are charged with mitigating their occurrences. In Nigeria, the incidence of such trafficking has been increasing in recent times, and the focus of concern is shifting in this direction. Its negative aspects are being publicised far more than ever before, particularly in destination countries. This has put pressure on the Nigerian government to address the incidence at home of trafficking of Nigerian children and women – across the country and in other countries. Consequently, the institutions handling this menace are very much in existence and are better known than those involved in other aspects of migration management (Federal Government of Nigeria 2004: 12).

In Nigeria, the following governmental authorities are responsible for addressing various forms of violence against children, in particular child trafficking: the Special Presidential Committee on Human Trafficking, Child Labour and Slavery; the Federal Ministries of Women Affairs, Labour and Productivity, Justice, and Information and National Orientation. Others are the Nigeria Immigration Service, the Nigeria Customs Service, the National Boundary Commission, and the Nigerian Police Commission (Federal Government of Nigeria 2004).

The coordination and monitoring of all issues and activities addressing violence against children lies essentially in the office of the President of Nigeria and is overseen by the Office of Special Adviser and the Special Presidential Committee on Human Trafficking, Child Labour and Slavery. The support of the government is also noticeable in the establishment of the Civil Rights Implementation and Monitoring Committees at national and sub-national levels. Civil society organisations (CSOs) have been involved in undertaking studies on the sexual exploitation of children in collaboration with development partners, setting up the Presidential Committee on Human Trafficking, and establishing drop-in centres for the rehabilitation of sexually abused child victims. They have also collaborated with other bodies in the promulgating into law of the 2003 Child's Rights Act.

Most state governments in Nigeria have passed the Child's Right Bills into law – as a direct result of the formation of a joint monitoring committee/advocacy group. This consisted of representatives of the mass media, CSOs, the NGOs, child's rights activists, legislators, judicial and law-enforcement officers, academicians and government officials (Federal Government of Nigeria 2004). Thus, the contribution in Nigeria of CSOs and other groups in advocacy, awareness-raising, research, abuse-prevention, rehabilitation and treatment of children harmed by violence, and the provision of services and resources cannot be overemphasised.

Also, children are now encouraged as actors in addressing violence against them, though they are not yet fully empowered. They have been involved thorough the Nigerian government taking many initiatives and supporting many programmes organised by and for children, including addressing violence against children. International agencies and other bodies, and bilateral donors, such as ECOWAS, the World Bank, UNICEF, UNIFEM, UNODC, USAID, the ILO and some embassies – including those of Belgium, Italy, Britain, the Netherlands and the USA – have also been providing resources for activities on addressing violence against children in Nigeria.

In addition, the National Human Rights Commission, based in Abuja, has a mandate from the Federal Government of Nigeria and the competence to receive and treat complaints in the area of children's rights violation, including any sort of violence against children. Also, there are special national and state Legislative Assembly Committees on Women and Children Matters, including human rights. A parliamentary initiative aimed at addressing violence against children was the passage into law of the 2003 Trafficking in Persons (Prohibition) Law Enforcement and Administration Act.

Some other institutions, groups and NGOs that play active roles in addressing violence against children in Nigeria include the Women Trafficking and Child Labour Eradication Foundation (WOTCLEF), the Nigeria chapter of the African Network for the Prevention and Protection against Child Abuse and Neglect (ANPPCAN), and Idia Renaissance. Others are the Heartland Child Care Foundation, the Nigeria Children's Parliament, the National Council of Women Societies, and various faith-based organisations. A review of the institutional framework for regulating trafficking of children and women cannot but cover the 2003 Anti-Trafficking Act that permits the *National Agency for the Prohibition of Traffic in Persons and Other Related Matters* (NAPTIP) to seek budgetary allocation and approval from the National Assembly, to accept gifts of land, money and other property, and to borrow money from banks with a view to carrying out the activities and objectives of the Agency.

Some of these agencies have been involved with research, others with awareness-raising, propaganda against the occurrence of incidents, notification of the nature and place of occurrence of incidents, and the rehabilitation of victims – among many others. ANPPCAN, for example, conducted research in 2000 on behalf of the ILO, which has served as baseline reference material on child trafficking in Nigeria, as well as providing figures for children who experienced sexual exploitation.[2]

WOTCLEF has spearheaded the struggle against human trafficking, child labour and sexual exploitation of children (see WOTCLEF 2001). It has also organised several national and international conferences, calling the attention of individuals and governments to the problem of trafficking of women and children into labour and prostitution. This NGO currently runs a shelter and an apprenticeship-training school for the rehabilitation of trafficked girls.

The Heartland Child Care Foundation, based in Imo state, uses advocacy

---

2   Information in this and the following paragraphs in this sub-section come from the Country Report on Violence against Children (Federal Government of Nigeria 2004: 11, 12).

strategies to fight the spread of trafficking and dissuade parents from collaborating with agents to traffic their children.

Idia Renaissance has responded to the rising incidence of drug abuse, drug trafficking, cultism on campuses, and prostitution. Other NGOs, such as Child Life-Line, the Women's Consortium of Nigeria, the Children's Rights Advocacy Group of Nigeria (CRAGON), the Children's Parliament, and various faith-based organisations and groups are involved in data collection, advocacy, campaigns, mobilisations, rehabilitation, and counselling, care and provision of services for children harmed by violence.

In addition, the federal government, through the Federal Ministry of Women Affairs, has undertaken sensitisation meetings for directors of the Child Development Departments at federal and state levels, in order to review and harmonise efforts to tackle child labour and trafficking. It also undertakes the distribution of copies of the UN Convention on the Rights of the Child, which has been simplified and translated into three major Nigerian languages (Yoruba, Igbo and Hausa).

The Nigerian electronic and print media have continued, persistently and relentlessly, to carry out advocacy programmes on issues dealing with the rights, welfare and protection of children, through articulate and provocative publications that have influenced behavioural changes, programmes and interventions for child victims of abuse and violence (Federal Government of Nigeria 2004: 12).

Also, Nigeria has signed bilateral agreements with countries addressing the issue of trafficking regionally and globally. These include ECOWAS countries such as Ghana, the Gambia, Benin, Gabon, Togo, Cameroon and Equatorial Guinea. Some others are Britain, the Netherlands, Italy, Saudi Arabia, Belgium and the USA. Other approaches to the problem are that Nigeria is a functional member of Interpol and has been creating massive sensitisation through workshops.

The institutional framework in Nigeria has, therefore, assisted in reducing the number of cases of violence against children, of which trafficking is a major part. For example, Sections 223–225 of the Criminal Code applicable in Southern Nigeria provide for sanctions against anyone trading in prostitution or facilitating the transport of human beings within or outside Nigeria. There has also been an increase in the level of arrest and prosecution of those involved in child trafficking and other forms of child abuse.

The Nigerian government also directly commissions studies from NGOs and other agencies, collaborating, for example, with UNICEF, the ILO and the UNDP to measure the effectiveness of policies and programmes. Examples of publications include the National Baseline Survey of Positive and Harmful Traditional Practices Affecting Women and Children in Nigeria (1998); the National Study of Sexual Exploitation of Children in Nigeria (2001) and the Country Report on Child Trafficking (2002). In addition, the government has set up desk officers for monitoring child protection issues at the Ministry of Women

Affairs – at both the federal and state levels – as well as at the Ministry of Police, and of the Ministry of Immigration and Customs Services. These desk officers are further engaged with ensuring compliance with the laws and policies dealing with violence against children.

There is thus already a viable institutional framework for regulating the trafficking of women and children in Nigeria. What needs to be done is a fine-tuning of cooperation between the different institutions, to avoid duplicate efforts. In this way, the management of irregular migration would be well-coordinated.

Institutional framework for managing forced migration

The most widely-accepted body for handling forced migration globally is the United Nations High Commissioner for Refugees (UNHCR). Many African countries, including Nigeria, are signatory to its 1951 United Nations Principles of *Non-Refoulement*[3] and its African counterpart, the 1969 Convention of the Organisation of African Unity.

In the absence of reliable government figures, the UNHCR must merely estimate the refugee population in many of the conflict-ridden African countries. The UNHCR extends protection and/or assistance to persons who are displaced – within their own country, or to another country – and to persons repatriated under the UN 1951 Convention, the 1967 Protocol (both relating to the status of refugees), and the 1969 OAU Convention, in accordance with the UNHCR Statute (UNHCR 1950).

The National Commission for Refugees (NCFR) was established by Decree 52 of 1989 (now Cap. N21 of the Laws of the Federation of Nigeria 2004). At inception, the commission was given the responsibility of initiating and executing policies and programmes aimed at efficient and effective protection and management of refugees in Nigeria. However, in 2002 the Federal Government assigned additional responsibility of managing internally displaced persons (IDPs) in Nigeria. For instance, after the withdrawal of care and maintenance from the Oru Refugee Camp by the UNHCR, the full responsibility of caring for the refugee population fell on the shoulders of the NCFR.

Joint ECCAS/ECOWAS Plan of Action against Trafficking in Persons, especially Women and Children in West and Central Africa (2006-2009)

Another elaborate plan involving two regional bodies, the Economic Community of Central African States (ECCAS) and ECOWAS, explicitly stipulates the different ministries, agencies and international organisations that are to handle

---

3 The principle that no contracting state shall expel or return *(refoule)* a refugee against his or her will to a territory where he or she fears persecution.

migration issues in the two regions. This is the Joint ECCAS-ECOWAS Plan of Action against Trafficking in Persons, especially Women and Children in West and Central Africa (2006–2009). The activities proposed for achieving its goals are very similar to those mentioned under the ECOWAS Initial Plan of Action, the main difference being that this document is much more explicit regarding the institutions responsible for each activity (ECCAS/ECOWAS n.d.).

The National Focal Point, the Ministry of Foreign Affairs and the Technical Ministry in Charge of Labour and Manpower Development (or their equivalents) of each of the member states are to execute the first step of the strategy: the legal framework and policy development. The national governments and the ECOWAS-ECCAS Secretariats are to ensure effective implementation of the legislative framework in compliance with international legal instruments. Also, a sub-set of the first strategy – inter-country cooperation agreements – is to be pursued by the individual national governments. The second strategy – protection and support to victims of trafficking – is to be addressed by the national government, the ECCAS/ECOWAS Trafficking in Persons Units and Secretariats, and the Joint Regional Commission. Others involved are ministries in charge of the technical components of the National Plan of Action, various decentralised authorities, CSOs, and UN agencies

The third strategy – prevention and awareness raising – is to be monitored by the National Focal Point, decentralised authorities and CSOs. The fourth strategy – the collection, exchange and analysis of information – is to be handled by national government, the ECOWAS Executive Secretariat and the ECCAS General Secretariat. The fifth strategy is specialisation and training, with the same responsibilities as for the fourth one, with the addition of NGOs.

Activities for managing travel and identity documents are the domain of the national government passport offices, immigration agencies, CSOs, consular services, health services, and law enforcement agencies, Interpol, border control agencies and various NGOs. The national governments are to see to the final strategy – monitoring and evaluation of the Plan of Action.

Evidence thus abounds that regional bodies are quicker in naming and allotting activities for *regulating* migration (in the form of trafficking in persons) than they are for *facilitating* migration – including legal (regular) migration. Their interest should, however, be in all the four areas covered in the management of migration, as stated earlier on, in order to keep in focus the comprehensive, cross-cutting feature of migration for development. This would bring out clearly the need for a central unit for coordinating the activities of the different institutions in charge of migration management.

An institutional framework for managing migration in Africa

The institutional framework for managing migration in the whole of Africa can be inferred from the many conferences, dialogues and documents on the issue, in particular from two of the documents of the Ninth Ordinary Session of the Executive Council of the African Union (held in Banjul in June 2006): the 'Migration Policy Framework for Africa' and the 'African Common Position on Migration and Development'. The first of these has since been endorsed by the Executive Council (AU Executive Council Decision EX.CL/Dec.305 (IX)), as it was adopted at the Banjul Summit in July 2006. The latter is yet to be implemented, and 'States are strongly urged to adopt the...broad decisions so as to properly manage migration with a view to optimizing its benefits while minimizing its negative impacts' (African Union 2006b: 43).

These documents highlight the need for considering migration. Migration is noted as an important development factor, occurring within Africa and towards Europe, North America and some Middle East countries. It is considered as taking the form of either legal or undocumented movement, and encompassing all social categories. The documents further reveal that Africa, with an estimated 16.3 million migrants, as well as close to 13.5 million internally displaced persons (IDPs), features both voluntary and forced movements (African Union 2006b: 3). The high level at which these forms of migration are generated and the dynamics of their causes are on a relatively large scale. Significant internal migratory movements, such as rural-urban migration, add to the complexity of the picture. Consequently an appreciation of the diverse international institutions that would be involved in the management of the various categories of migrants, the heightened scale of operation of migratory movements, and the information required in coordinating the activities would be in order.

In brief, the documents commented as follows:
Migratory flows are occurring, however, in an African context still marked by the inadequacy of institutional capacities of some African countries to address the problems individually and collectively. (African Union 2006b: 1)

Based on this premise, the documents made reference to the institutions that should be charged with responsibility for the various strategies put forward for managing migration in Africa. The names of institutions involved can be gleaned from the recommendations of the several seminars, workshops and conferences that African heads of state and government have made. For example:
...the Abuja Treaty (Abuja, June 1991)...established the African Economic Community (AEC), [which] urged Member states to adopt employment policies that allow the free movements of persons within the Community. This entails strengthening and establishing labour exchanges aimed at facilitating the employment of available skilled manpower of one

Member State in other Member States, where there are shortages of skilled manpower (Article 71 (e)), as an essential component for the promotion of regional co-operation and integration in Africa.

Further recognizing the important issue of migration and its consequences, a Seminar on Intra-African Migration was held in Cairo (1995). Heads of State and Government made several recommendations on legal, economic, political, social and administrative aspects of African migration. These were adopted during the 19th Ordinary Session of the OAU Labour Commission in 1996 and endorsed by the OAU Council of Ministers and Assembly of Heads of State and Government. (African Union 2006a: 4, 5)

The ministerial meetings aimed at commitment to a partnership between countries of origin, transit and destination; to better management of migration in a comprehensive, holistic and balanced manner, and in a spirit of shared responsibility and cooperation. These derived from:
- the outcome of the UN General Assembly High Level Dialogue on Migration and Development
- the outcome of the Euro-Africa Ministerial Conference on Migration and Development held in Rabat on 10–11 July 2006;
- the EU strategy for Africa adopted in 2005, and the shared commitment to work towards a joint EU-Africa strategy for Africa;
- the shared commitment to convene the second Europe-Africa Summit in Lisbon in 2007;
- the ongoing Euro-Mediterranean dialogue on Migration, and the Ministerial Meeting to be organised in 2007.

(AU-EU 2006)

The key recommendations were that migration issues be addressed regionally and that member states make every effort to utilise existing regional fora to discuss and resolve issues; that member states should have an efficient and advanced system of collecting information and statistics on labour migration, and that they cooperate more closely with regional economic communities (RECs) to achieve effective economic integration.

Often the institutions responsible for carrying out these recommendations are not explicitly named. It can therefore be inferred that the conventional ways of managing migrants, data and information, as outlined earlier on under consideration of the situation in regional units, would be the ones expected to take on this work. For example, for regulating irregular migration, the document (African Union 2006b: 17) recommended that:

The development of common regional countermeasures, based on the spirit of solidarity among States and with a focus on the human rights of trafficked victims, including harmonization of immigration laws; strengthened and modernized border management: co-operation and co-ordination between concerned ministries, particularly State security agencies; greater efforts to dismantle international organized criminal syndicates; signing of bilateral and multilateral agreements; and prosecuting traffickers and others involved in such activities.

The new major institutions that the documents specified at national and continental level include 'the full participation of the African diaspora in the building of the African Union'; 'strong cooperation framework for security between the RECs, the AU and the United Nations', and '[facilitating] technical co-operation activities with international agencies, including ILO, IOM, WHO, UNAIDS and other concerned entities' (AU-EU 2006b: 5, 6; 8).

An institutional framework for managing migration in southern Africa

The institutional framework for managing labour migration in most parts of southern Africa, prior to the establishment of a democratic government in South Africa, had for long been well-established and widely recognised. But since the dismantling of the apartheid system in South Africa by 1994, the framework has been less conventional. The earlier version managed the restrictive migration policies of the South African government, in which strict compliance with rules governing legal migration was ensured. But with the advent of democracy has come an increase in irregular, illegal migration – which could not hold back against the strong magnet of industrial development and relatively strong economies in South Africa and Botswana.

Contemporary studies of migration in the region show continuities and changes that reflect increased volumes and complexities (for example new directions) of border movements, restructuring of traditional contract labour systems, declining levels of legal migration to and from the region, and an expansion of trafficking and undocumented migration. Other changes are an increase in the volume of skills being drained from the region, a feminisation of cross-border migration, growth in informal intra-regional cross-border trade, rapid urbanisation, and, most recently, the development of xenophobia (Crush et al 2005: 6).

Management of these migration flows must be based on sound data and reliable information. In most cases in this region these are not exact, nor are they always available. This is a reflection of changes in the administrative system and a loss of coordinated effort on migration issues, as well as a far greater exposure to the outside world. Consequently the region has a less managed and less organised institutional framework that depends on less comprehensive data and information.

Considering some of the characteristics in more depth, although cross-border and internal migrations are prominent in the region, with a great deal of circular mobility, there is a perception, for example, that an overpowering percentage of people in South Africa are foreign-born. This has distorted relations between residents in the recent past. Xenophobia has been brewing and escalating on the premise of wrong data: of 25 per cent of South Africa's population being foreign, instead of a lower estimated percentage of about 10 per cent, that is about 5 million out of 49 million total population in 2008.

Data on remittances are also largely unavailable or inaccurate. This is a reflection, among others reasons, of variations in foreign exchange regulations, of differential exchange rates from country to country and of the use of formal systems as against the black market exchange rate, used especially by irregular migrants.

Another change is that brain drain has accelerated, in particular through the emigration of skilled professionals, though the actual number involved is more or less guesswork. In addition, most countries in the region have not pursued 'brain gain' strategies, in the form of proactive immigration policies. Regional migration policies, from the New Partnership for Africa's Development (NEPAD), which is continental, to local initiatives by the Southern African Development Community (SADC) have faltered in managing migration. Also, the attempt of the regional body to establish a free trade area in 2000 for mobility of persons was not successful, as South Africa, Botswana and Namibia opposed it. This was replaced by a Draft Protocol on Facilitation of Movement of People, which was shelved in 2000 by the SADC Council of Ministers. The launching of a Free Trade Area was the highlight of SADC Summit in 2008. There is yet, however, to be free mobility of persons in the region (Deborah Walter in the *Namibian*, 22 August 2008[4]).

In general, it can be said that no country in southern Africa has migration-friendly legislation, with the exception of Botswana, which has adopted the United Nations 1951 Convention relating to the status of refugees. Other countries have restrictive controlled migration policies – for example, permanent immigration both within SADC and from outside is said to be extremely difficult.

These are further indications as to why there has not been a clear-cut institutional framework for the entire region, which would ensure an up-to-date information database to assist migration policy formulation and implementation in the region. The conventional national institutions of the different southern African governments can be considered as carrying out different aspects of managing migration in the region. But these unilateral approaches would not make for the holist, comprehensive management that is required for a regional phenomenon of these dimensions – hence the continued attempts to improve the regional situation.

---

4 See allafrica.com/stories/200808220544.html

IOM's institutional framework in Africa: MIDWA; NEPAD

The IOM has collaborated with regional bodies, such as ECOWAS and SADC in establishing two Migration Dialogues: the Migration Dialogue for Southern Africa (MIDSA), formally constituted in 2000, and the Migration Dialogue for West Africa (MIDWA), established in 2001. MIDWA areas of interest cover border management, data collection, labour migration, development, remittances, rights of migrants, irregular migration, trafficking and smuggling, return and reintegration (IOM 2003). Also, as part of an increasing awareness of the importance of formulating and implementing a viable migration policy in many parts of Africa, the IOM supports projects in Benin, Burkina Faso, Ghana, Nigeria and Senegal. Moreover, it has special projects for women in Liberia, Mauritania and Niger, and offers technical assistance to some other ECOWAS member states.

In addition, the IOM has raised financial support for NEPAD programmes and projects at the regional level in many blocs of Africa, including West Africa (IOM 2004b; 2007). The IOM support to NEPAD includes the setting up of Regional Consultative Processes (RCPs), which operate on an informal and non-biding basis, in order to enable participating countries to improve considerably their levels of information exchange and, in many cases, contribute to the harmonisation of policy approaches.

IOM has also been involved in the AU/NEPAD health strategy on tackling HIV/AIDS, tuberculosis, and malaria. It has initiated an African Youth Exchange Programme to bridge the socio-cultural divide amongst African youth by mobilising the skills, potential resources and energies of African youth in diasporas. In the West African region, IOM has continued its support to projects in Benin, Burkina Faso, Ghana, and Senegal. Projects targeting women in diaspora have been developed for Liberia, Mauritania and Niger (IOM 2007).

The IOM has, however, not engaged itself in the institutional framework for managing the four main areas of migration (see Figure 6.1). Rather, its contribution has been in promoting workshops and dialogues aimed at the imbibing of culture of a well-managed migration in parts of Africa.

IOM and management of migration: MIDSA

The basics of an institutional framework for managing migration in the southern African region can be gathered from the IOM expertise in establishing the Migration Dialogue for Southern Africa (MIDSA). The agenda of MIDSA, as for MIDWA, is to foster cooperation among members of the regional body, SADC, on migration-related issues. Among its many objectives are migration management, border control, migration and development, causes, dimensions and impacts of migration, harmonizing systems of data collection and immigration policy and legislation, labour migration, irregular movements. MIDSA also aims to promote dialogue and interaction between governments and other agencies and institutions with migration-related interests and expertise.

In essence, these activities would involve the establishment of and/or continuation of the activities of relevant institutions charged with migration matters, in particular those coordinating issues at regional level – in the same way as those outlined for ECOWAS regarding the regulation of trafficking of persons.

Institutional framework offered by other international agencies on migration management in Africa

The different forms of international cooperation on migration have taken place in a variety of ways: through informal discussion and sharing of policy and programme information, and through formal operational and activity-based cooperation, including joint management, technical cooperation, and other forms of responsibility-sharing. Many of these have been mentioned in earlier sections of this chapter, but some are now highlighted again for emphasis, to demonstrate the general 'good will disposition' of international bodies towards the management of migration in Africa – though the outputs do not necessarily stipulate the institutions which should handle the different activities connected with it:

> Cooperation may be bilateral (between states: for example on labour supply and demand, conditions of employment, remuneration and social security, return and readmission of persons without activity as reason to stay, management of common borders), regional (multilateral: concerning movement of persons, RCPs), inter-regional or international.
>
> There are many sectors where cooperation exists, for example: data on trafficking, smuggling and irregular migration, trade, labour, development, health, entry and border control, labour migration, refugees, asylum, and technology.

In brief, many conferences, workshops, seminars and reports have dealt with migration issues. For example, the Cotonou Agreement (signed in June 2000 and entering into force in April 2003) – between the European Community and its member states on the one hand, and members of the African, Caribbean and Pacific Group of States (ACP) on the other – emphasises dialogue, cooperation, and partnership. It contains an article devoted to migration that recognises the rights of migrants between these regions and the link between migration and development. It also touches on the obligation of participating states to accept the return and readmission of their nationals (ACP-EU 2000).

The Second Ministerial Conference on Migration in the Western Mediterranean ('5+5 Dialogue') involves five European states on or close to the northern shore of the Mediterranean, and five North African states on or close to the southern shore. This Dialogue explores common principles for cooperation in managing cross-regional flows, while also tackling issues related to migration and development.

Although there is no global consensus on how to address the complexities of international migration, a number of significant global conferences have been held. Examples of principles arrived at these conferences include:
- Chapter X of the 1994 Cairo Declaration on Population and Development is on migration, refugees, asylum seekers and displaced persons, and offers a comprehensive overview of the challenges linked to the movements of persons;
- sections of the 2001 Durban World Conference Against Racism, Racial Discrimination, Xenophobia and Related Intolerance, which deal with migration issues.

In addition, multilateral cooperation that touches on migration and development in Africa is increasing – as shown, for instance, in the labour and trade sectors of the 1995 World Trade Organization's General Agreement on Trade in Services. Cooperation between countries concerning migration and development is often based on the close connection between these two factors. If properly managed this can lead to a relationship of benefit to the development of both sending and receiving states – for example as MIDSA and MIDWA seek to tap the potential of respective diasporas to develop the human capital of countries of origin.

The expected benefits of such cooperation are:
- for migrants: improved protection means greater social security;
- for emigration countries: facilitation of the transfer of remittances, making it harder for agents and recruiters to skim off profits from migration; regulation of recruitment activities through protecting migrants; thus, coming closer to meeting the national labour force requirements of emigration countries;
- for immigration countries: improved control of migration and the creation of a more stable and better-trained migrant workforce.

Conclusion

Migration issues have only recently become squarely addressed as a developmental policy issue in Africa. But adequate consideration is not yet being given to defining the institutions that would manage migration effectively. The first section of this chapter was, therefore, an examination of the IOM model for a comprehensive migration management.

As migration involves different elements of management at various stages, cooperation between the bodies dealing with the different activities involved is essential. An explicit institution is needed to coordinate the different activities that the management of migrants, data and information requires, rather than separate unilateral approaches to management. Since the onus for formulating policy – including migration policy – lies with the state, the state is the overarching unit which must synchronise and coordinate migration policy, within its broader activities, for the good of the nation and society as a whole.

As African states forge ahead to rectify the deficiencies of the past, they have to borrow from the expertise of the IOM in organising dialogues and formulating concrete migration policies. The Federal Government of Nigeria, for instance, proposes the establishment of an Agency/Commission for managing the different migration issues.

With respect to West Africa, the challenges of managing migration and the lack of a well-designed institutional framework at regional level have made ECOWAS prioritise the effective management of migration. Consequently, it has set in motion a flood of activities and institutions on regulating migration, with far fewer activities and institutions for harnessing or facilitating migration or for protecting those subject to forced migration. A case in point is the ECOWAS Initiative Plan against Trafficking in Persons for 2002–2003 and 2008–2011, which has an explicit institutional framework. The coordinating unit at national level is to be the individual National Task Force of each member state, whose activities are to be coordinated by the ECOWAS Trafficking in Persons Unit.

The Joint ECCAS/ECOWAS Plan of Action against Trafficking in Persons, especially women and children in West and Central Africa (2006–2009) explicitly stipulates the different ministries, agencies and international organisations which are to handle migration issue in the two regions. Again evidence abounds that the regional bodies are quick in naming and allotting activities for regulating migration (trafficking in persons) rather than for facilitating it (legal migration).

The agendas of the Migration Dialogue for Southern Africa (MIDSA) and the Migration Dialogue for Western (MIDWA) also address migration management, through regional dialogue and cooperation on migration-related issues, with the assistance of IOM.

Migration, as a cross-cutting issue, has been acknowledged in this chapter as demanding a well-structured management of the different issues, to achieve a more reliable, data-based migration policy. There is a need, therefore, for a central coordinating unit for the different institutions that have migration-related data to offer. An institutional framework, derivable from discussion, would be in a centralised form, rather than decentralised. The former would, however, require a complex infrastructure, which very few African countries have been able to establish, because of the very large amounts of data and information that would need to be collated and disseminated. Fortunately, modern information technology techniques offer a way out, if well-mastered and utilised to good purpose.

References

ACP-EU (African, Caribbean & Pacific – European Union). 2000. http://www.acpsec.org/en/conventions/cotonou/accord1.htm.

African Union. 2006a. Executive Council Ninth Ordinary Session, 25–29 June, Banjul, The Gambia. EX. CL/277 (IX). African Common Position on Migration and Development.

African Union. 2006b. Executive Council Ninth Ordinary Session, 25–29 June 2006, Banjul, The Gambia. EX. CL/276 (IX). The Migration Policy Framework for Africa.

Afolayan, A.A. 1988. Immigration and Expulsion of ECOWAS Aliens in Nigeria, *International Migration Review*, 22: 4–27.

AU-EU (African Union – European Union). 2006. Joint Africa-EU Declaration on Migration and Development, Tripoli, 22–23 November.

Crush J., V. Williams & S. Peberdy. (2005) *Migration in Southern Africa*. Paper prepared for the Policy Analysis and Research Programme of the Global Commission on International Migration. http://www.gcim.org/attachements/RS7.pdf

ECCAS/ECOWAS. n.d. Joint ECCAS/ECOWAS[5]Plan of Action against Trafficking in Persons, especially women and children in West and Central Africa (2006–2009). http://www.naptip.gov.ng/naptip/docs/PoA_new_copy_19_may00001.html.

ECOWAS (Economic Community of West African States). 2001. Initial Plan of Action against Trafficking in Persons (2002–2003). ECOWAS Executive Secretariat, Dakar, December.

ECOWAS. 2002. Joint ECOWAS/UNODCCP/CICP Regional Meeting of Experts on Trafficking in Persons. ECOWAS Executive Secretariat, Lomé, 2–3 December.

ECOWAS. 2007a. 59th Ordinary Session of the Council of Ministers, Regulation C/REG.28/12/07, extension of ECOWAS Plan of Action on the Fight Against Trafficking in Persons (2008–2011). Ouagadougou, 14–15 December.

ECOWAS. 2007b. ECOWAS Common Position on Migration. Abuja: ECOWAS Commission, 14 June. http://www.oecd.org/dataoecd/17/2/41400366.pdf.

ECOWAS. 2008. *ECOWAS Commission: Common Approach on Migration*. 33rd Ordinary Session of the Head of State and Government, Ouagadougou, 18 January.

Federal Government of Nigeria. 2004. *Country Report on Violence against Children*. Federal Ministry of Women Affairs, Abuja, July–August.

Federal Republic of Nigeria. 1989. Social Development Policy for Nigeria. Federal Republic of Nigeria, Lagos, October.

IOM. 2003. *IOM's role in enhancing regional dialogues on migration*. 86th Session of the Council, MC/INF/266. http://www.iom.int/jahia/webdav/shared/shared/mainsite/about_iom/en/council/86/MCINF_266.pdf (accessed 18 June 2009).

IOM. 2004a. Essentials of migration management: a guide for policy makers and practitioners. Vol. 1: *A Conceptual Model for Comprehensive Migration Management*.

---

5   Economic Community of Central African States; Economic Community of West African States.

http://www.iom.int/jahia/Jahia/about-migration/migration-management-foundations/conceptual-model-migration-management/model-comprehensive-migration-management.

IOM. 2004b. *Support to NEPAD* (May 2003 – August 2004). http://www.wwan.cn/africa/osaa/cpcreports/13.IOM_formatted.pdf (accessed 18 June 2009).

IOM. 2007 *Support to NEPAD* (July 2006 to June 2007). http://www.un.org/africa/osaa/reports/2007%20un%20folder%20IOM.pdf (accessed 18 June 2009).

NAPTIP. 2003. Federal Government of Nigeria: National Agency for Prohibition of Traffic in Persons and Other Related Matters, 14 July. See also http://www.naptip.gov.ng/ (accessed 13 June 2009).

UNHCR (United Nations High Commissioner for Refugees). 1950. *Statute of the Office of the UNHCR*. http://www.unhcr.org.au/pdfs/UNstatute.pdf (accessed 22 June 2009).

WOTCLEF (Women Trafficking and Child Labour Eradication Foundation). 2001. *The Rape of the Innocent*, Proceedings of the first Pan-African Conference on Human Trafficking, Abuja, Nigeria, 19–23 February.

CHAPTER SEVEN

Promoting Managed Migration through Bilateral and Multilateral Agreements between European and African Countries

Aderanti Adepoju

Introduction

In the last five years or so, various bilateral and multilateral agreements between poor sending and rich receiving countries (which have large concentrations of immigrants) have been established. Their purpose is to promote managed migration by addressing aspects such as admission procedures, flows, social security, family reunification, integration policy, and return; and to prevent and combat irregular labour migration. Other agreements – described below – are aimed at fostering an improved migration management mechanism through cooperation, capacity-building and dialogue between the countries concerned, the latter in the context of the 2001 Berne Initiative. Further initiatives aim at promoting managed migration for employment purposes – for instance by expanding avenues for regular labour migration – while at the same time having regard to labour market needs and demographic trends in the various countries. Yet other agreements are focused on issues such as the ethical recruitment of health professionals from poor countries.

The research project reviewed here describes the objectives of these bilateral agreements, how they were implemented, the lessons learnt and the best practices employed. It makes recommendations that take into account the interests and concerns of countries of origin and destination, as well as of the migrants themselves.

Three approaches were employed for data collection for this project: firstly, the researcher (this author) contacted the Ministries of Justice and Immigration of certain selected African countries with large emigrant populations, to solicit pertinent information on the bilateral agreements they had entered into with

European Union (EU) countries. From the Nigerian Ministry of Justice in Abuja we managed to secure information only informally.

Secondly, we contacted the embassies of Spain, the Netherlands, the UK, Belgium and other EU countries accredited to ECOWAS (the Economic Community of West African States) in Abuja, with a request for information on the bilateral and multilateral agreements their countries had entered into with African countries, and in particular with Nigeria. Only the UK Embassy responded.

The third approach involved an extensive search on the Internet. This has been the main source of the information included in this chapter, though a literature search of published materials was used to supplement the Internet source. We have chosen to use the situations in Nigeria, Senegal and Mali as illustrations: Nigeria being a major source of trafficked victims in women and children for sexual exploitation in Europe; Senegal as a major country of departure for irregular migrants attempting to cross to Europe via the Canary Islands; and Mali as a major source of irregular migrants but also as the site for the EU's pilot project on development and job creation to reduce poverty and help retain potential emigrants. Some detail is also given of the situation regarding the Maghreb region, in particular Morocco.

Nigeria

Nigeria is a major source, transit and destination country for trafficking women and children to Europe for the purpose of sexual exploitation, forced labour and child labour, especially to Italy (where there may be as many as 10 000 Nigerian prostitutes), Spain, Belgium and the Netherlands – as well as to other African countries (Adepoju 2004). Nigeria has endorsed most international instruments on human trafficking, played a key role in ECOWAS anti-human trafficking initiatives, and entered into bilateral agreements and memoranda of agreement on immigration matters with countries within and outside Africa on human trafficking, and on forced labour and migration in general. These agreements focus mainly on procedures for the repatriation of Nigerian nationals.

Key among the Nigerian bilateral migration agreements are:
- Agreement on Immigration Matters between the governments of Nigeria and Italy, signed 12 September 2000, ratified 30 November 2000;
- Agreement on Immigration Matters between the governments of Nigeria and Ireland, signed 29 August 2001, ratified 30 November 2002;
- Agreement on Migration Matters between the governments of Nigeria and Spain, signed 12 November 2001, ratified 30 November 2002;
- Cooperation Agreement between the governments of Nigeria and the United Kingdom to prevent, suppress and punish trafficking in persons especially women and children, signed June 2005, not yet ratified;
- Memorandum of Understanding on Migration between Nigeria and Italy, signed November 2003 (Federal Ministry of Justice, Abuja).

In recent years European countries have been seeking the cooperation of Nigeria in the readmission of undocumented migrants and rejected asylum seekers. Nigeria has become one of the most cooperative African countries on this issue and has readmission agreements with Italy, Spain, Ireland and Switzerland. In return, Nigeria has asked for immigration quotas in exchange for collaboration in readmissions (de Haas 2006).

Nigeria and Italy

Italy is a major country of destination for trafficking in women and children, and ranks among the top nine destination countries for sex trafficking in the world (*Associated Press*, 12 May 2003). Nigeria is the only sub-Saharan African country to have signed a readmission agreement with Italy (in 2000, as listed above). The agreement provides for the readmission of Nigerian citizens whose positions are found to be irregular, the provision by Italy of technical and material assistance, and training courses, to irregular migrants, as well as cooperation in the control of HIV and other sexually transmitted diseases – all of which form part of the integration process of the readmitted persons on their return home.

There has been a recent wave of repatriation of Nigerian girls (mostly victims of human trafficking) from Italy. The agreement with Italy does not make any specific mention of human trafficking, nor does it clarify the conditions under which victims of human trafficking are to be repatriated. Deported women have claimed that they were denied the opportunity of taking advantage of the legal provisions of the agreement. Many Nigerian women deported from Italy recount indignities that they suffered, having often been detained in holding centres prior to their expulsion and not being allowed to return to their places of residence to collect the belongings they had acquired during their stay (Nwogu 2006).

In the framework of bilateral cooperation in combating illegal immigration, Italy, in 2002, donated equipment and goods to the Nigerian government with a value of over US$2.5 million. A second round of donations took place in 2004 (of goods worth €786 000), and a third in 2005 and 2006 (with a value of about €4 million), for distribution among governmental agencies involved in immigration control, and the monitoring and investigation of human trafficking. (The agencies involved were the Nigeria Immigration Service, the Nigeria Police, the National Agency for Prohibition of Traffic in Persons – NAPTIP – and the Ministry of Foreign Affairs). In a determined effort to curb the trafficking of human beings, Italy financed a multi-lateral programme in 2002 costed at €776 000 to prevent and combat the trafficking of children and women from Nigeria to Italy. The project was implemented by UNICRI[1] and the UNODC (United Nations Organization on Drugs and Crime. During the first phase, covering 18 months, from the beginning of 2002 until April 2004, bilateral cooperation was strengthened by creating in both countries a task

---

1 The United Nations Interregional Crime and Justice Research Institute.

force to deal with human trafficking from Nigeria to Italy. The Memorandum of Understanding, signed in November 2003 by the Procurator General of Nigeria and the Italian Direzione Nazionale Antimafia, focuses on the fight against trafficking and organised crime. It established a National Monitoring Centre in Abuja, managed by NAPTIP, with the aim of exchanging information and creating a databank of victims involved in and/or rescued from trafficking. It also covered rehabilitation and reintegration activities in Benin City (Edo State), by providing micro-credit to help the victims acquire skills and set up small businesses of their own. The second phase of the project (for €1.9 million) was financed in 2006 by Italian Cooperation[2].

In 2002 a reserved entry quota of admittance into Italy was granted for the first time – to 500 Nigerian workers – in recognition of Nigeria's collaboration efforts on combating illegal immigration. This quota was continued and increased, starting from a low 200 in 2003, to 2000 in 2004 and 2005, and reaching 2500 in 2006, but the quota has not been fully utilised by Nigeria and has since been truncated/discontinued. Nevertheless, Nigeria is so far the only sub-Saharan African country to benefit from a such a quota.

Nigeria and Spain

The Nigerian agreement with Spain deals with victims of human trafficking and specifies joint measures to combat illegal migration, facilitate repatriation, exchange information on trafficking networks, and establish skills acquisition centres in Nigeria for those who have been repatriated. It also provides mechanisms for legal access to Spain for Nigerian workers.

Spain's pilot project for the Immigrant Voluntary Return Programme took off in September 2003 and provides a framework for similar schemes with African countries with large concentrations of immigrants in other parts of Europe. The project focuses on immigrants at risk: mainly those with integration problems, and the victims of trafficking. Beneficiaries are entitled to training for return, a free plane ticket and seed money at destination to help them reintegrate 'at home'.

Spain's bilateral agreements with some African countries focus on the readmission of irregular immigrants and for the management of migratory flows. On 12 November 2001 Nigeria signed a draft agreement with Spain and over 1000 illegal immigrants were repatriated in humane conditions in both 2002 and 2003, and about 900 in 2004. Similarly, a draft agreement signed with Ghana in Madrid on 21 February 2003 led to the repatriation of 370 migrants. The terms of the Agreement on Immigration, signed with Guinea-Bissau on 7 February 2003, were provisionally implemented, pending its later ratification. A similar Agreement on Immigration was signed with Mauritania on 4 July 2003 (Casado 2004).

---

2 See http://www.cooperazioneallosviluppo.esteri.it/pdgcs/inglese/intro.html.

Nigeria and the United Kingdom

The 2005 Memorandum of Understanding between the UK and Nigeria focuses on efforts to combat human trafficking and addresses the issue of poverty – the root cause of trafficking. It calls for greater sensitivity on the part of the UK's immigration and law-enforcement officers, and includes strategies to ensure the protection of trafficked persons, as well as for technical and institutional capacity-building to prevent trafficking, protect victims and prosecute offenders. Other aspects are related to programmes providing counselling for the physical, psychological and social rehabilitation of trafficked victims.

Remarks

Nigeria should negotiate bilateral agreements to protect its nationals abroad and regularly review the implementation of these agreements, ensuring that readmissions comply fully with international standards for the protection of the rights of migrants and trafficked persons. The country's consular offices in destination countries should provide information to migrants about their rights and obligations. In addition, the governments of destination countries should guarantee the humane treatment of victims of human trafficking during repatriation, and assist more actively in capacity-building and institutional support to the Nigerian government agencies responsible for tackling the problem of human trafficking (Nwogu 2006).

Senegal

During his visit to Senegal in 2006, the EU's Commissioner for Development and Humanitarian Aid called for a 'closer dialogue' between the EU and the countries of origin of irregular migrants, in order to combat the seemingly intractable problem of migration, and the human tragedies it provokes. Two short-term cooperation projects between the EU and Senegal were put on the drawing board: a contribution to surveillance operations and to repatriation and rehabilitation (about €1.8 m), and local support for activities of non-state actors engaged in the migration arena (€1 million). This was in recognition of the fact that aid for economic development was necessary to supplement efforts at strict migration controls – to achieve a lasting solution to the problem of irregular migration. The medium-term plan is investment in public projects (€19.8 m to €27.4 m) to create about 4000 jobs in a year (EUbusiness 2006).

Senegal and Spain

So far, Spain has signed migration control and development aid agreements with the main countries of departure of irregular migrants – Morocco, Mauritania and

Senegal. These countries have also received logistic aid in controlling borders. The success achieved in Morocco – by Spanish and EU authorities – in closing the main migration routes into Europe through economic and diplomatic concessions to Morocco contributed to the harsh crack-down on Africans trying to use that country as a base to migrate to Spain. (Libya and Tunisia are taking similar action against irregular migrants heading for Italy.) (Belguendouz 2006)

Spain and Senegal also agreed to bolster surveillance in the Canary Islands of illegal migrants arriving from Senegal, in a bid to stem the flood of more than 24 000 illegal migrants, mostly on board rickety boats, who arrived there in 2006, risking death in a bid to enter Spain in the hope of finding work in Europe. Rescue services estimate that 550 people may have died in 2006 in unsuccessful attempts to reach the Canaries. In an agreement signed in August 2006, Senegal pledged to discourage people from migrating illegally, and to provide logistical help for Spain in monitoring Senegal's coasts. A month after the agreement was signed, Senegal's president criticised Spain for slowness in sending adequate patrols to Senegal. Spain's response included plans to send planes to scan the coast of Senegal for migrants trying to sail to Europe.

Irregular migrants from Mauritania, Senegal and Cape Verde have thus forced the EU to intensify patrols in West African waters and increase police cooperation – in return for generous development aid packages. These measures have managed to limit, though not entirely halt, the flow out of Senegal. The tougher anti-migration efforts in Senegal resulted in Senegalese traffickers moving their main departure point further south, to Guinea-Bissau, prompting Bissau authorities to ask Spain for economic assistance to stop the new flow. This fresh spate of uncontrolled immigration from West Africa has prompted Spain, in cooperation with the EU, to intensify diplomatic action and increase development aid to Guinea-Bissau.

Senegal and France

The Franco-Senegalese Protocol Agreement, initially signed in 1975 and revised several times thereafter, encourages the voluntary return of Senegalese migrants in France, to enable them to contribute to the development of their communities of origin (Diatta & Mbow 1999).

In 1975 France launched a programme to finance professional training for Algerians living in that country who would then return to Algeria, to replicate the training locally. For sending countries such as Senegal, this indicated a shift in the French objective: from encouraging legal or illegal migrants to return, to promoting 'stay-at-home' development and reducing migration flows. Nevertheless, a series of programmes launched between 1977 and 1992 to promote 'stay-at-home' attracted very few participants – in spite of offers of travel expenses, a three-month paid professional traineeship in France, and a three-month multiple-entry visa for illegal migrants from Mali and Senegal who left France, on condition that their reintegration into their home country was successful (Magoni 2004). These unsuccessful schemes probably informed the Regularisation Act of June 1997 which granted legal status to 80 000 previously irregular migrants.

In an agreement made with Senegal in December 2003, the French government's 'reciprocal assistance' enjoined Senegalese authorities to simplify the deportation of illegal Senegalese migrants living in France by facilitating their readmission to Senegal. Under the agreement, France would increase the number of entry visas issued to Senegalese nationals, cover travel and accommodation costs of highly-skilled Senegalese nationals residing in France who wished to undertake temporary development missions in Senegal, and double the assistance for the voluntary return of those who wished to undertake small development projects at home. This agreement included the establishment of mechanisms to prevent irregular emigration, and increased bilateral police cooperation through the creation of a border police unit and a national security department in Senegal, as well as the training of local immigration officials (Magoni 2004).

Mali

Mali is a landlocked Sahelian country, with few natural resources and an impoverished population. As one of Africa's poorest countries, it is a major source of emigration: in 1993 it accounted for at least a quarter of all inter-African emigration.

Despite the problems experienced by Malians living abroad (xenophobia, racism, expulsion, etc.), their commitment to migrate remains strong. The government has created a ministry to assist emigrants and to provide potential emigrants with information about living conditions abroad, as well as employment and residence requirements. Emigrants are encouraged to remit money home regularly, and Malian consular offices in the major receiving countries have increased staff numbers to deal with the problems faced by nationals (Findley et al 1995).

Mali and France

Since 1997, based on a Franco-Mali Agreement, France's visa policy has required French consulates to monitor closely the visa applications of parents of French citizens and foreign nationals studying in France. In return for adherence to this close monitoring procedure, France increased the number of visas issued to Malians to 25 000 in 2001 – up from 7000 in 1997. As a reward for facilitating the free circulation of bona fide migrants, France urged Malian authorities to cooperate in reducing corruption in visa-issuing. The 1997 agreement resulted in the apprehending, indicting and jailing of a former Malian sports minister in October 2001 for trafficking in visas (Magoni 2004).

The 1999 'Cooperative Efforts to Manage Emigration' project between France and its former colonies in sub-Saharan Africa focuses on how countries of origin, transit, and destination can work together to coordinate migration movements and reduce emigration pressures. In that context, Mali, Comoros and Senegal have been targeted for 'co-development', to link migration policies and development policies.

As part of this co-development, Mali and France established a Consultation on Migration, signed in December 2000, which involves an annual bilateral discussion at ministerial level, dealing with issues such as the integration of Malians who want to remain in France; the co-management of migration flows to allow migrants to circulate between their home countries and abroad; and cooperative development in core emigration localities in Mali. The agreement targets core emigration regions, helping build infrastructure, stimulating job creation, and supporting education, health care and infrastructure development, as well as income generation. Malians abroad are mobilised for their country's economic development through small enterprises; their skills are registered and the information is co-managed by a Franco-Malian committee. A contract with a local Malian bank guarantees loans to small businesses that require additional funding for expansion. The agreement has also helped some migrants return voluntarily and become self-supporting (Magoni 2004).

The cost of repatriation from France to Mali was used to encourage voluntary return in a more humane manner, while also providing livelihood for the returnees – mostly unskilled migrants. The realisation that encouraging voluntary 'assisted returns', rather than relying on mandatory deportation, would better meet the interests of both sending and receiving countries partly informed the ongoing voluntary assisted return of Malians living illegally in France. In 2001, about 500 immigrants agreed to return voluntarily to Mali in exchange for US$3600 each to start businesses such as agriculture, hairdressing, importing used auto parts and sewing traditional clothes (Martin et al 2002). More than two years after the start of the project, 80 per cent of these returnees were still in business. Although many returnees lack the local guarantees required for bank loans, this foreign support helps to re-integrate migrants, and some of them do manage to become self-sustaining.

The Maghreb

Since the European Union eliminated internal borders between its members in the mid-1990s, and extended its reach into Eastern Europe, it has become a particular magnet for immigrants. The political backlash that followed the increase in immigration from African countries forced the EU to tighten controls at its external borders, especially on the Mediterranean coast.

The introduction of tougher rules regarding entry and residence of foreigners in Europe for regular migration, has inadvertently pushed irregular West

African migrants to use complex routes to reach the Maghreb as a transit region, in order to enter Europe clandestinely (Adepoju 2006). In the process, Morocco has become a major transit-migration country for migrants from West Africa and beyond. They enter the country from Algeria, at the border just east of Oujda, after crossing the Sahara through Niger, and hope to enter the EU via the Strait of Gibraltar (separating Morocco from Spanish Andalusia) or via the Strait of Sicily (which separates Tunisia from Italy), and, increasingly, via the 240 kilometres that separate the Canary Islands from the Spanish mainland. About 2000 Africans are believed to drown in the Mediterranean or the Atlantic each year while attempting illegal crossings to Europe.

The issue of irregular migration gained political urgency in Europe as television footage vividly captured the rising surge of arrivals in Spain and Italy of destitute youths in overcrowded boats – fuelling discontent, fear, racism and xenophobia.

Observers and human rights organisations accuse the EU of 'outsourcing the responsibility' of stopping migrants from further south from moving into the Maghreb countries, which they transit – even though these countries lack the means to do so. Recently, however, emphasis has been slowly shifting from repressive measures to cooperation by boosting African economies and opening more channels for regular migration to the EU, and encouraging circular migration[3].

Morocco and Spain

Spain and Morocco signed an agreement on 30 September 1999 to permit Moroccans to take up employment in Spain, in agriculture and construction. This bilateral agreement served as a model for agreements with other countries such as Mali (as well as Colombia, Ecuador, Romania and Poland). Under this 'guest worker' programme, up to 300 000 Moroccan workers a year may enter Spain for up to nine months. After four years of seasonal work, these migrants can become regular immigrants. All migrants in Spain are protected by minimum wage and other laws, and can accrue social security and retirement benefits, and earn vacation benefits. Spanish employers are responsible for providing transportation, food and lodging for these workers. This has been acclaimed as a new approach – managing migration into Europe by admitting workers on temporary basis. Morocco aimed to conclude similar agreements with Italy, Belgium, the Netherlands and France.

Morocco and the European Union

From July 2006, the EU's new approach has been to push for re-admission

---

3 Migrants coming to the receiving country only for a certain length of time, intending from the outset to return home at the end of the work period

agreements under which African countries will take back illegal migrants, in exchange for economic assistance. An agreement has been negotiated with Morocco for the readmission of migrants: as well as taking back its own nationals, Morocco also agreed to EU demands that it return those from other countries who had transited to Europe through its territory. A promise was also made to extend this scheme to other African countries.

The Maghreb and the European Union

The following bilateral agreements between Morocco and Spain, Tunisia and Italy, and Libya and Italy are indicative of the growing interest in curtailing irregular migration and ensuring the return and readmission:

- Bilateral agreement between Morocco and Spain for the return of Moroccan nationals;
- Bilateral agreement between Morocco and Spain in September 1999 to curb irregular migration of nationals and those who had transited Morocco;
- Bilateral agreement between Libya and Italy in 2003 in which Italy pledged financial support to Libya for combating smuggling and providing sea-rescue operations;
- Bilateral agreement between Libya and Italy, signed in 2005, for Libya to hold African refugees and irregular migrants in detention camps to prevent them from crossing to Europe.

The new spirit of cooperation between Tunisia and Italy is also manifested in other measures, which include the training of coastal surveillance staff, the provision of logistical support for maritime security forces, and joint police and naval patrols with Italy in Tunisian territorial waters.

In the wake of the deaths of irregular migrants attempting to penetrate the fence around Ceuta (an enclave of Spain on the African coast) on 29 September 2005, the EU Commission's technical mission to Morocco which visited Ceuta and Melilla (a similar Spanish enclave) a week or so later concluded that the mounting migration pressure from Africa on Morocco and the EU would intensify in the coming years. Although Morocco and Spain are making efforts to control this challenge, the EU has found it necessary to provide substantial assistance to ensure the long term sustainability of the control efforts; to intensify cooperation with and assistance to Morocco; to launch a dialogue and initiate cooperation with Algeria, and to develop a comprehensive migration policy for the main countries of origin and transit in both West and sub-Saharan Africa (EC 2005).

Irregular migrants in Morocco, lacking legal status, and probably carrying false travel documents, are vulnerable to social and economic marginalisation and rarely have access to decent employment. The Moroccan media have intensified negative sentiments by comparing these people to 'black locusts', prompting the authorities to round them up to be deported to the Algerian border (A. Obisesan, Deportees: Widespread Killing of Black Africans in Libya, *Agence France Press*, 5 October 2000).

The authorities in Libya and Morocco bully and expel these people, often sending them to desert border posts where they face hunger, torture and even death. In a forest near Morocco's border with Ceuta, encampments were set up by destitute Africans, who are reported to have been attacked and arrested by Moroccan police. Libya has stepped up efforts to crack down on illegal migrants from North and sub-Sahara African countries – at least in part to appease the North, by meting out heavy punishments for victims and traffickers, including imprisonment and deportation.

In June 2005, Libya signed an agreement with Italy to hold African refugees and irregular immigrants in detention camps, to prevent them from crossing to Europe. The head of France's Information and Support Group for Immigrants called the policy 'the most symbolic example of European cynicism…externalising its asylum and immigration policy by getting third countries to take responsibility for the flow of migrants before they arrive at its borders' (Amnesty International 2005). Non-Libyans have been picked up by police, thrown into camps and expelled en masse, without human rights protection. The European Parliament noted that Libya 'practises arbitrary arrest and detention', and speaks of 'the detention, [and] massive repatriation of foreigners in conditions which do not guarantee their dignity or survival' (EC 2004).

Morocco and Spain, as well as Tunisia and Italy, have mounted joint naval patrols aimed at catching migrants smuggled by boat to Spain and Italy. In July 2003, Libya signed an agreement with Italy for financial support in combating smuggling and in providing sea-rescue operations. This is one outcome of talks between the two countries on collaborative efforts to curb irregular migration (Delicato 2004).

In all, bilateral agreements and cooperation in coastal areas and along land borders, aimed at curtailing and controlling irregular migration and readmission of repatriated immigrants, remain the dominant strategy between European countries bordering the Mediterranean and the Maghreb countries of migrant transit and origin. Critics argue that the implementation of bilateral agreements ignores migrants' rights and accuse Morocco of bowing to pressure from the EU to play the role of 'Europe's policeman' in North Africa (Belguendouz 2006). The lesson to be learnt from reinforcing security around Europe's borders is that the problems of irregular migration are not solved by these measures, but simply pushed further south, with Europe using Maghreb states in an attempt to keep irregular African migrants and refugees out of its territories.

Other multilateral agreements

Europe and Africa

As part of the 2001 Berne Initiative, Portugal signed a series of bilateral and multilateral agreements on immigration with lusophone African countries with which it has colonial, cultural and historical ties. These included the multilateral agreement on the 'Establishment of Specific Desks in Border Entry Gates for Reception of African Portuguese Speaking Countries Nationals', signed on 30 July 2002. The agreements are designed to facilitate the entry of immigrants in regular situations and prevent irregular migration.

An Africa-Europe expert meeting on trafficking in human beings, sponsored by the governments of Sweden and Italy in September 2002, called for a number of measures to be taken in both origin and destination countries. These involved the prevention and combating of trafficking, and awareness-raising; the protection of and assistance to victims; the creation of a legislative framework for dealing with human trafficking and law enforcement; and cooperation and co-ordination within and between states and regions. In Turin, Italy – one of the main destinations of trafficked Nigerian women – an outreach unit has assisted 1250 victims, 60 per cent of them Nigerians, with access to health and other welfare services (Nwogu 2006).

Europe and ACP countries

The Cotonou Agreement, which was signed on 23 June 2000, aimed at building a partnership between the EU and 77 countries situated in Africa, the Caribbean and the Pacific (ACPs), in order to reduce and eventually eradicate poverty – by promoting sustainable development, capacity building, and integration into the world economy (IOM 2003). This agreement, based on the principle of equality between all the countries involved, stressed the ACPs' ownership of development strategies, and the concluding parties agreed to emphasise political dialogue, development cooperation and trade relations as specific areas of concern.

Migration is an important element of on-going political dialogue, which seeks to explore different dimensions of cooperation. Moreover, management of migration is one of the priorities in the field of technical cooperation, which should assist the ACP countries. Article 13 of the Cotonou Agreement sets out a framework for migration management which includes the following:
- Respect of the rights of migrants shall be guaranteed. Rooted in international law and human rights dispositions, an important component of this is commitment to fair treatment (absence of discriminatory practice) of migrants who reside legally in the territories of the concluding parties.
- Strategies to tackle root-causes of massive migration flows: these should aim at 'supporting the economic and social development of the regions

from which migrants originated'. The training of ACP students is an explicitly-mentioned element of such strategies.
- Regulation to counter irregular migration: the parties are committed to return or re-admit all nationals who are in an irregular situation. To this end, bilateral readmission and return agreements shall be concluded.
- Based on the principles of cost-efficiency and ownership, technical cooperation should enhance the transfer of knowledge, develop national and regional human capacities and promote exchange between EU and ACP professionals. As an integral element of technical cooperation, the EU is committed to support the ACP's efforts to reverse the brain drain.

Management of labour migration

The EU's project on 'the management of labour migration as an instrument for development in Africa', spanning the period from March 2004 to February 2006, was implemented by the International Labour Organization. The project promoted the adoption of new policy frameworks and mechanisms for managing labour migration as an instrument for development. It aimed to promote social dialogue and raise awareness among stakeholders regarding regional labour migration issues, and to facilitate engagement in policy debates, with a view to developing regional policy frameworks and enhancing cooperation between Europe and the different African regions. It also provided a forum for engaging regional partners in core activities concerning labour migration. Seminars were organised in each region on capacity-building and social dialogue, and two sets of studies – on the situation of labour migration and on the relevant legislations – were conducted in thirteen sub-Saharan African countries. Advocacy campaigns followed the publication of the studies in the different countries (EC 2007). These apart, little information is available to assist in the evaluation of the implementation of the project, or lessons learnt from it.

A new approach: circular migration with development

An effective and novel approach to slowing down emigration seems to be the concept of investing in development in Africa. Rather than fighting the trend of people leaving an area they view as less desirable, the aim is now to make places of origin more attractive to stay in. Economic development as a long-term solution implies reducing crushing poverty and offering Africa's youth a future of dignity, rather than risking death attempting – usually fruitlessly – to enter EU countries.

During a ministerial meeting of 57 African and EU countries in Rabat in July 2006, it became apparent that efforts to increase border security have had only limited success and the strategy of zero-immigration has not succeeded. Recognising that some immigration is necessary, the EU made pledges to help develop African economies, urging African ministers to work together to fight illegal migration, in order to facilitate legal migration (France-Diplomatie 2006).

Mali as a pilot project

In recent times, poverty and misery in Mali have intensified to such an extent that over ten per cent (2800) of the 26 000 irregular migrants arriving in Spain in the first months of 2007 were Malians. This number does not include Malians using the Saharan route to Italy via Algeria. One estimate puts the number of Malians living in Europe, mostly in France, at 200 000.

On 22 January 2007 the EU Immigration Commissioner, Franco Frattini, unveiled a pilot project of a new 'guest worker' scheme for Africa which aims to boost local economies, enhance the earnings potential of migrants and (hence) stop – or very significantly reduce – irregular migration. A pilot project for this flexible scheme is designed to coordinate job offers in the EU with job seekers in Mali. It aims to boost the EU's workforce – diminished in an ageing population – and assist the economies of developing countries by allowing workers to develop skills and earn money. In this way it forms part of an EU strategy to combat illegal immigration. In return for assistance with legal circular immigration, Mali is expected to increase its cooperation in the fight against illegal immigration to the EU and to sign a treaty with the EU on the repatriation of illegal immigrants.

In pursuance of the new strategy – aiming both to fill jobs in areas of labour shortage and to stem the tide of irregular immigration – the EU Development Commissioner announced in early February 2007 that the EU planned to follow up the Mali pilot project by setting up job centres for African migrants in Senegal and Mauritania. The aim is to help migrants find jobs in the EU in sectors such as the labour-short areas of agriculture, construction and sanitation services. So, although the EU is increasing border patrols against *illegal* immigration, both on land and sea, the current strategy is to offer more avenues for *regular* migration (Afrik.com 2008).

Mali was chosen for this scheme because of its functional national employment agency and its experience of bilateral accords, especially with France. The scheme is to involve farm labourers, construction workers and seasonal tourism employees, and is modelled along the lines of a project in Spain's southern province, which receives 1000 agricultural workers from Morocco for six months each year. The EU commissioner aims to find job quota offers from member states for Mali workers, and plans, eventually, to establish a network of job centres across Africa. (Observers are, however, cautioned by a similar scheme introduced in Germany in the 1960s for Turkish guest workers. The intended circular migration never materialised, and tensions erupted in the 1980s when Turkish migrants, many of whom had been born and brought up in Germany, demanded citizenship rights.)

At the end of September 2006, the EU and Mali signed a development-aid-for-migration-control agreement. Under this agreement, the EU promised to grant Mali €426 million over the period from 2008 to 2013, with the funding going mainly into government poverty reduction projects, to help the country control migratory flows. The EU's expectation is that economic growth, productive investment, the private development sector, and regional integration could substantially boost job creation, halt the flow of irregular migrants, at the same time as strengthening efforts to fight the mafia networks organising illegal migrations. As mentioned above, Spanish and EU operations in Senegal have already been effective in dismantling these trafficking networks.

Another development is the Migration Information and Management Centre project for Mali, which was set up in Bamako, and is funded by the EU's European Development Fund and was expected to be functional in late 2007. The aim is to implement the joint Mali–ECOWAS–EC–France–Spain Declaration of February 2007 as a follow-up to the 2006 Tripoli EU–Africa Ministerial Conference on migration and development. The general objective of the Centre is the definition and implementation by Mali of a migratory policy adapted to both regional and European policies and dynamics, implementing and coordinating the various elements of Mali's migration policy. To help Malians emigrate legally and temporarily, the Centre informs them about job and training opportunities both at home and abroad, as well as about the dangers of illegal migration. Expected outcomes – aimed primarily at the prevention of irregular migration – include the definition and implementation of an information and communication strategy regarding legal conditions for migration, and an analysis of migratory flows of relevance to Mali. In addition, the Centre aimed to put in place a mechanism for welcoming, orientating and accompanying new (legal) migrants coming into Spain and France, and productively using the human, financial and technical capital of the diaspora. The EU Development Commissioner Louis Michel remarked early in 2007 that the Centre 'goes in the direction of the "third (alternative) way" that we are proposing to find realistic and humane solutions to migration problems' (Afrik.com 2008).

Conclusion

A summary of the attitudes and actions of the EU towards migrant-sending countries in Africa can be given as having occurred in five phases:

Firstly, the initial concern in Europe was with rounding up irregular migrants and victims of trafficking and deporting them from Europe back to their countries of origin. In most cases this was done without consultation with the countries of origin and often effected in inhumane conditions and in breach of the rights of the expellees.

In the second phase, emphasis shifted to some form of dialogue and consultation between the host countries with the sending countries, with the objective of guaranteeing the readmission at home of the irregular persons to be expelled. A part of this strategy was the tightening of border controls in what became 'fortressed Europe', and an aim of zero tolerance of irregular migration.

The third phase – outsourcing responsibility for the policing of borders, and halting irregular migrants from the EU to Morocco, Libya and Algeria – was a strategy that is both unrealistic and unsustainable. These Maghreb countries include those with poor records of human rights which also lack the financial and logistical facilities essential for carrying out the defence of their borders against the surge of irregular immigrants from other parts of Africa and beyond.

The fourth phase involved rewarding cooperative sending countries with donations of technical and operational equipment – to make 'home' more desirable, and thus contain irregular emigration from source. The 'carrot' part of the 'carrot and stick' strategy also rewards sending countries that cooperated by granting work quotas (albeit only of token size) for their nationals in receiving countries.

The last and most recent phase recognises that strict control does not produce the desired results – instead it inadvertently spurs trafficking. The EU countries have thus proposed investing in job creation, economic growth and poverty alleviation schemes in Africa, in order to stem the tide of irregular emigration. This strategy also includes some form of guest worker scheme and circulatory migration that allows Africans to work in specified sectors of labour shortage in EU countries, in regular situations. Mali is serving as a pilot for the new strategy.

In all these phases, the receiving countries of the EU have been the prime architects of the schemes, initiating the bilateral agreements, their contents, the modalities for their implementation, and providing funds to cajole sending countries to fall in line and implement the agreements. Sending countries do not seem to have sufficiently critical inputs in the negotiations leading to the agreements – which are therefore mostly Eurocentric. Little wonder then that some of the earlier agreements have not been implemented in either the letter or the spirit of these accords.

Bilateral and multilateral agreements between countries sending and receiving migrants must also address the issue of depleting Africa of its scarce skilled-manpower resources. It is important that the residential laws of rich countries be made flexible, to give skilled professionals the opportunity of relocating for extended periods to their countries of origin without losing their residence rights in those countries.

African countries need to ensure that their specific interests and concerns are adequately reflected in any bilateral or multilateral migration negotiations. Issues relating to the treatment of their nationals living and working in regular situations in EU countries, the rights of irregular migrants to basic services, and the need to review the unfair trade regimes which impoverish millions of their nationals who are engaged in farming at home should assume centre stage in future migration agreements. Efforts should be made to revisit existing agreements in order to review and amend unfavourable conditions.

Above all, African countries' embassies and missions in destination countries should provide their nationals with appropriate information on the rules that guide entry, residence and work – in short their rights and obligations in receiving societies.

This chapter has been adapted from my 2007 report titled *Bilateral and multilateral migration agreements between European and ECOWAS and Maghreb countries*, being a research project on promoting managed migration through bilateral and multilateral agreements between European and African countries, undertaken by the Research Group Migration and Development at Radbound University, Nijmegen, Netherlands and the Human Resources Development Centre, Lagos, Nigeria. I appreciate the comments received from my colleagues especially Annelies Zoomers, femke van Noorloos, on the draft report.

References

Adepoju, A. 2004. *Regional Migration Processes, Multilateral and Bilateral Migration Agreements in Sub-Saharan Africa*. IOM: Berne Initiative Policy Research Paper. Berne: International Organisation for Migration.

Adepoju, A. 2006. *The challenge of labour migration flows between West Africa and the Maghreb*. ILO Migration Research Papers. Geneva: International Labour Organisation.

Africa Union. 2006. Report of the Joint Africa-EU Declaration on Migration and Development. Sirte, 22–23 November. www.africa-union.org/root/au/conferences

Afrik.com. 2008. EU to create job search in Africa to stop illegal migration. 6 October. Afrik.com website: http://en.afrik.com/article14630.html.

Amnesty International. 2005. Spain/Morocco: The authorities must be held accountable for the violation of migrants' rights. Press Release, 26 October.

Belguendouz, A. 2006. *Enjeux Migratoires Maghreb-Europe-Afrique Subsaharienne: Un regard du Sud*. Sale: Imprimerie Beni Snassen.

Casado, L. 2004. Inter-state cooperation in the Kingdom of Spain in managing migration. Berne Initiative Policy Research Paper, Inter-state Cooperation on Migration, unpublished paper.

De Haas, H. 2006. *International migration, national development and the role of governments: the case of Nigeria*. Proceedings of Expert Meeting on International Migration and National Development, Migration and Development series, Report No. 6. Nijmegen, Netherlands.

Delicato, V. 2004. *National legislation and good practices in the fight against illegal migration – the Italian model*. Rome: CARDS Programme.

Diatta, M.A. & N. Mbow. 1999. Releasing the development potential of return migration: the case of Senegal. *International Migration* 37 (1): 243–266.

EC (European Commission). 2004. Report of Technical Mission to Libya on illegal immigration, 22 November – 6 December. Memo 7753/05 Brussels: EU.

EC. 2005. Visit to Ceuta and Melilla: Report of Technical Mission to Morocco on illegal immigration, 7–11 October. Memo/05/380. Brussels: EU.

EC. 2007. *Circular migration and mobility partnerships between the European Union and third countries*. Memo/07/197. Brussels: EU.

EUbusiness. 2006. http://www.eubusiness.com (accessed March 2008).

Findley, S.E., S. Traore, D. Ouedraogo & S. Diarra. 1995. Emigration from the Sahel. *International Migration* 33 (3 & 4) 469–520.

France-Diplomatie. 2006. Regional Euro-African Conference 2006, Migration and Development, Rabat, 10 July. www.diplomatie.gouv.fr.

IOM (International Organisation for Migration). 2003. *2003 World Migration Report*. Geneva: IOM.

Magoni, R. 2004. *International Migration and Relations with Third Countries. Country report: France*. Brussels: Migration Policy Group.

Martin, P., S. Martin & P. Best. 2002. Best Practices Options: Mali. *International Migration* 40 (3): 87–102.

Nwogu, V.I. 2006. Nigeria: Human trafficking and migration, *Forced Migration Review*, 25: 32–33. http://www.fmreview.org/text/FMR/25/20.doc (accessed May 2007).

CHAPTER EIGHT

Conclusion

Aderanti Adepoju

As several authors have emphasised in this volume, intra- and inter-country movements continue to be a central feature of life for the people of Africa. Much of this movement takes place in diverse political, economic, socio-ethnic and ecological settings but remains essentially intra-regional. These configurations are changing dynamically – to the extent that no country remains unaffected by international migration flows, with some serving concurrently as countries of origin, or transit, or destination for migrants. Stressful economic conditions, especially the absence of sustainable livelihood opportunities, poverty and unemployment, endemic conflicts, and the general perception of a bleak future have fuelled the emigration of both young and old, males and females alike, increasingly to regions outside the African continent, in search of greener pastures. Consequently many countries are concurrently experiencing challenges with respect to the emigration of skilled professionals, the diaspora's links with their country of origin, and migrant remittances from within and outside Africa, as well as irregular migration and human trafficking. Africa is burdened with poverty, unemployment and socio-economic insecurity, which have drawn more people into circular or temporary migration to a variety of destinations. Some of the migration that would otherwise take place internally has emerged as sequential intra-regional and international migration.

Many of these dynamics are set to change, especially in the face of on-going global financial and economic turmoil. As the world's worst economic crisis since the end of the second world war unfolds, it is now obvious that its impact is rapidly spreading beyond the coasts of the rich countries where the crisis began to those of emerging market economies, and to poor economies as well. The speed and depth of the spread makes poor countries very vulnerable.

The emerging and fast-growing economies of Brazil, China and India are now facing severe economic difficulties, and the South African government announced at the end of May this year (2009) that that country is currently experiencing the worst economic depression since 1992. South Africa is Africa's economic giant, and the impact of the recession there will be felt acutely by the labour-sending countries of the SADC – Zimbabwe and Mozambique especially – whose economies are very largely dependent on that of South Africa. Even Botswana's economy, among the best managed in Africa, has been hard hit, forcing that country to borrow US$1.5 billion from the African Development Bank to shore up a fiscal deficit as export earnings from diamonds are hit by the recession (Guardian 5 June 2009).

Observers are worried that migrant-sending, poor countries, whose economies depend heavily on migrants' remittances, are the ones set to suffer most from the financial and economic crisis. The discourse on migrant remittance – its volume, use, resilience and its impact on recipient households and communities – is most topical in this era of global economic and financial crisis. It is even more topical given the uncertainties surrounding continued migrant remittance flow from rich to poor countries, even as development assistance to poor countries is set to dwindle.

Migrant remittance to Nigeria has been increasing steadily in recent years, has overtaken official development assistance, and is second only to receipts from oil revenue. Indeed, in 2007, Nigeria received the largest volume of remittances in sub-Sahara Africa: nearly 65 percent of official recorded remittances flow to the region and about 2 per cent of global flow. Depending on the definition, remittances to Nigeria are estimated to have increased from US$2 billion in 2003 to $2.3 billion in 2004, and by 2007 remittances to the country reached over US$17.9 billion. These are underestimates because the figures exclude informal remittances which observers believe constitute over 20 per cent of total remittances.

Remittances have lifted many families and individuals out of poverty, enhanced educational enrolment and the health status of migrants' household members left behind in countries of origin, and are also beneficial at community and national levels. They play crucial role in developing local-level infrastructure as well as increasing the effective demand for local goods and services. But will this trend continue in view of the massive job losses in host regions across all professional cadres, including those that employ migrants?

Unlike rich countries, no African country is able to launch robust stimulus plans – owing to financial and institutional constraints – thereby exposing their already poor people to further hardship. For many aid-dependent countries – Uganda, Rwanda, Malawi and so on – the flow of development aid is set to decline, just as are private capital flows. Ghosh, writing in the Wall Street Journal (Europe edition, 23 March 2009), observed that most private foundations are planning to spend less on aid than previously, and humanitarian organisations are already downsizing their staff and projects. Above all, migrant-receiving countries are closing their doors, and local populations are increasingly xenophobic as job competition increases between migrants and nationals, with government ministers enforcing the implementation of strategies to ensure that the few existing jobs are reserved strictly for nationals – in Britain, for example, proposing new measures to make it tougher for outsiders to enter in regular situation (Economist, 17 January 2009: 52). Without opportunities for regular entry, more migrants are likely to try irregular channels, often through dangerous scams organised by unscrupulous human traffickers.

As the *Economist* (17 January 2009: 51) noted, 'The economic slump is battering migrants. For tens of millions of people working outside their homelands, life is becoming much more precarious'. Many industries where migrants predominate (such as tourism in Ireland, construction in Spain and North America, financial services in Britain) have been among the first to shed jobs. More recent arrivals in Europe are distressed by the tightened global labour market and the increasing difficulty of finding even menial work. With unemployment running at a high 12 per cent in Spain, and over 7 per cent in the USA – in most cases the highest level in fifteen years – prospects for immigration are dim. The predictable impact of the slump in rich countries is that some potential migrants may be discouraged altogether from making the move, some may have to return voluntarily, or be forced to take that decision, while yet others may opt for migration instead to emerging economies such as China. With a projected global loss of about 20 million jobs in 2009, migration is bound to slow down. Yet the cost of living is on the increase, making savings and remitting a mirage.

For so long, African leaders have faced the challenge of how to retain, attract back and effectively utilise the rare skills of nationals for national development. As this volume suggests, given favourable working conditions, skilled professionals, both men and women, would prefer to remain in their home countries, and those in diaspora would opt to return home to contribute to local development. Leaders must now put in place policies that are designed to ensure that industrial establishments operate at optimum capacity, provide an enabling environment for the private sector to thrive, promote democratic governance and popular participation so that its returning nationals can be more effectively inserted into domestic economies.

Sub-regional economic organisations can foster dialogue and enhance the management of labour mobility in Africa. The African Economic Community and NEPAD advocate programmes aimed at fostering labour mobility within and between the countries of the region, as well as encouraging sustained development. For countries that have hitherto remained ambivalent regarding the principle of free movement of persons and reluctant to modify domestic laws and administrative practices, now is the time to realign national laws with sub-regional treaties to facilitate intra-regional labour mobility, establishment and settlement. Lessons learnt from ECOWAS in creating a borderless sub-region should be replicated by other sub-regional organisations.

Although migration is increasingly a global phenomenon, in Africa it remains largely regional and should be addressed by NEPAD, which could play a larger role in the management of intra-regional labour migration, and strengthen regional economic groupings. It is in this context that regional dialogues and consultative approaches are required, to help balance the interests of sending and receiving countries, and of migrants themselves.

About the Authors

Ben hadj ABDELLATIF, a Tunisian economist-statistician and demographer, received his PhD in Demography in 1990 from the Paris Institute of Demography (Sorbonne). He spent several years in the Tunisian National Institute of Statistics dealing with statistical issues (vital registration, census and surveys etc.) and about ten years in the General Commissariat of Regional Development in Tunis, as Director of Regional and Rural Development Planning. He was recruited by the African Union as Chief of Population and Development, where he promoted the population programmes and activities – in particular the creation of the African Population Commission. He was also a focal point of migration research, strengthening relationships with the IOM and other international agencies. He initiated the Migration Policy and Strategy in Africa. As a consultant, he worked with the African Development Bank and the Islamic Bank on many population and development issues (Millennium Development Goals, consultant on census etc.). He is a member of the Hague Process on Refugee and Migration Policy; and of NOMRA (Network of Migration Research on Africa).

Aderanti ADEPOJU, a Nigerian economist-demographer, received his PhD in Demography in 1973 from the London School of Economics. He spent several years researching issues of internal and international migration as Professor of Demography at the University of Ife, now Obafemi Awolowo University in Nigeria (1980), then as Research Professor and later Dean, Faculty of Business Administration, University of Lagos in 1988. He worked for the ILO, UN and UNFPA from the mid-1970s to the mid-1980s, and from 1988 to 1998. He also served on United States National Academy of Sciences Committee on Population, and is on the editorial advisory boards of *International Migration*, *International Migration Review*, and the *Journal of Migration and Refugee Studies*. A former President of the Union for African Population Studies, he is now Chief Executive at the Human Resources Development Centre in Lagos, a member of the Hague Process on Refugee and Migration Policy, and Co-ordinator of the Network of Migration Research on Africa. Leader of the IOM-UNFPA Research Team on Emigration Dynamics in Sub-Saharan Africa from 1992 to 1996, he was recently appointed a member of the World Economic Forum's Global Agenda Council on Migration. He has published extensively on international migration in Africa.

Adepoju's most recent books include *Migration in Sub-Saharan Africa* (Nordic African Institute, Uppsala, 2008), and *International Migration and National Development in Sub-Saharan Africa: viewpoints and policy initiatives in the countries of origin* (co-edited with van Nearseen and Zoomers; Leiden: Afrika-Studiecentrum Series, 2007).

Adejumoke AFOLAYAN, a Nigerian population geographer, received her PhD in Geography in 1972 from the University of Ibadan, Nigeria. She has spent several years researching issues of internal and international migration in her current position as Professor of Geography at the University of Ibadan. She is a fellow in Peace and Conflict Studies at the Institute of African Studies and in the Center for Peace and Conflict Studies (CEPACS) at the University of Ibadan, where she handles courses and does research on refugee and repatriation issues. She was one of the four members handling the Nigerian Migration Project (NESMUWA) at the Nigerian Institute for Social and Economic Research, and a researcher-author on Emigration Dynamics in Sub-Saharan Africa from 1992 to 1996, sponsored by the IOM-UNFPA Research Team. She is a consultant to IOM National Migration Policy, and to the National Population Commission on Internal Migration Survey, among others.

Afolayan has published extensively on international migration in Africa.

Anthony BARCLAY, a Liberian development economic planner and governance specialist, received his PhD in Urban and Regional Planning with a minor in Economics in 1986, and an MA in Public Policy and Administration in 1977, both from the University of Wisconsin-Madison in Madison, Wisconsin, USA. He worked as a trainer and researcher in Public Administration at the Liberian Institute of Public Administration from 1978 to 1980, and at the University of Liberia, serving simultaneously as Assistant Professor in Regional Development Planning and Director of the Office of Planning and Institutional Development from 1988 to 1990. He also worked with the UNDP-Liberia from 1990 till early 2000. Following a brief stint with the Central Bank of Liberia, he joined the African Capacity Building Foundation in Harare, Zimbabwe, working as Programme Officer from 2000 to 2004. Subsequently, he moved to the Economic Community of West African States (ECOWAS) Commission in Nigeria – from 2005 till early 2009. While at ECOWAS, he served as Advisor, Poverty Alleviation and Human Development and as Chairperson of the ECOWAS Task Force on Migration.

Barclay has produced several publications on development issues, including various aspects of the migration-development nexus, and has made presentations on migration issues at many international conferences. He is a member of a number of professional organisations including the Network of Migration Research on Africa. Currently he is at the World Bank in Washington, DC, USA where he works as Senior Advisor to the Executive Director for Africa Group 1.

CHAPTER EIGHT About the Authors

Eugene CAMPBELL, a Botswana demographer, received his PhD in Population Studies in 1990 from the University of Ghana. He is currently an associate professor at the University of Botswana, and was Deputy Dean of Social Sciences there from 1999 to 2005. Before 1998 he spent several years researching issues of internal migration and fertility in both West Africa and Botswana, and since 1998 he has been investigating international migration. He worked at the University of Liberia, from 1978 to 1983, as a United Nations Volunteer demographer and lecturer, and from 1983 till 1986 as a lecturer at Obafemi Awolowo University in Nigeria. He was an Associate and the Coordinator of the Botswana section of the Southern African Migration Project from 1998 till 2006.

Campbell has published extensively on international migration and fertility in Africa. His most recent publications include 'Brain drain potential in Botswana' in *International Migration*, (Vol. 45 No. 5 of 2007), and 'The role of remittances in Botswana: does internal migration really reward sending families?' to be published in *Population, Space and Place* later this year (2009 – and currently available online through the journal website).

Theophilus O. FADAYOMI is an economist-demographer who is currently Professor of Demography and Social Statistics in the Department of Economics and Development Studies, Covenant University, Ota, Ogun State, Nigeria. He taught at the University of Ife (now Obafemi Awolowo University) in the department of Demography and Social Statistics, and at the University of Ibadan in the departments of Sociology and Agricultural Economics in the 1970s and 1980s. He was a researcher in population and development studies at the Nigerian Institute of Social and Economic Research (NISER), Ibadan, where he was later a Research Professor, and became head of the Social Development Department in 1988. In 1992, he joined the African Development Bank as a demographer/socio-economist and retired as a Principal Demographer in the Bank's Environment and Sustainable Development Unit in 2006. He has worked as a consultant to many international public and non-governmental organizations, including the United Nations in New York, UN-DTCD in Tanzania, the World Bank, UNESCO, the ILO, the African Center for Applied Research and Training in Social Development (ACARTSOD) in Tripoli; the Population Council in Dakar, and the African Institute for Economic Development Planning (IDEP), also in Dakar.

Fadayomi has published several papers, books and technical reports related to population and development studies.

John OUCHO is a geographer-demographer who holds a PhD in Population Geography and was a Ford Foundation post-doctoral fellow of the Carolina Population Center in the University of North Carolina at Chapel Hill, USA in 1982 and 1983. He has taught at the Universities of Nairobi, Ghana and Botswana. He was elected a Fellow of the Kenya National Academy of Sciences in 1989, and of the World Academy of Art and Science in 2003. He was Secretary-General of the Union for Population Studies (UAPS) from 1987 to 1991, and from 1987 to 1999 was Secretary of the Population Association of Kenya, becoming its Patron in 2000. He is a member of several other population associations with regional and global constituencies. He is an accomplished researcher on internal and international migration, forced or voluntary, and on population-development interrelations in Africa, and Afro-European relations. As a professor, and holder of the European Commission's Marie Curie Chair, at the Centre for Research in Ethnic Relations in the School of Health and Social Studies at the University of Warwick since March 2007, he has undertaken training of doctoral candidates, as well as continuing his research, and organising conferences on African migration to Europe.

Oucho has authored several books, book chapters, and refereed journal articles and conference papers. Two of his books – *Urban Migrants and Rural Development in Kenya* (Nairobi: Nairobi University Press, 1996) and *Undercurrents of Ethnic Conflict in Kenya* (Leiden & Boston: Brill Academic Publishers, 2002) are in wide circulation. In August 2008, he founded the African Migration and Development Policy Centre, based in Nairobi and serving mostly the Greater Horn of Africa region.

www.ingramcontent.com/pod-product-compliance
Lightning Source LLC
Chambersburg PA
CBHW080246030426
42334CB00023BA/2722